THE DISCOVERY OF PASTA

THE
DISCOVERY
OF PASTA

A History in Ten Dishes

LUCA CESARI

TRANSLATED BY JOHANNA BISHOP

PEGASUS BOOKS
NEW YORK LONDON

THE DISCOVERY OF PASTA

Pegasus Books, Ltd.
148 West 37th Street, 13th Floor
New York, NY 10018

First Pegasus Books cloth edition January 2023

ISBN: 978-1-63936-316-2

10 9 8 7 6 5 4 3 2 1

Printed in the United States of America
Distributed by Simon & Schuster
www.pegasusbooks.com

CONTENTS

INTRODUCTION

Anyone who cooks up a dish of pasta, anywhere in the world, can't help thinking of Italian cuisine. Even if they live on another continent and the food has been in their diet for generations, it makes no difference: the *Bel Paese* is a touchstone by default.

Yet pasta does not just belong to Italy: in the Western world alone, there's Moroccan couscous, Spanish fideuà (a paella made with short, thin noodles instead of rice), and all kinds of filled pasta – German maultaschen, Russian pelmeni, Ukrainian varenyky, the uszka and pierogi of Eastern Europe and so on – which have nothing to do with the Italian tradition and developed on their own.

If you think about it, it's a little strange that a single country in the heart of the Mediterranean developed a culture with hundreds of pasta dishes, up and down the peninsula, that characterise its cuisine more than anything else. In the end, pasta is just one way of eating a dough of water and flour: bake it, and it's a pie, flatbread or pizza; dip it in boiling oil, and it's a fritter (plain or filled), but boil it in water, and you've entered the vast world of pasta.

Definitions are not set in stone, however, and that is why, for the first few centuries of its existence, pasta was not considered a culinary category unto itself (see, for instance, the chapter on lasagne). The circumstances of its birth are also rather hazy, and although we know that Sicily was a centre of production for dried pasta as early as the twelfth century, the thread of its origins gets lost somewhere back in Classical Greece and the Near East.

Seen from the outside, Italy is one nation united under pasta: families cook it almost every day at home, and very few restaurants fail to offer at least one kind on the menu. There are famous recipes that can be found everywhere and have become true national symbols, like spaghetti with tomato sauce, but most have an extremely local connotation. You can probably find a good carbonara in Milan, or excellent trenette with pesto in Rome, but these dishes are still closely associated with the place where they were invented. If we look a little closer, we will notice that every place has its own speciality, and that the next town over has a different way of cooking what is *more or less* the same dish. Italian cuisine is built from a myriad of recipes forming an intricate mosaic, whose tiles aren't easy to make out; the differences are sometimes minimal, and may even hinge on individual family traditions.

It's a bit like looking at an Impressionist painting: seen from afar, it seems clear enough, but as you get closer the overall picture splits apart and the brushstrokes become an indistinguishable blur.

Since pasta is a food so deeply tied to identity, it becomes a factor distinguishing those who cook it, or rather 'know how to cook it', from those who don't; in short, the classic dividing line of 'Us and Them', which more or less falls along national boundaries. When Italians go abroad, they can't help being amazed by how pasta is eaten in other countries, and two common errors in particular draw the fiercest criticism. The first is cooking it too long, that is, not al dente: that characteristic consistency where the core is still firm to the bite. A dish of spaghetti or macaroni that is too soft is thought of as a mortal sin, and in Italy would justify sending the food back to the kitchen, although that rarely happens.

The other mistake that 'They' often make is serving pasta as a side to meat. Those noodles nestled alongside a bit of roast, or maybe a beef stew? To an Italian, they're completely incomprehensible, because pasta is a *primo piatto*, a first course, and meat is a *secondo*, and never the twain shall meet.

What many fierce Italian champions of orthodoxy do not realise is that these two ways of serving pasta were once quite common even back home, and it was from here that they spread abroad over a century ago. 'Overcooked' pasta – you'll find various examples in the last chapter – was standard in northern Italy until the early twentieth century; the fashion of cooking it al dente sprang up in the South, and took a long time to work its way up the peninsula and become the national standard. Just a few generations ago, it was normal for a Neapolitan to cook pasta differently compared to someone in Milan.

The habit of using it as a side dish was also quite common. From the Renaissance up to the late nineteenth century, one finds many cookbooks that suggest covering boiled meat, especially poultry such as duck or capon, with macaroni or filled pasta. In Italy, this custom almost completely disappeared over the course of the twentieth century, as pasta carved out its own place on the menu, both at home and in public settings.

Essentially, when Italians criticise this sort of thing, they are revealing the cultural divide that separates them not only from foreigners, but from their own ancient culinary roots.

In countries such as Germany, Britain, France or the United States, pasta was brought by Italian immigrants. Initially considered an interloper at the national table, it took quite a while to be assimilated into those cuisines. And as we know, immigrant communities tend to be protective of their traditions, which they rightfully consider a fundamental part of their identity. So this – along with the fact that contact with their homeland was only sporadic – may be why their cooking preserved some older habits, continuing down a path that Italy diverged from. In much the same way that a language cut off from its country of origin tends to evolve separately, holding on to some archaic patterns of speech.

This led to hybridised cuisines that have every right to exist, but almost never reflect contemporary Italian usage.

For instance, Italian American cooking, with its spaghetti and meatballs, chicken Alfredo or macaroni and cheese: recipes that all evolved out of traditional Italian ones, but are now only distantly related to those original delicacies and have no real counterpart in Italy. The famous macaroni dish so common in the US and UK actually echoes the oldest way of eating pasta – topped with cheese alone – but remains a speciality of the English-speaking world, and you'd never find it on a restaurant menu in my country.

Pasta becomes entangled with cultural identity not just in relation to foreigners, but even – and one might say above all – when Italians are talking to other Italians. Endless arguments over the 'authentic' recipe for a given speciality are par for the course. This maniacal attachment to our foods usually causes considerable amusement among non-Italians, who can't see why, say, the very notion of breaking spaghetti in half to fit it in the pot, or of adding a spoonful of tomato sauce to carbonara, should be such hot-button issues.

In Italy, there have always been foods associated with a given region, and examples can be found all the way back to the Middle Ages, although they are often individual products rather than actual dishes.

Even in those days certain foods had a special relationship with their place of origin, but there was nothing resembling the fanatical attachment to tradition that we see today. The fierce battle against real or imagined

threats to our national cuisine is a rather recent phenomenon. And the particularly inflexible attitude of the people
I call 'food purists' in this book took shape around the
beginning of the 1960s, during Italy's frenzied industrialisation. If you read the newspapers of the time, they
convey a clear sense that Italian culinary traditions were
in jeopardy: according to commentators, an incredible
legacy was at risk of disappearing for good.

The model they were looking to was France, which
had been keenly aware of its national culinary heritage
for some time and was working to protect certain skills,
terroirs, and products through research and publications.

So the years that followed brought a concerted effort
to record and preserve Italian foodways, but the link to
thousand-year-old traditions that gourmets are always
invoking was still missing from the picture. And the quest
for (or rather, invention of) the ancient roots of Italian
cuisine unleashed a debate that is not only still open, but
has taken on gigantic proportions.

The stories we hear today about the origins of a dish
almost never reveal the true circumstances surrounding
its birth. They do, however, shed light on the values that
people are trying to preserve by holding on to tradition.
In these narratives, the past is utterly transfigured and
constantly rewritten, painting imaginative pictures of
a rural world where peasants lived off the fruits of the
earth, or else of sumptuous courts in an era when it was
Italy that taught the rest of Europe how to eat. These two
scenarios suggest a powerful longing for vanished roots,
and the hope of recovering them through traditional
cooking.

In the end, my true motivation for writing this book has been to bring a little clarity to the discussion, because legends can teach us quite a bit, but should not be confused with historical fact.

Alongside ancient cuisine, I have another longstanding passion: historical fencing. These two interests may seem to have little in common, but are both spurred by a desire to learn more about everyday life in the past, since such details have fascinated me since childhood. In that field, too, one comes across many clichés and fanciful reconstructions. So along with other scholars and enthusiasts, I began to focus on analysing primary sources such as fencing treatises and manuals. It is an approach that has proven to be of fundamental importance for launching a serious study of the ancient martial arts and their practical applications.

When it comes to food history, my research has concentrated on cookbooks as a primary source of information, but in order to interpret them correctly it has been necessary to explore many other fields, such as access to ingredients, production techniques, transport, food prices and every other aspect of the ancient diet.

These studies have revealed that many popular beliefs about the origin and evolution of classic Italian dishes, particularly pasta specialities, are flat-out wrong. When I began to publish my first findings, *Gambero Rosso* magazine invited me on to their masthead to write articles about food history and recipes for ancient dishes. This is how I found my calling, so to speak, and I still write a newspaper column for *Il Sole 24 Ore* titled 'Indovina chi sviene a cena' ('Guess Who's Succumbing to Dinner'), where I tell curious, little-known anecdotes about food – like the ones that turn up throughout this book.

Writing about food in Italy is often complicated enough as it is, but proposing variations on traditional recipes could be thought of as an extreme sport in this country. It's far safer to wave around a sharp sword than to serve friends a carbonara made with cream.

But to be honest, Italians are not the only people deeply attached to their own culinary specialities. To cite just one recent example: in January 2021, when the Spanish chef David Muñoz – who can boast three Michelin stars – dared to offer his own take on Spanish paella, calling it 'Madrid Paella', all hell broke loose on the internet. His recipe was even called a 'sacrilege'.

Nor are the neighbours to be outdone. The battle to defend French cuisine began long ago and shows no sign of slowing: in other headlines from 2021, the Confederation of French Bakers nominated the baguette for inclusion in the UNESCO list of intangible cultural heritage. Such appeals to the UN are nothing new in Italy, either, where the art of Neapolitan pizza-making was granted ICH status in 2017.

As a rule, in Italy, cooking is a phenomenon that flows out of the kitchen into every aspect of conviviality and social life. Food is an opportunity to strengthen family ties and friendships, the consummate binding agent. And this is true of pasta in particular, because it can be easily prepared in large amounts to share with others, at relatively little expense. If it's homemade pasta, which fortunately still exists in many parts of Italy, the whole family is often summoned to take part in the preparation of some beloved dish, especially for special occasions. It is not uncommon for everyone to gather around a big table to make the lasagne, tortellini, orecchiette or ravioli that will become part of a festive meal. And on such occasions, the fun starts long before everyone sits down to dinner, as friends and relatives all pitch in to concoct complex dishes. These customs reveal a deep love of cooking that I would like to convey to my readers abroad, hoping that the stories and recipes in this book will inspire them to visit Italy and, fork in hand, sample its vast spectrum of regional specialities.

Foreigners are often surprised to learn that over dinner, Italians like to discuss what they're eating, what they've eaten, and what they plan to eat or cook in the future. Of course that's not *entirely* true: sometimes we just make small talk, or chat about literature, music, philosophy, history and so on.

But only if the food is mediocre.

1

Fettuccine Alfredo

A history of Italian pasta can only start here, with the legendary fettuccine Alfredo. A very simple dish, with just three ingredients, that has been wildly successful: it turns up in over 800 American cookbooks published from 1933 to the present.

So why will your Italian friends tell you they've never heard of the stuff?

It's not their fault. Alfredo is by no means a household name in our country, which is why those of us who *have* heard of it put it in the same category as spaghetti and meatballs – which we've only ever seen in *Lady and the Tramp* – or carbonara with bacon, garlic, mushrooms and cream: some shoddy imitation of an Italian dish, seemingly unrelated to our traditional cuisine.

This goes to show that fame has a way of ruining old friendships. Because although the average Italian may not know it, the 'original' fettuccine Alfredo goes back centuries, and is actually the most ancient pasta dish in our tradition. But I'll get to that later.

Nowadays, in the United States, fettuccine Alfredo has become a dish of tagliatelle in a cream and cheese sauce, sometimes seasoned with garlic and parsley. It may be served in this simple version, or gussied up with other ingredients – the most common being chicken or prawns. But the most extreme form is the Alfredo sauce found in American supermarkets, either in packets – to be mixed with water and butter – or in jars, ready to pour on your pasta (or pizza, as some labels suggest). It comes in dozens of brands, including organic and vegan options. In the better ones the main ingredient is cream, which is sometimes outweighed by products like modified cornstarch, maltodextrin, partially hydrogenated soybean oil and other such delicacies.

At first glance, this seems like a classic example of a carefully constructed, Italian-sounding fake, a dish that has reached the height of popularity in the US (and other countries) without ever setting foot in the *Bel Paese*. A marketing ploy by some cunning multinational corporation intent on pleasing palates used to creamy, mouth-filling sauces, with no link to real Italian cuisine.

And it's true enough that at some point, that's more or less the direction the dish took. Yet its early history is surprising, because it takes us to the heart of Italy at the dawn of the twentieth century, when a cook discovered – or rather, rediscovered – a fabulous dish that uses a few simple ingredients to magical effect. Believe it or not, in those days Rome had not yet developed the pasta recipes we all know and love. Amatriciana was just starting to appear in a few eateries; cacio e pepe – which we'll discuss later in this chapter – was not yet considered a local speciality; and carbonara and gricia had yet to be invented.

Back then, the most famous pasta dish in the Eternal City was – you guessed it – fettuccine Alfredo.

The *majestic* fettuccine al doppio burro

Alfredo di Lelio, inventor of the fettuccine that bears his name, was born in Rome in 1883 and got his start at the family restaurant in Piazza Rosa, which later vanished to make room for the shopping arcade now known as Galleria Sordi. He was still a child when he began helping out at the family business run by his mother, Angelina. The establishment was rather anonymous, one of the many restaurants dotting the capital, and that's how it would have stayed had it not been for the arrival of Armando, Alfredo's eldest son. This was in 1908. After giving birth, the mother, Ines, was so weak that Alfredo strove to come up with a food that would be nourishing yet easy to digest, to help get his wife back on her feet.

So here's what he did: 'he personally prepared some fettuccine, using a semolina dough, and mixed it with very fresh butter and parmesan cheese. Then he said a prayer to St Anne (patron saint of new mothers) and served it to Ines, saying, "if it's not to your taste, I'll eat it!"'[1]

It was to her taste, all right.

So much so that she suggested putting the dish straight on the menu of their little trattoria. A simple recipe, with butter and parmesan perfectly blended to create a velvety sauce enveloping the fettuccine. What was so special about it, as opposed to just dumping butter on noodles? The quality and freshness of the ingredients, of course, but above all the method of emulsification used by Alfredo, whose skilled hands imparted an extraordinary texture to the sauce.

Two years later, his parents' restaurant, where fettuccine Alfredo first saw the light of day, disappeared as the city underwent all kinds of transformations. But in 1914 Alfredo managed to open a new restaurant – also in Rome, but this time in the very central Via della Scrofa – which he named after himself. Just how the fame of his dish travelled so far outside the Italian capital and rippled across the Atlantic is still a mystery. To be sure, some part was played by the fact that foreigners were enthralled by the histrionics of the owner, and that his fettuccine perfectly suited American tastes in pasta.

One of the first American references to the dish turns up in the 1922 novel *Babbitt*, by Sinclair Lewis, which was quite popular in its day. At one point in the story, the protagonist meets an upper-class American lady who confesses her infatuation with Rome. But the object of her affection is not the city's paintings, music or antiquities: rather, it's the 'little trattoria on the Via della Scrofa where you get the best fettuccine in the world'.[2]

This was just the beginning.

A few years later, in 1927, the restaurant was reviewed in the *Saturday Evening Post* by George Rector – a food expert, prolific essayist and host of a CBS radio show – whose long article launches into an admiring description of 'Maestro' Alfredo di Lelio's handiwork. It starts, obviously, with a recipe for the fettuccine, which calls for a kilo of flour, five egg yolks, a glass of water and a pinch of salt. But the real key, according to Rector, is the next step: when it is served, or rather *how* it is served. Coming to the table himself, Alfredo brandishes a large spoon and fork, sprinkles parmesan on the fettuccine, and 'turns it over and over. Now, that's simple enough, but, as Eva Tanguay* used to say about her dancing, it's not what he does but the way he does it.' The secret to his fettuccine is finally revealed, and the author can barely contain his enthusiasm for Alfredo's artistry, as we read in his priceless closing words: 'The recipe for the making is very simple. But so is the formula for painting a Rembrandt. Just get oils, canvas and brush, and go to it.'[3]

By this point it's not only clear that the dish was exquisite, but that Alfredo was a master at winning over his guests by showcasing the preparation of his speciality. What normally would have been done in the kitchen was now paraded before a roomful of diners anxious to see ordinary pasta transformed into Alfredo's 'majestic fettuccine with double butter sauce',[4] as it was advertised in the papers of the day.

But it was only in 1927 that this Roman speciality got its true consecration, an investiture presided over – and how could it be otherwise, given the theatrical flair that went into the dish – by two Hollywood stars: Mary Pickford and Douglas Fairbanks. Actually, the pair had already eaten at Alfredo's in 1920, while on their honeymoon. Seven years later they came back, bearing an unexpected gift with enormous publicity potential: a

---

* Eva Tanguay was a famous singer and dancer known as the 'Queen of Vaudeville'.

gold fork and spoon engraved with the dedication 'To Alfredo the King of the noodles'. It's hard to convey the colossal popularity of these two silent film idols by comparing them to celebrities of our era. Douglas Fairbanks was known as 'the king of Hollywood' and starred in the first adaptation of *Zorro*, as well as a famous *Robin Hood* that set box office records for 1922, and *The Black Pirate*, one of the first all-colour films in history. As if that weren't enough, he was one of the thirty-six founding members of the Academy that created the Oscars in 1929. Mary Pickford was one of the best known and best paid actors in silent film, famous for playing cheerful teens with golden ringlets. Dubbed 'America's sweetheart', she teamed up with her husband and with figures like D. W. Griffith and Charlie Chaplin to found United Artists, an independent production company that still exists today. Their wedding not only marked the union of two demi-gods, but created what at the time was probably the most famous couple in the Western world.

No amount of advertising could have equalled this endorsement from the Fairbanks, and Alfredo milked it for all it was worth without changing a comma in his recipe. Famous figures visiting Rome from all around the world made an obligatory stopover in Via della Scrofa, where the owner, always smiling under his prodigious handlebar moustache, would prepare the famous dish for them directly at the table.

In 1943, at the darkest point in the city's history, Alfredo sold his historic restaurant and all the photos of stars on the walls. But as soon as the war ended he opened a new place in Piazza Augusto Imperatore, calling it Il Vero Alfredo ('The Real Alfredo'). Both restaurants cashed in on Alfredo's distinguished name and there was a fierce rivalry between them, but it doesn't really matter which was the true hub of the *dolce vita* in those years. By then the dish was already on the road to fame, travelling far beyond the city walls.

Given that the recipe was so closely identified with its inventor, fears of straying into plagiarism may have hindered its spread in Italy, where it never achieved the popularity of classic Roman dishes like amatriciana, carbonara, or cacio e pepe. There could be other reasons, too: the fact that Italians tend to think of pasta with butter as 'hospital fare', or the impossibility of making variations on a sauce with just two ingredients, or the choice of parmesan rather than pecorino, which made it harder to think of the recipe as a Roman speciality. Whatever the reason, back in its homeland, fettuccine Alfredo remained a phenomenon almost wholly confined to those two restaurants in the capital.

Starting in the 1940s, however, some cookbooks did offer sporadic instructions on how to make the famous fettuccine at home. They never mentioned Alfredo, only the amount of butter, which seemed to keep growing. The 'Tagliatelle al burro'[5] (tagliatelle with butter) in *Tesoretto della cucina italiana* in 1948 thus became 'Tagliatelle doppio burro'[6] (with double butter) in *Annabella in cucina* in 1964; it then reached the 'triplo burro' level and stayed there, in the versions proposed by Luigi Carnacina in 1961,[7] Vincenzo Buonassisi in 1979,[8] and finally Luigi Veronelli in 1985.[9] But let's have a look at Carnacina's, as an example:

> *Fettuccine (tagliatelle) with triple butter*
>
> [For 6 people]. 420 gr homemade fettuccine (make a dough using 9 eggs for each kg of durum wheat flour and a little semolina). About 200 gr of pure cream butter, set in cold water for a few hours to soften. 200 gr of parmesan (from the centre of a semi-aged wheel, grated at the last minute). Cook the fettuccine in lightly salted boiling water, drain it al dente, transfer it to a warm china bowl, sprinkle immediately with grated parmesan and with the butter in small pieces, mix well and serve very hot.

The promise of 'triple butter' in the name is fulfilled by the 200g of butter used here for just over 400g of tagliatelle, a proportion that rises to 250g for 400g of pasta in Veronelli's version.

The appeal of the recipe definitely lay in its simplicity and in the ease of preparation, since it was well within the capabilities of anyone who could turn on a cooker.

At first, Americans tried to reproduce the original version of the dish, as we can see from a 'Fettuccine all'Alfredo'[10] that is perfectly identical to the Italian fettuccine with double butter. It turns up in *Cook as the Romans Do* (1961) by Myra Waldo – one of America's most prolific cookbook authors, and a great fan of European cuisine. But other versions that began to catch on around this time in the United States were much more 'democratic', in the sense that they tried to ensure a good outcome even for cooks with very few real skills.

And so some versions appeared that added quite a bit of cream, sometimes along with egg yolks, and ingredients like garlic and parsley that had never been in the Roman recipe.

This American take on Alfredo sauce began to be popularised not only through cookbooks, but through other, more ubiquitous channels, like the box of 'Fettuccine Egg Noodles' that the Pennsylvania Dutch brand began to market in 1966, which had a recipe on the back calling for cream and Swiss cheese (in addition to the classic butter and parmesan).[11]

Its definitive success in the United States, however, came with industrialisation and mass distribution, as companies began producing packets or jars of ready-made sauces that could be poured directly on pasta, adding other toppings at whim. As is almost always true of processed foods, quality took a back seat to practicality, and even a recipe as seemingly simple as pasta, butter and cheese had to bow to the laws of the supermarket shelf.

The same approach was taken by the Olive Garden restaurants, specialising in Italian American dishes. Their menu introduced a cream, butter and cheese-based fettuccine Alfredo to which other toppings could be added, creating the variants we mentioned earlier: 'Chicken Alfredo', 'Seafood Alfredo', or 'Shrimp Alfredo'. The chain now has over 800 locations across North America, and has played a key role in shaping the image of Italian American food since the 1980s.

One need only take a look at the leading American recipe sites to see that not much has changed even today, although in recent years Americans have developed a much keener awareness that quality ingredients do indeed matter. Influenced in part by thousands of cooking blogs and TV shows, a segment of the population has raised their standards for food and become willing to devote more time, energy and attention to what they eat. Encouraged by this trend, some chefs have been trying to reintroduce the original recipe for fettuccine Alfredo in the United States.[12]

Il cacio sui maccheroni

But let's stop for a minute and go back a step. A step that, as we are about to see, spans several centuries.

For now, let's set aside the ritual of preparing fettuccine at the table, the famous guests and the golden utensils from Pickford and Fairbanks. What's left? A dish of noodles, butter and parmesan. A pasta dish that may look at first like nothing special, but is the only one with a history going back over half a millennium.

Since the Middle Ages, there have been at least two other general approaches to cooking pasta in Italy: it could be baked in the oven, or boiled and served in broth (or milk). But what Italians now call *pastasciutta*, 'dry pasta' – which does not necessarily mean *dried* pasta, but pasta that has been boiled, drained and topped with something – has always been sprinkled with cheese.

First of all, let's do away with a fairly common misconception. One shouldn't imagine that pasta dishes were as common as they are today, or that pastasciutta was the primary form. Actually, the opposite is true: for centuries pasta played only a tiny part of the role it fills in contemporary Italian cuisine.

If we look at the earliest references to pastasciutta, cheese was not considered an extra ingredient, but the one irreplaceable topping. *Cacio sui maccheroni* ('cheese on macaroni', now an expression meaning 'just the thing' or 'the perfect match') was an obvious pairing even to the medieval mind, and a famous example turns up in Boccaccio's *Decameron*, written in the mid-fourteenth century. In the third tale of the eighth day, Bruno and Buffalmacco are trying, as usual, to pull a prank on the gullible Calandrino, with Maso's help. To attract the attention of their chosen victim, Maso starts making up fanciful stories about an imaginary land, Bengodi (usually translated as Cockaigne), where Boccaccio imagines macaroni and ravioli being rolled down a mountain of parmesan, so that they arrive at the bottom perfectly coated in cheese and ready to eat: 'there was also a mountain made wholly of grated Parmesan cheese, on which dwelt people who did nothing but make macaroni and ravioli, and cook them in capon broth, and then throw them down for anyone to catch as many as they could'.[13]

Boccaccio's Bengodi is just one version of the 'Land of Cockaigne', the literary trope of an ideal place where people can gorge themselves on food and indulge their every whim, with no work and no effort. If in a land where anything was possible, macaroni and ravioli were covered only in cheese, we can deduce that this was one of very few ways in which it was conceivable to eat them.

In about the same era, we find the earliest examples of recipes confirming this state of affairs, such as the *Libro de la cocina*, which has a wonderful recipe for lasagne.

We'll look at the full history of lasagne in another chapter, but for now let's just say that it was initially served as simple rectangles of pasta boiled in broth and layered with grated cheese.

Lasagne

Take good white flour; temper it with warm water, and make a firm dough; then roll it out thin; leave it to dry; it should be cooked in broth from a capon, or from other rich meat; then put it in the dish with rich grated cheese, in layers, as you see fit.[14]

One should note that at the time, no one even envisioned adding butter, which began to be used on pasta only in the fifteenth century.

The first thorough description of this new method is found in the *Libro de Arte Coquinaria* by Maestro Martino de Rubeis (or de Rossi).[15] Universally celebrated as the 'prince of cooks',[16] he wrote what are considered to be the most important recipe books of his era, with an approach to the culinary arts that is much more precise and systematic than medieval authors, and fully integrated with the humanist culture of his time. Here the author suggests only grated cheese and spices as a condiment for 'Ravioli in tempo di carne' and 'Vermicelli', while he calls for adding butter to 'Maccaroni siciliani' and 'Maccaroni romaneschi'.

To make Roman macaroni

Take some good flour and add water and make pasta a little thicker than for lasagne, and having rolled it around a stick, slip out the stick and cut the pasta to the width of your little finger, so it is like ribbons or laces, and let it cook in rich broth or in water depending on the season, and the rich broth or water must be boiling when you put it in. And if you cook it in water, put in fresh butter, and a little salt, and when it is done put it in dishes with good cheese and butter and sweet spices.[17]

If it weren't for the fact that Maestro Martino's pasta is eggless and calls for the addition of spices, this dish would sound exactly like the one that Alfredo di Lelio whipped up almost five centuries later. And interestingly, both were from the area of Rome.

During the Renaissance, that golden age of Italian cuisine, pastasciutta continued to be associated only with butter and cheese, but the addition of sugar and spices (especially cinnamon) was increasingly common – at least for the lucky few who could afford them, but we'll discuss that later on.

The centuries that followed saw no significant changes, and even at the dawn of the nineteenth century, although major innovations were on the horizon, the basic idea remained the same.

In 1803, Vincenzo Agnoletti managed to condense three ways of serving pastasciutta, which in that era were still the only standard ones, into a single recipe.

The basic condiment for 'macaroni' – which at the time was a generic term for pasta – was still butter and parmesan, to which one could add pepper and cinnamon, cream and béchamel, or the liquid from stewed meat (a very important innovation, as we will see in later chapters).

Several ways of cooking macaroni in the Italian style

Entrée, and Terrine [baked dish]. In a pot, melt a large piece of butter, put in macaroni cooked in salted water and well drained, stir it a bit over the fire, and add grated parmesan (and if you like, a hint of pepper, or ground cinnamon); then pour it on to the plate, sprinkle over more grated parmesan and melted butter; and serve it quickly piping hot. You can also serve macaroni in another way, that is, after mixing it as above, you can put a little coulis [reduced broth], or liquid from a stew, or from beef braised with cloves, and serve it with plenty of cheese and butter as before. Or instead of the coulis or gravy, you can put in cream, or béchamel, and serve it as described above. You can also, after dressing the macaroni in any of the ways described, put it in a dish, or terrine; bake it until

{ slightly browned in a rather hot oven, and serve it
{ straight away.[18]

Although there are dozens of recipes describing pasta with butter, it is hard to know exactly what the resulting dish was like, due to the lack of specific instructions about the quantities to use.

A very rare description of pasta in the eighteenth century comes to us from none other than Giacomo Casanova, in the account of his daring escape from the Carcere dei Piombi in Venice.

As you may know, in 1755 this famous adventurer was thrown into prison, from which he escaped by using a sharpened iron bar to chip out a hole. When it was almost ready, his plans were almost dashed by a change of cells. But Casanova managed to communicate with the friar in the cell above his, bringing him in on the scheme. In order to pull it off, he needed to smuggle the bar to the monk, and the only person who could be turned into an unwitting go-between was Lorenzo, the prison guard. So Casanova decided to hide the tool in the spine of a bible, but the ends were left visible. He therefore decided to send it to the friar with a large dish of buttered pasta sitting on top. His bizarre stratagem was that the dish – so full of butter that it threatened to slop over on to the cover of the book underneath – would distract the guard and keep him from noticing the protruding bar.

On St. Michael's Day Lorenzo appeared very early in the morning with a great kettle in which the macaroni were boiling; I at once put the butter on a portable stove to melt it and I got my two dishes ready, sprinkling them with Parmesan cheese, which he had brought me all grated. I took the pierced spoon and I began to fill them, adding butter and cheese with each spoonful and not stopping until the big dish meant for the monk could hold no more. The macaroni were swimming in butter, which came up to the very edge of the dish [. . .] holding it on the palms of my hands with the spine toward Lorenzo I told him to put out his arms and spread his fingers, and I admonished him to carry it with the greatest care and slowly so that the butter would not spill out of the dish and run over the Bible.[19]

Of course, this situation was unusual to say the least, and can't be taken as a general rule. Yet the idea that Casanova could fill the dish with macaroni that were literally floating in fat, without the guard being surprised, suggests that this must have seemed relatively normal at the time.

Pasta and spices

Let's head back to Rome for a minute. When talking about Rome, and pasta with cheese, one can't help being reminded of that close cousin of Alfredo's: cacio e pepe – another extraordinary dish that is now firmly established on the list of the city's specialities, along with carbonara, amatriciana and gricia.

It is not hard to see that fettuccine Alfredo and cacio e pepe share the same roots, both deriving from those medieval pastas that were served with cheese alone. The difference, however, is that cacio e pepe has preserved the memory of a key addition used to give it extra depth and flavour: spices.

All through the Middle Ages and at least until the end of the seventeenth century, these powdered seasonings were a precious ingredient, and as such, were priced out of most people's reach.

This may seem like a side note to history. But in point of fact, it is no exaggeration to say that the spice trade played a pivotal role in building the splendour of Venice – whose merchant fleets were the first in the Old World to trade with the East – and then in encouraging European expansion to the coasts of South Asia and the Americas.

In 1498, when the Portuguese fleet of Vasco da Gama reached Kozhikode (Calicut), India after circumnavigating Africa, they were met by some incredulous Tunisians who asked what they were doing in such a distant port. Their answer was telling: 'We are looking for Christians and spices.' No Christians were on hand, but pepper was truly abundant. From the late fifteenth century on, all the great European explorers shared the mission of finding an alternative route to the Indies, which were the source of many exotic goods, but above all of spices that could not be grown back home. The journey across Asia by land via caravan routes was long and dangerous, and merchandise went through many changes of hand, with vast price hikes each time. Once new types of vessels were developed that made ocean voyages possible, many expeditions set off in the hope of finding safe new passages that would permit a steady flow of spices and other precious goods at less expense. Christopher Columbus himself headed west across the Atlantic in search of another way to reach the same lands (and goods) as the Portuguese. In short, if the history of the Americas was changed forever, it was due in part to these exquisite seasonings.

In the centuries that followed, as they became easier to obtain, spices began to lose value – symbolically as well as economically. In just a few hundred years, with the aid of new plantations, what had once been a product worth its weight in gold became relatively affordable, and thus lost its role as a precious status symbol reserved for the elite.

By the nineteenth century the price of pepper had definitively plummeted, and it could be found even in the humblest kitchens. Among many other signs of this devaluation, a particularly interesting one can be found in the observations of a young doctor who was treating peasants with pellagra in the countryside around Radicofani, a small town in the Val d'Orcia, near Siena, around 1830. These people on the bottom rungs of the social ladder could not afford bread or even pasta, so they survived almost entirely on polenta, which they seasoned with 'cheese and pepper' – that is, 'cacio e pepe'.[20]

This ancient topping, which by then had become a humble one, could be adapted to dishes ranging from soups to pasta, and was used all the time in everyday life, even though it didn't show up in cookbooks. It was a 'non-recipe' that we can imagine was very widespread, and hard to associate with any one place.

Even in the early twentieth century, in the years leading up to the Great War, cacio e pepe was never numbered among Rome's traditional dishes. This can be seen from the failure to mention it in the first three cookbooks that attempted to catalogue the regional specialities of the peninsula.[21] Only in the 1930s did the Touring Club's *Guida gastronomica d'Italia* finally list 'Spaghetti cacio e pepe: that is, generously dusted with pepper and pecorino'[22] as a Roman speciality. From then on, this recipe too began to take on a new life as a hallmark of the city's cuisine.

A sprinkling of parmesan

To sum up this historical overview, one might say that Italians basically ate pasta with Alfredo sauce for hundreds of years. Pasta with butter and cheese was not *a* pasta dish, it was *the* pasta dish.

But then, if it was so common, why did anyone make such a fuss over the fettuccine in Via della Scrofa? And above all, why did no one, until just over two centuries ago, realise that you could top a dish of pasta with all kinds of other things?

The introduction of pasta sauces dates more or less to the end of the eighteenth century: a shift that brought about a true revolution in Italian cooking, transforming a rather monotonous dish into a category of food that now includes hundreds of specialities.

The first steps in this direction came when a few spoonfuls of meat juices or gravy began to be added to cheese pasta. This was followed by a rapid acceleration in which all kinds of new recipes carved out a place for themselves, like the spaghetti with tomato sauce or tagliatelle with clam sauce that were described by Ippolito Cavalcanti as early as 1837.[23] Nowadays we are so used to serving pasta with sauces of every ilk, traditional or creative, that it seems 'natural' to use it as a neutral base to be flavoured at whim.

Although that's not quite true, because even today many pairings are considered unacceptable to Italian tastes, and aside from a few wild experiments, no one would dream of serving spaghetti with mayonnaise or chocolate. But looking back, it seems as if Italians, for hundreds of years, ate only what they now call 'pasta in bianco': the standard dish of children, invalids, or anyone who had overindulged the night before.

Yet strange as it may seem, even simple cheese pasta had its rules – or preferences, anyway – especially when it came to the choice of cheese.

The earliest recipes tend to specify a kind called piacentino or lodigiano, which must have been quite similar to modern-day parmesan or grana padano. It's not any old cheese, or even any generic aged cheese, but rather a specific product, whose modern incarnation still tops the list of cheeses to be grated on pasta.

Thanks to the Italian doctor Pantaleone da Confienza and his *Summa lacticiniorum* of 1477, we have a consummately detailed description of what this cheese was like in the late Middle Ages. Having gathered together all the information at his disposal about dairy products, both in Italy and abroad, the author spoke very highly of the kind from Piacenza.

The cheeses of Piacenza are called parmesan by some because similar ones are made in Parma, not much different in quality. The same is true in the area of Milan, Pavia, Novara and Vercelli [. . .] but to be honest, piacentino cheeses are far superior to the rest. The wheels are big, and wide, and sometimes weigh a hundred pounds or more, but normally fifty pounds or thereabouts. [. . .] As for quality, they are pleasantly flavourful, especially those made in the spring and properly aged, that is, for about three or four years, depending on their size, because, as mentioned above, the largest ones will keep longer [. . .] These cheeses are made from cow's milk, so they are fatty. They are also creamy, even though a considerable amount of butter has been extracted from the milk.[24]

According to the *Summa*, piacentino cheeses weighed on average about 15–16 kg, but could even exceed 30 (the lowest weight limit for modern wheels). Like the cheese grated on pasta today, they were made with semi-skimmed milk, and the finest were aged for three or four years.

All told, they must have been not unlike the big wheels of parmesan or grana that Italians are now used to seeing, aside from differences due to the breeds of cattle and the way they were raised and fed.

Pantaleone da Confienza was the first to write an entire treatise on cheese, which still had the reputation it had borne for most of the Middle Ages: a humble foodstuff, suited at best to people who got by on a rustic diet.

After a gradual evolution, in the fifteenth century it was starting to find a place on other tables, even those of the aristocracy.[25] The author himself spoke out against this centuries-old prejudice:

> No argument can persuade me to accept the idea that all cheeses are contemptible, as some authors say [. . .] personally, I have seen kings, like the most Christian Louis of France, and innumerable dukes, counts, marchesses, barons, soldiers, nobles, merchants, and simple folk of both sexes, who willingly partake of cheese.[26]

The cultural elite was beginning to realise that cheese was a food worthy of attention, which could sometimes be truly outstanding. Their doctors, however, would not completely approve of it for at least two more centuries, since its characteristics were deemed unwholesome by the medical theories of the time.

Nonetheless, cheese truly caught on in every diet when it came to be paired with pasta, which was instead – again, from the perspective of the time – considered to have various benefits, at least two of which are difficult to imagine today.

The first is that it was a food considered acceptable for 'fast days', that is, the dates on the liturgical calendar when Christians were obliged to abstain from meat.[27]

There were actually two kinds of fast-day regimes: the first, more common, called for avoiding meat on certain days of the week and at certain other times of year, for instance on Christmas Eve; the second was 'strict' or 'Lenten' fasting, because it was usually for the forty days before Easter, when the ban extended to include almost all foods of animal origin, including milk, dairy and eggs. In both diets one could, however, consume seafood and some amphibians (such as frogs). These dietary rules followed a specific calendar that had already appeared between the first and second century of the Christian era, and had a major impact on what people ate: in any given year, there might be up to 150 or 160 fast days. In the eighteenth century, Lenten fasting began to become more elastic in various ways, allowing previously forbidden foods such as butter, and eventually blurred into the more ordinary fast-day diet. Nonetheless, in the late nineteenth century one still finds cookbooks geared towards accommodating a centuries-old diet that we would now call dairy-free pescatarian.[28]

Many have correctly pointed out that one of the reasons for the success of dried pasta in Italy is the fact that it was a food permitted year-round, even on the strictest fast days, since it is completely plant-based. Likewise, dietary rules played a role in the popularity of the cheese and vegetable fillings so common in stuffed pastas, or the traditional sauces based on vegetables and seafood (which was always allowed), or what is still the country's best-known dish, spaghetti with tomato sauce.

A second factor was exclusively aesthetic, but still quite important.

In the Middle Ages and Renaissance, there was a particular fondness for foods that were white or golden in colour, since these two hues, in food, denoted luxury and wealth. While yellow could be obtained by adding spices – first and foremost, saffron – white could only come from carefully selected ingredients. There are many references in cookbooks to this chromatic aspect, and one of the most famous ancient dishes is of course 'blancmange', identified by its colour rather than its ingredients, which could vary quite a bit.

Yet in the Middle Ages and Renaissance there were dozens of sauces used to flavour foods, mainly meat, which from a modern perspective could easily have been paired with pasta to create new dishes. So why was pasta topped only with cheese for almost half a millennium, adding spices or sugar at most?

At this point I ought to underscore an important principle: the development of taste is a cultural phenomenon. It is not based solely on the availability of ingredients and whether they are already in use, or at any rate, those things are not enough to yield a new recipe. The tongue and the mind are closely connected and culturally mediated by the society we live in, which teaches us to distinguish between good and bad, right and wrong.[29]

Freedom of action is as limited in gastronomy as it is in other fields of human knowledge. To make a parallel with painting, any artist with a paintbrush, in any era, could theoretically have painted like Michelangelo, Gauguin or Pollock. But that's just not how things work. There are barriers that progressively fall, giving rise to new creations, new schools of thought and habit, in cooking as well as in art.

Although pasta is now served in all kinds of ways, an almost 'genetic' memory of old customs has survived.

Here's an example. Whether or not cheese will actually improve the taste, the act of sprinkling on some parmesan – or ricotta salata, or pecorino, etc. – before digging in is a constant in almost all Italian pasta recipes, from north to south. It's simply that instead of first coating the pasta in cheese and then (much later) putting on sauce, as people used to do, the order has now been reversed. Yet it's the same ancient ritual, which we unwittingly perform every time we greet a steaming bowl of pasta by reaching for the cheese.

2
Amatriciana

Now let's picture a situation almost all Italians have found themselves in at some point. One that's fun, but also – might as well admit it! – fraught with risks: throwing together a spaghetti dinner for a dozen friends.

What's the first dish that comes to mind, one that everybody's sure to like?

No question about it: I think the perfect choice is an amatriciana.

Not as ho-hum as plain tomato sauce, more nourishing than garlic and olive oil, easier to get right than a carbonara and much, much faster than any meat sauce or pesto (unless one resorts to opening a jar).

Just four ingredients: guanciale, tomatoes, chilli and pecorino.

Of course, the old rule applies that the fewer ingredients a recipe has, the more carefully they must be chosen. A well-aged guanciale, from free-range pigs if at all possible, will ensure stunning flavour; as for the pecorino (black rind, please), your best bet is to seek out an artisanal one

37

from Lazio. There aren't many farmers who make it, but good cheese is worth some detective work.

Next, the method.

The guanciale should be cut into fairly thick slices, then into little strips, and sautéd over low heat in a cast-iron skillet. When it has a golden crust, but is still soft, remove some of the fat that has melted off, but not too much – it will help flavour the pasta. As for the guanciale, take it out and keep it warm. The tomatoes (make sure they're firm and fleshy) should be blanched for a couple of seconds in boiling water, skinned, seeded and chopped; throw them into the same pan as the fat from the guanciale, along with a piece of chilli pepper, preferably fresh. Turn up the heat and when the tomatoes begin to soften, put the guanciale back in. After just a few minutes, the sauce is ready. Add al dente spaghetti or mezze maniche and toss it all in the pan for a moment with a generous handful of grated pecorino romano. The fresh tomatoes can be replaced with tinned plum tomatoes, or with very high-quality passata (strained, uncooked purée), but of course it's not the same thing. One tip, though: adding a few spoonfuls of passata to the fresh tomatoes will help you achieve the perfect consistency. For half a kilo of tomatoes I use about 200g of guanciale, but the proportions are variable, and everything else is a matter of taste.

So far, so good, and this all seems agreeable and uncontroversial enough. But what I've ventured into here is not a recipe, it's a war zone. Need proof? Let's go back a few years.

To most of you, 7 February 2015 is not a date that means much. You certainly won't remember where you were or what you were doing. Yet that day will go down in history for one of the most tragic (or comic, depending on how you look at it) episodes in Italian food culture: when celebrity chef Carlo Cracco, appearing on the programme *C'è posta per te*, publicly stated that an unpeeled clove of garlic – sautéd with everything else and then removed before serving – is an ingredient that can go into amatriciana.

Now, this was not any old chef: it was Carlo Cracco, who trained under Gualtiero Marchesi, Alain Ducasse and Alain Senderens – to name just three giants – who has been awarded multiple Michelin stars, and who was a famously harsh judge on the country's most popular cook-off show.

A crime so heinous could not be ignored.

The blowback was swift. The first reaction came from the official website of the municipal government of Amatrice, no less, which struggled to control its emotions.

> We should point out that the only ingredients in a true amatriciana sauce are guanciale, pecorino, white wine, San Marzano tomatoes, black pepper and chilli pepper.
>
> To ensure the authenticity of the recipe, we would like to remind everyone that Amatrice has established a DE.CO [denominazione comunale d'origine] mark, and that this municipal designation of origin was granted just a few weeks ago to the first local products, including guanciale Amatriciano and pecorino di Amatrice.

We are sure that this was just a slip-up on the part of the eminent chef, given his professional background and also his willingness to joke around a bit, even advertising a well-known brand of crisps.

Again, we are certain that this famous chef meant well, and know he is free to use garlic in any sauce he prepares. We are even more certain such a sauce may be good, but it cannot be called Amatriciana.

The City of Amatrice would be delighted to have Chef Carlo Cracco as its guest, if he would like to visit the place where the world's most famous pasta dish got its start.[1]

Let's analyse this post. The municipal council of Amatrice starts off by setting everyone straight about the ingredients in the 'true' recipe, which is even safeguarded by an official certification (the DE.CO mark). Only then do they seem to hold out an olive branch to the chef who has sullied the name of amatriciana (perhaps it was just a 'slip-up'), although they also throw in a little barb about his willingness to endorse 'a well-known brand of crisps', as if to say: don't mix the sacred with the profane. But the strongest message – and also the most interesting, since it is a recurrent weapon in this kind of dispute – is the final one: if Cracco puts garlic in his sauce, he can't call it 'amatriciana'.

The news travels around the world.

It even gets a write-up in the *Guardian*, under the headline: 'Italian birthplace of amatriciana denounces chef's "secret ingredient": Town of Amatrice, where pasta dish originates, accuses Carlo Cracco of lapse in judgement for adding sautéed garlic to recipe'.[2]

The scandal, which is now international in scope, forces the president of the Region of Lazio, Nicola Zingaretti, to try to calm the waters with a Facebook post – but not even he can resist taking a potshot at the chef: 'Garlic in amatriciana, never. And no onion either, whatever some may say.'[3]

At this point, on his own Facebook page, the mayor of Amatrice, Sergio Pirozzi, thanks Zingaretti for supporting their 'battles' for the true amatriciana: 'I just got a phone call from President Zingaretti expressing his sympathy with our battles to protect our famous recipe, a traditional product of the Region of Lazio.'[4]

As if sparking an international crisis weren't enough, Cracco refuses to give in, and a few days later restates his point of view: 'I might use it, what's wrong with that? [. . .] Regional Italian cuisine is so complex . . . It's not about following a recipe to the letter, you have to make it a living thing, interpret it as you like. And in this case I happened to like garlic.'[5]

There's something surreal about this whole exchange, as if putting an extra ingredient into a recipe were something that could undermine the very existence of a traditional dish and shake regional and municipal institutions to their core.

But at the end of the day, there's a question left on the battlefield that no one has really tried to answer: who is right? The locals, or rather, the local authorities of the town that the recipe is from, or the famous chef who offered his own unorthodox version? This is the eternal dilemma affecting almost all recipes considered corner-stones of Italian cuisine, from carbonara to aubergine parmigiana: is there any group of people, large or small, who can rightfully claim to possess the 'true' recipe for a traditional dish? What variations, and how many, can be introduced without misrepresenting a speciality?

Before trying to answer that, as always, let's look at the history.

The birth of *amatriciana*: history and legend

As with most traditional recipes, the circumstances sur-rounding the invention of amatriciana are shrouded in mystery. According to legend – at least the one that turns up in the regulations for producing 'traditional Amatriciana' published in the *Official Journal of the European Union* – it grew out of the rural world of Central Italy and the food used during the long periods of transhumance, when livestock was moved to higher pas-tures in summer and lower ones in winter. Supposedly:

> shepherds [. . .] took with them some foodstuffs which could be easily kept for long periods, such as cured pork jowl and flour. With these simple ingredients the shepherds were able to cook in a long-handled pan their frugal but hearty pasta dish. The people of Amatrice, by recreating and enrich-ing this very basic rural dish, particularly with the addition of tomatoes in the early 19th century, gave

life to one of the most popular dishes of the Italian tradition.[6]

Needless to say, this story is not backed up by historical sources, and as reconstructions go it is more than a little naive. The idea of eighteenth-century herders packing pork jowl and flour for transhumance may be plausible, but only modern-day campers would picture them using these things to make pasta.

To start with, the very notion of pastasciutta was not particularly widespread in the eighteenth century. But even when it was prepared, it was not something people of every class could afford, and above all, it was not topped with much more than butter and cheese.[7] The diet of peasants and shepherds in the eighteenth and early nineteenth century was primarily based on soups, where pasta might be an ingredient, but always cooked in broth.

In general, this story is used to establish the presence of the basic ingredients of amatriciana – though actually just the pork jowl – in the area around Amatrice prior to the spread of tomato sauces. This is a cautious move prompted by the fact that the culinary adoption of the New World fruit is well documented, so anyone with even a smattering of food history can date all 'red' (tomato-based) sauces to some point after the turn of the nineteenth century.[8] So according to this reconstruction, amatriciana supposedly derives from a drier sauce – almost a gricia, that is, just guanciale and pecorino – to which the people of Amatrice later added tomatoes, creating the dish we all know and love.

But actually, tomatoless sauces with just pancetta, guanciale or lardo – like the 'Pasta condita col lardo rosso'[9] or the 'Spaghetti al guanciale'[10] that we find in the cookbooks by Giulia Lazzari-Turco and Ada Boni – show up only much later, around the middle of the twentieth century. One might therefore imagine people topping pasta with grated cheese, but replacing the normal butter with pork fat; this would be the only example of such a thing happening, however, and there is no historical record of it.*

Instead, it seems more likely that what really paved the way to amatriciana was a recipe similar to the 'Vermicielli co le pommadore'[11] described by the Neapolitan writer Ippolito Cavalcanti in 1837. Here we find only three ingredients: tomatoes, lard (or oil) and garlic. It's a simple, very modern sauce that leaves out additional liquids like broth or gravies from stewed meat, and limits its animal-based components to pork fat. But around the same time that Ippolito Cavalcanti was writing down his recipes, Italians also began to flavour their sauces with small pieces of meat. This was a true breakthrough, which would yield many of the pasta dishes we still enjoy today.[12]

It was probably thanks to this new climate, which accepted and actually encouraged experimentation with pasta sauces, that the first recipe for amatriciana was conceived.

---

* The widespread use of lard as a cooking fat might have led some people to put it on pasta along with cheese as a substitute for butter. But this is a practice that fails to turn up in any cookbook of the time, so it remains a conjecture, or at any rate an idea that calls for further investigation.

Wherever it got its start, we know that amatriciana began to grow truly famous only after it arrived in Rome, where it became popular with the working-class clientele of the city's inns and taverns. Perhaps with the help of cooks from Amatrice, who were building a reputation for themselves in the local culinary world.

An early sign of the dish's migration turns up in a booklet from the mid-nineteenth century that records a few curious details about Roman *osterie*. One of them, located at 22 Via della Pilotta, is of particular interest: '*Osteria della Matriciana* – It got this name because it was always run by a woman from Matrice, in the Kingdom of Naples.'[13] Of course there's no way to know just how many women from Amatrice were managing Roman eateries at the time. This note seems to suggest that her presence was more an exception than the rule. But it could be that their number or prestige grew over the years. This seems to be hinted at, around the turn of the century, by the valuable account of an eyewitness with excellent credentials, though he was only twelve at the time: Luigi Carnacina, who grew up to be one of the most famous cooks and gourmets of the twentieth century. He got his start in Rome, first as an innkeeper's boy in 1900, then by working his way up at the finest restaurants of Europe and America; just twenty years later, the great Auguste Escoffier tapped him to head his Restaurant de l'Ocean in Ostend. In 1960, reminiscing about his youth, he tells of an early encounter with 'spaghetti all'amatriciana [. . .] one of the first dishes to spark my enthusiasm.

> 'The osteria drew carriage drivers, hotel workers [. . .]
> and, above all, the carters who delivered wine from the
> Castelli Romani villages just outside the city. These
> were robust men with robust tastes, and after unloading
> their goods, they would visit all the inns in Rome, where
> they invariably ordered the same meal: a pound of spa-
> ghetti alla Matriciana (which cost 12 baiocchi)* and a
> litre of wine (4 to 8 baiocchi, depending on quality).
> I remember their arguments about which innkeeper
> made the best spaghetti alla Matriciana, and above all
> who made it the right way, according to the specific
> regional standards. Our cook, a little man of about
> sixty, born and bred in Amatrice, made it just right.'[14]

Not only was amatriciana well known at the time, at least in Rome, but there were already debates about who kept to 'regional standards', and Amatricians were already seen as having a certain authority in the matter.

Though Carnacina's memoirs could easily be coloured by the kind of nostalgia that mythologises the past, there is at least one other account pointing to the role and reputation of Roman transplants from Amatrice. It turns up an article from 1903, in the monthly supplement to *Corriere della Sera*, which describes the tradespeople of the capital and tells us that the 'salumeria clerks are from Amatrice and Norcia'.[15] It was no small achievement to be named

---

* In that place and time, a pound was about 340g, and 12 baiocchi were about 50 pence in today's currency.

in the same breath as the natives of Norcia, so famous for their cured meats that pork butchers came to be known as 'norcini'. Amatricians must also have become experts in the field, perhaps owing in part to their connections back home, since the region produced outstanding salumi for Roman shops. This automatic association of people from Amatrice with pork products might explain why the key ingredient in amatriciana is guanciale.

Workers, herders and brigands

The article in the *Corriere* supplement – which was rather evocatively titled 'The Bowels of Rome' – is important for another reason. It contains one of the first recorded references to 'spaghetti all'amatriciana' under this name, in a list of characteristic turn-of-the-century Roman dishes:

> The working class [. . .] mainly eats pasta and vegetables. The dishes most frequently prepared by the city's 725 taverns that serve food are gnocchi, tripe, rice supplì, beans with pork rind or beans in sauce, salt cod, rolls filled with porchetta, roast lamb, spaghetti 'at any hour' and, as a speciality, spaghetti 'all'amatriciana'. If one also adds rigatoni with olive oil; fried artichokes 'alla giudia', Jewish style; crostini made with provatura cheese; beignets; and vast amounts of broccoli and fennel, there you have it: the classic menu of Roman cuisine, which is based on lard.[16]

Amatriciana is listed as a speciality, but a speciality of modest establishments. An occasional treat for the working-class people of Rome.

This window on to popular cuisine offers a glimpse of some dishes that are still very famous and others that are now only vaguely remembered. You may notice that the list leaves out the two other cornerstones of modern Roman cuisine, carbonara and gricia. For a simple reason: they didn't exist yet.

If amatriciana fails to show up in any of the three most important cookbooks of regional Italian cuisine published between 1908 and 1910 (the anonymously authored *100 specialità di cucina italiane ed estere*, Vittorio Agnetti's *La nuova cucina delle specialità regionali* and Alberto Cougnet's *L'arte cucinaria in Italia*),[17] the reason is probably different: the dish may have still been considered too plebeian. The only Roman pasta specialities in those three books are either baked ('gnocchi'[18] and 'pasticcio di maccheroni'[19]) or in broth ('gnocchi in brodo'[20]), and there are no recipes for pastasciutta.

The lower-class associations of amatriciana are also confirmed by another source, a most unusual one. It is a book, published in Florence in 1911, that profiles Italy's most famous bandits, depicting them as ruthless but courageous adventurers – solitary rebels against the laws of God and man. The title is *Briganti celebri italiani* ('Famous Italian Brigands') and the author is Eugenio Rontini. One chapter towards the end describes the deeds of Domenico Tiburzi, 'king of the outlaws', who had chosen the area between Lazio and the Maremma as his raiding ground. On the evening of 23 October 1896, he was in the vicinity of Orbetello, lodging with a family of goatherds who shared their dinner with his band.

> Sitting around the fire, after eating spaghetti alla matriciana (seasoned only with pepper and pecorino cheese), after drinking ten litres of wine, as a violent wind raged outside and the rain crashed down, the brigands lit their Toscano cigars and played the role of villainous heroes in the conversation with the shepherds and their wives.[21]

Surprising, right?

The two main elements, guanciale and tomatoes, are obviously missing, but Rontini nonetheless seems confident about what the dish should be called. This little 'linguistic incident' allows two hypotheses: the author might of course be only vaguely familiar with the Roman speciality; but it is just as possible that the term 'matriciana' still had a fluid meaning, a more flexible one, that eludes us today – perhaps a cacio e pepe with some form of pork fat as a base? The mystery remains unsolved.

All of these doubts about the canonical ingredients can only be cleared up when the first recipes appear.

The House of Savoy, America and Rome

Pellegrino Artusi and other culinary authorities of the time say nothing about amatriciana (even though, as we have seen, it was already a well-known dish in Rome). To find the first written recipe we must move up the peninsula, all the way to Turin, and peek into the royal kitchens of the House of Savoy. They were run at the time by Amedeo Pettini, unquestionably the most important chef in the whole country, a luminary of fine cuisine. His position in the royal household had obviously made him a leading name in the food world, to the point that even some famous companies like Knorr, or the olive oil producer Carli, tried to exploit his image to peddle their products (just like those celebrity chefs of today who appear in adverts for crisps, spaghetti or hamburgers).

Aside from the Carli cookbooks that he began to edit in 1935, his most famous work remains the *Manuale di cucina e di Pasticceria*, published in 1914, which is the first to give a recipe for amatriciana:

> *Spaghetti all'amatriciana*
>
> Cut a nice piece of ventresca into small pieces, sauté it for a few minutes, and add some good tomato sauce, diluting with broth. Cook your spaghetti and toss it with this sauce and grated cheese.[22]

However brief the description, there can be no doubt this time that the dish is the classic amatriciana we all know. One detail is striking, however: it contains no guanciale, but rather (surprise!) ventresca – pork belly, or in other words, pancetta.*

---

* The choice of pancetta must also be due to the rarity of guanciale in northern Italy. Another curious deviation from the recipe we are used to is the dilution of the tomato sauce with broth: a holdover from nineteenth-century cooking that was imitated by almost no later authors.

In just a few years amatriciana achieved dazzling success, becoming a symbol of Roman popular cuisine in Italy and abroad. Like fettuccine Alfredo and carbonara after it, in the early 1920s amatriciana began to appear – timidly, at first – in American cookbooks as well.

As early as 1921 we find an article in *Outing*, an American magazine about outdoor recreation, that includes various recipes for Italian 'pastes'. Sandwiched between tales of moose-hunting and a plug for the latest rifle model is 'Camping and Cooking in Italy: How You Can Be Your Own Italian Chef on Your Next Trip into the Woods',[23] the story of Mr Augusto Frank's expedition in the Apennines near Terni.

The ingredients it lists for 'Pasta all'amatriciana' are a generic 'salt pork', cheese (advising readers to look for pecorino in Italian American groceries, and even listing a few addresses in New York), tomatoes – fresh or tinned – and an onion. The recipe calls for browning the diced meat with the onion, adding the chopped tomatoes, letting it simmer until cooked, and topping pasta with the sauce along with plenty of pecorino.

This recipe is significant not only because it documents the dish's arrival in America, but because it is the first to describe the guanciale being chopped and fried with the onion that is now considered outrageous. One shouldn't take this for some American whim, however; onions, as we are about to see, turn up in many, many Italian recipes for this sauce up to the 1960s.

Let's head back to Italy. The recipe truly took off in 1927, gaining official recognition as a distinctive Roman speciality when 'Spaghetti all'amatriciana' was included in *Il talismano della felicità*. This cookbook by Ada Boni (a food expert, born into an upper-middle-class family in Rome, who will be frequently mentioned here), was a wildly successful bestseller – comparable only to Artusi's – and gave what was perhaps the biggest boost to the spread of the dish.

> Spaghetti alla amatriciana, though named after
> a provincial town, is a classic of Roman cuisine,
> and a sought-after speciality in many of the city's
> taverns and trattorias. It couldn't be simpler. For a
> kilogram of spaghetti, chop an onion along with a
> hectogram of guanciale and put this mixture into
> a frying pan with a spoonful of lard. When the
> guanciale and onion are sautéd but not brown, add a
> kilo of peeled, seeded and chopped tomatoes. Season
> with salt and pepper – not too much of the former,
> since the guanciale is quite salty – and continue to
> cook over high heat for several minutes, until the
> tomatoes are soft but not a pulp. Meanwhile cook
> the spaghetti, and as soon as it is done, toss it with
> the sauce and 100 grams of grated pecorino romano.
> The traditional recipe calls for pecorino. But if
> you do not like the sharp flavour, you may use half
> pecorino and half parmesan, or all parmesan. Black

pepper should be the most prominent note in this
spaghetti dish.[24]

As you can see, Ada Boni also calls for guanciale and
onion to be chopped together, then browned in a spoonful of lard. If we look at the proportions, chopped fresh
tomatoes are the main ingredient, a full kilo as opposed
to just 100g of guanciale – which is thus only there to flavour the pan, along with the lard and onion.

Even today the relative proportions of the ingredients
vary enormously, but the ratio of guanciale to tomatoes
suggested by Ada Boni in *Il talismano della felicità* is
definitely the lowest ever. By 1934, just a few years later,
the situation had been reversed, and we find almost equal
amounts of the two ingredients – more specifically, 450g
of guanciale for half a kilo of fresh tomatoes – which
even today remains the all-time high.[25] But overall, the
average amount of guanciale tended to increase over the
years. Up to the 1960s it was around 250g for every kilo
of fresh tomatoes, and in the thirty years that followed
it grew by about 100g, to more than 350g per kilo of
tomatoes.

The true recipe for amatriciana

To trace the evolution of amatriciana, I have compared
twenty-five Italian recipes from the first fifty years of the
recipe's existence, 1914 to 1964.

The picture that emerges is an eclectic one.

For instance, it was perfectly acceptable to use pancetta

in place of guanciale: in fact, the recipes are almost split down the middle in terms of their preference for one or the other. Although one should also note that if we look at the explanations in some old cookbooks, almost no distinction is made between the two: 'What is called guanciale in Rome is known in northern Italy as "pancetta", the best, leanest, softest cut of fatty pork';[26] or even 'pancetta (which in Rome is called guanciale)'.[27] As if jowl and belly could be synonyms!

Luckily, other authors tend to specify that the two meats are different, providing explanations such as 'guanciale (barbaglia, pork cheek)',[28] or 'in Abruzzo "guanciale" is preferred, but you can make do with an ordinary lean pancetta'.[29] In any case, for a long time pancetta was thought of not just as a perfectly good substitute for guanciale, but as part of the canonical recipe from the get-go. Here and there we even find variations on these two ingredients, including, surprisingly, the 'capocollo' suggested by French chef Henri-Paul Pellaprat in 1937.[30]

Nor can all authors agree on how the meat should be cut: though most use a dice and some prefer strips – which would become the norm only in the 1990s – a minority continue to chop it finely even in the 1960s.

As for the tomatoes, the overwhelming preference is for fresh ones – peeled and seeded – rather than tinned plum tomatoes or purée, which are often permitted, but only as a fallback.

Likewise, there is a near unanimous tendency to choose pecorino over parmesan, which is sometimes mentioned as a possible substitute, or, more rarely, mixed in with the pecorino to mitigate the latter's sharpness.

One even sees a clear shift between black pepper and chilli pepper: in the first fifty years there is a general preference for the former – in about three times as many recipes, in the sample I analysed – whereas after the 1960s there is a sudden switch, with chilli pepper taking over.

〰〰〰〰〰〰〰〰〰〰

Onions and garlic are ingredients that deserve special attention (remember the Cracco scandal?). Nowadays, as we saw at the start of the chapter, they are seen as completely foreign to the 'original' recipe. And yet, however shocking some people may find this, they were part of almost every recorded recipe for amatriciana from the outset.

Let's take a look at the numbers.

Among the twenty-five cases analysed, only four fail to include any onion, and one considers it optional.[31]

Out of these, the first is 'vegan' long before the term existed, a purely 'vegetable sauce of celery, carrots, tomatoes, parsley, etc.';[32] then comes a rather surprising variant that adds beaten eggs to the tomatoes (a sort of crossover with carbonara);[33] while the third describes 'A simple version of spaghetti all'amatriciana',[34] that is, a much faster one, with no sautéing, and tinned tomatoes rather than fresh. The only onionless recipe at all similar to the 'canonical' one is actually the version described by Amedeo Pettini in 1914. And what's more, out of these twenty-five recipes, no fewer than twelve add garlic to the sauté, sometimes whole and sometimes chopped along with the onion.

Based on this data one can go so far as to say, without a shred of doubt, that in the first half-century of the recipe's history, onions came just after tomatoes as the most consistent ingredient. They appear even more frequently than pecorino and guanciale, which were more often replaced by parmesan and pancetta. So although a strange hostility has led to their definitive ousting in recent years, onions were right at home in the historical recipe for amatriciana.

Their disappearance is part of a broader, more complex trend. In the 1950s and 60s a growing movement took shape among lovers of Roman and other regional cuisines, devoted to preserving and protecting Italian culinary traditions; and thus the quest (or battle) for the 'true' recipe began.

The battle lines are drawn

This change of climate first became perceptible in 1959, when a heated debate took place in the pages of the magazine *Il gastronomo*. On one side was its editor-in-chief, Luigi Veronelli, a key figure on the Italian culinary scene of the day. Profoundly knowledgeable about the entire world of food, from the field to the table, he was a journalist, editor and essayist whose life's mission was to codify and champion Italy's culinary heritage.[35] On the other was Felice Cunsolo, who had written the cookbook *Gli italiani a tavola* (Italians at the Table).[36] Veronelli launched a direct attack on the author in an open letter, accusing his recipes of containing 'hordes' of mistakes:

[. . .] and so, riffling through its pages, we come across hordes, flocks, myriads of colossal errors and strange horrors – from the gastronomic standpoint, of course. Care for a few examples? [. . .] this recipe for spaghetti all'amatriciana, what is it saying? A full kilo of tomatoes? But in amatriciana the tomatoes serve at most to give a little colour, and are optional. One onion? You must be joking, at most a quarter of an onion, and even that can be left out. Pancetta? Of course not. Lard? Of course not. On the other hand, after such a lavish use of ingredients that have no place here, we're missing the only two that are the hallmarks of the dish: guanciale (part of the jowl) and chilli pepper.[37]

These scathing words were being levelled at a recipe for amatriciana that was, in point of fact, quite similar to the ones that had circulated in magazines and cookbooks up to the late 1940s. The only difference is that in the meantime, the world of food criticism had changed.

After giving Cunsolo an earful, Veronelli wanted to set the record straight, with his own recipe for the 'true' amatriciana:

Would you like the true recipe for spaghetti all'amatriciana? Here you are, no more and no less. Ingredients: 600 grams of spaghetti – 150 grams of very lean guanciale cut into fairly large pieces – two spoonfuls of oil – ¼ onion, finely chopped (optional) – 1 clove of garlic, crushed (optional) – the flesh of a few tomatoes, free of juice and cut into small pieces – a piece of chilli pepper – 100 grams of pecorino.

Put the guanciale in a pan with the oil; brown it over high heat, drain, keep warm. Using the same oil, sauté the onion, garlic and chilli pepper. When the onion and garlic are golden, add the tomatoes; season with a little salt. Stir, and after 8–10 minutes the sauce will be ready – add the crisp guanciale. While the tomatoes are cooking, drop the spaghetti into a potful of lightly salted boiling water; drain while still al dente, transfer to a fairly large serving bowl, top with sauce and grated pecorino. Mix and serve.[38]

Cunsolo attempted to defend himself, citing his sources, the research he had done: 'I can prove to you that my recipe is traditional. See the authoritative *Guida gastronomica d'Italia* from the T.C.I. [Touring Club Italiano] and the much-admired books *Il cucchiaio d'argento* and *Il talismano della felicità*, the first as regards ingredients, the other two as regards the method of preparation.'[39]

Unfortunately for Cunsolo, Luigi Veronelli was not prepared to give an inch and instead doubled down, even denying the authoritative nature of those works (which, objectively, are pillars of Italian culinary culture).

You are citing three books, dear Cunsolo, whose authority I no way acknowledge; the first is excellent for tourists, the other two are fine for housewives, but none of them will do for the experts you yourself meant to address. Still, if you read more closely, you will see – what a surprise – that all three explicitly mention guanciale, and one, as if that weren't enough, also mentions chilli pepper. So this really won't do. Bluffing is for the poker table. Try harder, dear Cunsolo, try to challenge the substance of my recipe for spaghetti all'amatriciana, without fear of abusing your right of reply. The effort will help you see how, as in every exact science, there is only one correct culinary precept to follow here. If nothing else, it will help you prepare the second edition (if your book makes it that far).[40]

This vitriol was capped off by a peremptory note from Luigi Carnacina, who described how amatriciana was made in Rome at the turn of the century: 'a few small tomatoes, peeled and chopped, a small piece of finely chopped onion (optional), none of the garlic that people toss in everywhere nowadays, a piece of chilli pepper, pecorino cheese, and, as the primary, hallmark ingredient, guanciale, very lean and cut in a large dice'.[41] His input concludes with a phrase that by now has become almost the rallying cry for defending traditional recipes: 'Nowadays people tend to be creative; no harm done, if they would only refrain from using the original names.' Remember the municipal council of Amatrice and its response to Cracco's amatriciana with garlic? 'We are [. . .] certain such a sauce may be good, but it cannot be called Amatriciana.'

A cooked-up tradition

As we saw earlier, Italian food critics – with Luigi Veronelli in the lead – were trying to lay the groundwork for the recognition and protection of the country's food and wine specialities. Their task was quite complex, especially in a patchwork context like Italy, where dishes tend to change names, ingredients and cooking methods if you move just a few kilometres away, and where even in a recipe's birthplace, different traditions may peacefully coexist, constantly overlapping and influencing each other.

Mid-century gourmets found themselves faced with the difficult task of reconstructing the ideal recipe for each dish, with some possible intersection between the different currents of Italian cuisine. Otherwise there would be only personal opinions, family preferences or neighbourhood customs, forming a dust cloud of recipes impossible to catalogue. When Veronelli says 'there is only one correct culinary precept' he means there can be only one recipe for every speciality; everything else is a deviation, or at best a variation on the theme, with nothing 'authentic' about it.

These were the years that marked the rebirth of the food sector, the relaunch of tourism and the rise of Italian products, driven by the industrial boom. There was a very real risk that Italy would forever lose the traditions of a rural world that was rapidly crumbling, and the urgent need to preserve them inspired a take-no-prisoners approach. Experts and institutions sprang into action. Associations were created like the Accademia Italiana della Cucina, set up in Milan in 1953, or the Accademia Gastronomica Italiana, founded in Bologna in 1957 on the idea 'that a wine, an andouille, a raviolo are symbols of a food culture that must be preserved, through the symbols and sacred rites of the table'.[42]

Given this context, it becomes easier to understand how the mission of bringing order to the motley universe of food took on the dogmatic traits we have seen, elevating one version of a dish over all possible variants, even when they were just as traditional. As a corollary, this meant repudiating all previous cookbooks, no matter how authoritative, that deviated from the new gospel, and rejecting every historical study that highlighted the complexity of culinary specialities.

But history could not be completely ignored, since only a recipe's antiquity could furnish definitive proof that it alone was the original one. Stories about the invention of dishes soon became an alibi, however. It didn't matter whether they were grounded in historical fact; actually, unassailable.

The aim was purely ideological, a true 'invention of tradition', to borrow Eric Hobsbawm's term,[43] that overlooks, or rather, is forced to overlook the variability of recipes so that it can confidently state 'this is the way it's always been done'. The search for the 'true' tradition thus went hand in hand with the concoction of legends about the origins of regional specialities, while avoiding the kind of serious historical inquiry that would have proved fatal.

Yet the existence of different versions of the same dish is deeply inscribed in many recipes, especially those that can boast a long history, and amatriciana is no exception.

Actually, given its popularity, it was to be expected that sooner or later it would inspire artistic minds. In the 1970s, for instance, although the attitude towards more creative interpretations was growing rigid, some truly surprising recipes appeared. An example comes from the brilliant pen of the famous actor and comic Aldo Fabrizi, born and bred in working-class Rome, who dedicated an entire book of sonnets in Roman dialect to pasta. One of them, of course, describes his own priceless, unconventional version of amatriciana.

My Matriciana

Fry up in a seasoned skillet
onion, garlic, chilli pepper
fifty grams of smoked guanciale
fifty more of rolled pancetta.
When you've crisped up all that meat,
splash on fragrant vinegar,
let it burn off on high heat,
add some dense paste from a jar.
Then a stock cube to give savour,
fresh tomatoes (San Marzano),
basil leaves for extra flavour.
Once it's bubbling good and steady,
grab some parm and pecorino,
pop it all on your spaghetti.[44]

To recap, his ingredients are: onion, oil, chilli pepper, smoked guanciale, rolled pancetta, vinegar, tomato paste, stock cube, fresh tomatoes, basil, pecorino and parmesan cheese. Yet it seems Aldo Fabrizi could roam through the streets of Trastevere without armed bodyguards. If he'd posted it on social media today, I'm not sure that would still be true.

The suppression of the onion

In Luigi Veronelli and Luigi Carnacina's view there could be no doubt. The ingredients of the one true amatriciana are: chunks of guanciale, olive oil, chopped onion (optional), crushed garlic (optional), chopped fresh tomatoes, chilli pepper, and to top it off, a dusting of pecorino. All other recipes, even if they had made it through two world wars, were to be scorned, as good enough for housewives and tourists but unworthy of the name 'amatriciana'.

Another half-century has gone by since the two Luigis presented this recipe, and as a result, their 'true' amatriciana no longer rings so true. What has not changed, on the other hand, is the hardline stance that inspired it. If anything, it has grown harder over the years, as Italian cuisine has definitively shaken off French influence, acquiring fame and markets that were unimaginable just a few decades ago.

Today, the push to preserve such recipes has been exacerbated by another tool. The protection and promotion of food and wine heritage have become watchwords not only for Italy, but for all of Europe, as one can see from the creation of protected geographical indications (PGI), protected designations of origin (PDO) and traditional specialities guaranteed (TSG).

With this institutional turn, the need to choose a single recipe within the broader culinary landscape is no longer just an ideological choice, but an obligation imposed by laws and regulations; such protectionism sometimes risks creating huge distortions in the sphere of food, from the way ingredients are produced to the way traditional dishes are prepared.[45]

Amatriciana has met the same fate as many other specialities: pared down to its bare basics, to minimise the variables that would otherwise inevitably become points of conflict. Reduced to the lowest common denominator of all possible recipes, it was thus pruned of non-essentials, starting with onions and garlic – which, again, had always been permitted as ingredients.

If we look at more recent cookbooks, a majority of versions up to the 1990s still contained some chopped onion, but it was no longer as ubiquitous as it had been in the first half-century of the recipe's existence. Some authors began to consider it optional, while others left it out altogether. It definitively disappeared at the turn of the millennium and now almost no trace is left, except as something to be harshly criticised – like cream in carbonara, that other great outcast (which we will look at in the next chapter).

The reduction of ingredients to tomatoes, guanciale, chilli pepper and pecorino is thus a result both of the City of Amatrice's institutional and media campaign, and of the dish's admission to the Italian register of traditional food products (PAT) in 2005.[46] This was followed by the publication of production specifications for 'Salsa all'Amatriciana' in 2015, and finally by its registration as a TSG by the European Union on 6 March 2020.[47]

As a result, the 'true' amatriciana of today is no longer the 'true' amatriciana of the 1960s, nor the 'true' amatriciana of the early twentieth century. Instead, it is the outcome of a culinary (and political) evolution that has taken over a hundred years. Or perhaps, rather than evolution, one should call it a process of 'selection', just as when humans intervene to accentuate certain traits in plants and animals and breed out others.

It remains to be seen whether the selection of amatriciana has really reached its peak – which is difficult to imagine – or whether it will continue, with ingredients and methods different from the ones we know today. To be honest, I hope so, because a cuisine that stands still, sacrificing creativity in the name of some mythical, ahistorical 'tradition', is doomed to disappear.[48]

3

CARBONARA [1]

Now let's talk about a true flagship of Italian cuisine, one of the world's best-known and best-loved pasta dishes, and at the same time, one of the most hotly debated: carbonara.

Browsing the web, you'll run across many cooking sites offering the 'original' recipe for carbonara. They flood you with hundreds of tips, but almost all focus on the three ingredients considered canonical: eggs, guanciale and pecorino, plus an abundant sprinkling of pepper.

Many also seem to enjoy narrowing the field even further. The guanciale has to be from Amatrice (because carbonara and amatriciana, as we know, are kissing cousins); the pecorino has to be black rind pecorino romano; the eggs have to be one per person (some use them whole, others just the yolk) plus one 'for the bowl'; pepper is something everyone can agree on, but it has to be ground on the spot. Cooks, food bloggers and ordinary pasta lovers, united by a single recipe, speak with one voice in defence of tradition.

The origin myth is pretty much the same as for amatriciana: a few wholesome, filling, tasty ingredients that the legendary shepherds and charcoal burners (*carbonai*) of the Central Apennines would stuff in their packs before setting off at dawn to go tend their herds or their kilns.

A few vague doubts crop up from time to time, however, bringing memories of different recipes.

Some Italians seem to recall that until just a few years ago, many people used pancetta instead of guanciale to make carbonara at home – but that must have been an informal lapse. Others, though few to be sure, will confess: in the 1980s, the recipe also included that infamous ingredient, cream – but in those days cream popped up everywhere, from penne alla vodka to filetto al pepe verde, so once again, that couldn't be considered an 'authentic' carbonara.

In short, to trace the recipe back through time we have to sidestep various 'impostors' to arrive at the 'authentic' version used by those shepherds, and who knows, maybe even those charcoal burners.

A terrible doubt creeps in.

What if there is no original recipe? Or rather, what if no one ever wrote it down?

In that case, Italians will say, it ought to be easy enough to reconstruct. After all, the few animal foods in our ancestors' diet were from the livestock they raised at home: cured pork from the pig, cheese from the sheep and eggs fresh from the coop. And spaghetti? Well, that was always around, we're talking about Italy. The ingredients were all there, they just had to be put together, simple as that.

With carbonara, as with the other dishes described here, history and legend intertwine and their boundaries become blurred. There are no old written records to cite, so some people swear that their great-grandmother was already making carbonara in the early 1900s. Others have heard that it's named after the Carbonari: back in the nineteenth century, Roman members of this secret revolutionary society would request the dish as their last meal before the infamous executioner Mastro Titta deprived them of their heads.

But maybe there's a different story behind carbonara. And maybe it tells us more about our new globalised world than the peasant one of legend, however hard it may be to dispense with the bits of myth that embellish this unique and special recipe.

'Listen, do you know how to make carbonara?'

'You've got to come over to dinner, I've made a carbonara that's to die for: garlic, pancetta, Gruyère and eggs scrambled in the pan with the spaghetti, just like the original recipe.' If that's the preamble to the carbonara you're about to eat, then your friend is a sadist – or a food historian, which may be worse.

But let's not get ahead of ourselves. Shocking as it may seem, even carbonara, in its brief history, has gone through major changes to arrive at the current version, made with just guanciale, pecorino and creamy, unscrambled eggs. As always, older recipes offer a very different and sometimes surprising picture of how much the ingredients used to vary.

The invention of carbonara is a widely debated topic, and the absence of any written record of the dish in the first half of the twentieth century makes it even more contentious. In any case, there seem to be no reliable sources pointing to its existence until the 1950s.

At the very dawn of that decade, on 26 July 1950, the first reference turns up in the Turin-based newspaper *La Stampa*, in an article titled 'Il Papa ha "passato ponte"' ('Pope Pays a Visit "Across the Bridge"'). Describing the Trastevere district of Rome, the journalist mentions a restaurant, Da Cesaretto alla Cisterna, which had apparently built a reputation years before as a place where American officers could find spaghetti alla carbonara.[2]

Another reference from around the same time, also in Rome, appears in a film: *Cameriera bella presenza offresi . . .*, from 1951. It comes from a scene where Aldo Fabrizi – in the role of Giovanni Marchetti, a man trying to hire a housemaid – gives an impromptu job interview on his doorstep to Maria (Elsa Merlini).

Giovanni: Hold on a minute. Listen, do you know how to make carbonara?
[The maid shakes her head.]
Giovanni: What sauces can you make for spaghetti?
Maria: Well, meat sauce, tomato sauce, butter and cheese.

Giovanni: Oh, that's hospital food . . . can you make it with tuna?

Maria: Sure, sure.

Giovanni: With a leaf or two of basil?

Maria: Basil, sure.

Giovanni: Ah . . . and amatriciana? Can you make that?

Maria: Of course.

Giovanni: Careful now: which goes in amatriciana, guanciale or pancetta?

Maria: Aren't those the same thing?

Giovanni: Oh no, they're not the same, because guanciale is this [pointing to his cheek] and pancetta is this [pointing to his belly].

Maria: [laughing] That's too big to call 'pancetta'.

Giovanni: Well, no, pancetta is what you buy, I'm not selling this one, heh. [Clears his throat, embarrassed] I'm losing my voice. Last question: aside from tomatoes, what do you put in amatriciana for flavour, garlic or onion?

Maria: Nothing!

Giovanni: Good! Very last question: the black pepper . . . careful now, do you put it in the sauce or the pasta?

Maria: No black pepper in amatriciana! Just chilli pepper!

Giovanni: Then come in![3]

This scene offers an extraordinary yardstick of how popular certain dishes were at the time. We should note one thing in particular: Maria the maid says she doesn't know how to cook carbonara, yet when it comes to amatriciana her expertise gets her hired on the spot. That's no coincidence. It's proof that while amatriciana had been around since at least 1914, and achieved definitive success with Ada Boni's *Il talismano della felicità* in 1927, carbonara was just getting off the ground.

In the same year we find a reference to carbonara in *Lunga vita di Trilussa*, Mario dell'Arco's biography of a famous Roman dialect poet: 'Our hero almost never attacked a dish of spaghetti "alla carbonara" or "alla carettiera" without the aid of two or three equally gluttonous friends. Epigrams seemed to come to him more easily over a steak (he ate at Dal Bolognese in Piazza del Popolo).'[4]

Current research suggests that these were the first instances in which carbonara sauce was mentioned anywhere. All three are closely linked to Rome: no recipes had yet been printed, but the dish must have been well known by that point in the capital, at least.

The first recipe is American

For some clue of what carbonara was like early on, we have to wait until 1952, when the first recipe was finally published.

The place it turns up is disconcerting, to say the least. It's not in Rome, as one might expect, but rather in the

United States. More specifically, in an illustrated guide to Chicago restaurants, by Patricia Brontë, titled *Vittles and Vice: An Extraordinary Guide to What's Cooking on Chicago's Near North Side*. The book describes various establishments in this neighbourhood, including one, Armando's, that served carbonara.

The author not only gives the recipe, but briefly recounts the family history of one of the owners, Pietro Lencioni.

A few years earlier, he and his business partner had purchased an old house that used to be a gambling den, and after fixing it up, turned it into an elegant gourmet restaurant. So far, nothing particularly strange – aside from finding the first recipe for carbonara on the wrong side of the ocean. But when Brontë talks about Pietro Lencioni's background, a rather odd coincidence comes to light.

Pietro Lencioni's father was originally from Lucca, and here's the real tidbit – his youth in Tuscany had been spent mining coal, *carbone*! He later moved to Iowa, where he had the same job. Unfortunately, all that is said about his son Pietro is that he studied cabinet-making in Florence and then went back to the United States, where he waited tables for over sixteen years before opening his own restaurant with fellow waiter Armando Lorenzini.

It could be a mere coincidence, and in any case it is very hard to link Pietro Lencioni's father's profession to the name of the recipe, given the chronology – the dish had already been around for some time, at least in Rome. (We'll get back to the name later.) Still, since the circumstances surrounding the invention of the dish are such an enigma, one can't wholly rule out a Tuscan origin. And unsolved mysteries aside, the first written recipe for carbonara is unquestionably worth looking at. Here it is:

Pasta carbonara

Boil 1½ pounds of *Tagliarini* (thin wide noodles) according to the directions on the package. Meanwhile, chop and fry half a pound of *Mezzina* (Italian bacon). Drain the noodles and the bacon. Take 4 *eggs* and ¼ pound of *grated Parmesan cheese* and lightly whip together. Mix everything together and toss over a flame. Serves four.[5]

First, let's single out a few linguistic details: 'tagliarini' and 'mezzina' are local terms that definitely suggest an origin in Tuscany or at least Central Italy, where 'mezzina' meant pancetta. Using 'tagliarini', which probably implied egg noodles, is also a rather unusual choice for carbonara.

What is interesting to note for now is that even in this first recipe, the outlines of the dish are already quite clear in the handful of ingredients that are listed (one shouldn't be surprised by the pancetta and parmesan, a pairing that lingers on until the 1960s, as we shall see). The story of carbonara – and this is why it's so fascinating to reconstruct – was thus intercontinental from day one, a factor that would play a pivotal role in its rise to fame.

Chilli pepper, ham, mushrooms and clams

Let's move on to 1954. That year brought a bevy of carbonara sightings, references and recipes, especially abroad. In response to its instant popularity with Americans, the 'News of Food' column in the *New York Times* on 12 July featured the article 'When in Rome You Eat Magnificent Meals in Simple Restaurants'. After reviewing several famous eateries – including Il Fagiano in Piazza Colonna, Il Passetto in Piazza Navona, Alfredo's original restaurant in Via della Scrofa (which we encountered earlier) and his new one in Piazza Augusto Imperatore – it moves on to La Trattoria al Moro:

> 'Spaghetti al Moro,' as a matter of fact, is a variation of the newest fashion in spaghetti sauces – spaghetti alla carbonara. It is not really new, but there is a sort of fad for it now, a sauce whose peculiarity is chopped bacon, not to mention the usual eggs, butter and cheese. For the best spaghetti alla carbonara – or at least as good as you can get – one goes to another Alfredo, the one in that marvelous old square near the Vatican in an ancient part of Rome, Piazza di Santa Maria in Trastevere.[6]

The funny thing is that 'Spaghetti alla Moro' can still be found on the menu of that Roman restaurant, which has never stopped serving it. Even today, this variation on carbonara is made with eggs, smoked bacon, parmesan and chilli pepper. Aside from this last ingredient – which must have been its signature twist on the classic recipe – we're looking at a version that is very close to the carbonara of the 1950s. According to the journalist, the addition of pancetta ('chopped bacon') to the 'usual' sauce of eggs, butter and cheese was a fairly recent, faddish variation on a classic recipe that was already well known, 'cacio e ova'.

That same year, carbonara was included in the cookbook *Italian Food*, published in London and based on extensive research carried out in Italy by Elizabeth David with the help of the Italian tourist bureau. In her acknowledgements, the author even includes a hat tip to Signor Osvaldo from the restaurant Il Buco di Roma, who probably gave her this recipe:

Maccheroni alla Carbonara – Macaroni with Ham and Eggs

A Roman dish, and a welcome change from the customary *pasta* with tomato sauce. It can be made with any shaped *maccheroni*, spaghetti, or noodles. Cook the *pasta* in the usual way, in plenty of boiling salted water. Strain it and put it into a heated dish. Have ready 4 oz. (for four people) of ham, bacon, or *coppa* (Italian bacon) cut into short matchstick lengths, and fried gently in butter. When the *maccheroni* is ready in its dish add to the bacon 2 beaten eggs and stir as you would for scrambled eggs, pouring the whole mixture on to the *maccheroni* at the precise moment when the eggs are beginning to thicken, so that they present a slightly granulated appearance without being as thick as scrambled eggs. Give the whole a good stir with a wooden spoon so that the egg and bacon mixture is

{ evenly distributed, add some grated Parmesan, and
{ serve more Parmesan separately. Sometimes *rigatoni*
{ (short, thick, ribbed macaroni) are used for this dish.[7]

The unique thing about this carbonara is its openness to alternatives in both the type of pasta – macaroni, spaghetti or tagliolini – and the cured meat, allowing three variations that would make today's stricter food purists clutch their pearls: 'ham, bacon, or *coppa* (Italian bacon)'. In short, the height of laxity, and what's more with a clear preference for ham, judging by the recipe title. As you will have noticed, the most surprising thing is that guanciale is not mentioned at all among the options.* (Whereas the choice of parmesan is intentional: in the recipe for amatriciana [see below] she recommends pecorino romano.)

Another excellent demonstration of how elastic the concept of carbonara still was can be found in an unusual version published, that same year, in the American magazine *Harper's Bazaar*. The ingredients? Eggs, parmesan and clams. Can't believe it? Here you go:

{ *Spaghetti alla carbonara*
{
{ While the spaghetti is boiling make a sauce as follows in
{ a double boiler or chafing dish. Combine 1 stick butter,

---

* The last sentence in the recipe currently reads '[. . .] and streaky salt pork rather than ham or bacon', but this was added in a later edition (and still fails to specify guanciale).

> 1 cup chopped clams, the well-beaten yolks of 3 eggs,
> ½ cup grated Parmesan, 1 teaspoon saffron, salt and
> pepper. Stir as sauce thickens and pour over drained
> spaghetti.[8]

Having tried it (oh yes indeed), I have to say the pairing is not as awful as one might think – except the rather incomprehensible decision to chop the clams. Although this is an isolated example, it gives a sense of how much wild experimentation went on with this recipe, even in its first few years of existence.

While it's almost impossible to say where this maverick version of carbonara came from, there's no such doubt about another recipe collected that same year by the Chamberlains, directly in Rome. Samuel Chamberlain was a food critic, and his wife Narcissa a photographer. In March 1954, they embarked on a two-year pilgrimage around Italy in a Peugeot 203, armed with pen, paper and a 5x7 camera, to taste the specialities of every region for a series of articles in the American magazine *Gourmet* (tough job, but somebody had to do it). In addition to the articles, their tour yielded the book *Italian Bouquet*, published in 1958, which describes an interesting visit to the Tre Scalini restaurant in Piazza Navona. The recipe for carbonara that it gives was roughly outlined by Signor Ciampino, the owner. It features two kinds of cured meat: pancetta stesa ('lean bacon') and prosciutto, along with thinly sliced, quickly sautéd mushrooms. And to top it off – cited here for the first time as preferable to parmesan – we find the now classic choice of pecorino, along with the beaten eggs.

Spaghetti Carbonara

Signor Ciampini's recipe was nothing but a brief description. We hope the following more explicit directions do not stray too far from his original.

Boil 1 pound of spaghetti in salted water for 9 to 10 minutes, or until it is cooked but still firm. In 2 tablespoon of butter and 4 tablespoon of olive oil combined, sauté on a low fire ½ cup each of julienne of ham and lean bacon and ½ cup of thinly sliced mushrooms, without allowing them to brown. The sauce must remain 'blond'. Remove the pan from the fire and stir in 3 tablespoon of grated Pecorino cheese and 2 large well-beaten eggs. Mix this combination quickly into the drained hot spaghetti. (If you cannot get Pecorino, use Parmesan.)[9]

It's hard to say how much influence this approach to carbonara had elsewhere. What we do know is that outside of Italy, the mushroom version became a sort of 'official' variant.

Shades of Gruyère

Interest was growing, references to the dish multiplied.[10]

In 1954, the year that carbonara exploded around the world, the first recipe was also printed in Italy. And if you think the liberties taken by those early recipes were an American prerogative, get ready to think again.

In the August issue of *La Cucina Italiana*, we finally find 'Spaghetti alla carbonara'. After the title, in parentheses, a note: 'by request'. The author doesn't seem completely at ease with the recipe, and even suggests using Gruyère, a favourite cheese of international chefs, better suited to a grand hotel than to what was supposedly tavern fare.[11] The result is a rather stringy (but not at all unpleasant) dish, even though the recipe suggests allowing the eggs to set.

In addition to Gruyère, the ingredients include pancetta and garlic – much as this will dismay all the food purists who clamour for a return to the original recipe every time the slightest variation on carbonara appears. Here it is in full:

Spaghetti alla carbonara (by request)

For 4 people
Ingredients:
Spaghetti, 400 gr.
Pancetta, 150 gr.
Gruyère, 100 gr.
A clove of garlic – two eggs – salt – pepper.
Cooking time: about half an hour.

Put a large pot of salted water on to boil.

Chop the pancetta and dice the Gruyère.

When the water begins to boil, put in the spaghetti, stir and allow to cook for about 15 minutes (depending on the thickness) then drain well; remember that spaghetti is best when served rather al dente.

Break the eggs into a bowl, both yolks and whites, and beat as if preparing an omelette.

In a large pan, fry the pancetta and the crushed clove of garlic (which you will then remove), add the spaghetti, eggs, Gruyère and plenty of pepper. Mix well, continuing until the eggs are slightly set. Then transfer the spaghetti into a dish and serve immediately.[12]

In the mid-1950s, allusions to carbonara continued to proliferate – in the US, too, where the dish kept gaining ground. Its characteristics were not yet fully defined, however, nor was its provenance clear, as we can see from a 1955 guidebook published in New York that lists it as a Sicilian speciality: 'delicate fettuccini al burro, served in Rome's restaurants, the full-flavored lasagne al pesto, eaten in Genoa, the tortellini of Bologna, the ravioli of Florence, the Sicilian spaghetti alla carbonara.'[13]

The year 1955 also marked carbonara's first appearance in an actual cookbook, *La signora in cucina* by Felix Dessì, a Milanese intellectual who dabbled in culinary matters. Unlike other recipes, this was a simple one, limited to the basic trio of ingredients: smoked pancetta, parmesan and eggs. The eggs were also cooked only by the heat of the freshly drained pasta, avoiding the notorious 'scrambled' effect of some previous versions.

Macaroni alla carbonara

Here, too, the pasta will need to be tossed in a large, warm bowl; while the pasta is cooking, beat together in this bowl, as if preparing an omelette, one egg per 100 g of pasta, a spoonful of parmesan per egg and a pinch of pepper.

Separately, in a small pan, render and brown some smoked pancetta cut into small cubes. The proportion should be about 50 g per egg.

When the pasta has been cooked and drained, toss it in the bowl so that it is well coated in the egg, which will cook slightly in the heat, then pour in the pancetta and rendered fat and mix again.

For a zingier flavour, the parmesan can be replaced with a good pecorino.[14]

Until the end of the decade, pancetta continued to be the key ingredient in the dish. Guanciale ('pig's cheek') appears for the first time in the American guidebook *Eating in Italy*,[15] from 1957, but only as an alternative to pancetta and prosciutto.

For some reason, at least in the first few years of the recipe's existence, the United States was always a step ahead of Italy, which picked up new trends in carbonara but almost never launched them. Of course, this could have been due to the greater vigour of the American publishing industry, which at the time was churning out magazines and books at a rate that Italy could never possibly match. Whatever the reason, this once again goes to show that carbonara is both Italian and American.

The Dolce Vita of carbonara

Although it had yet to settle on one form and had been around for little more than a decade, by the end of the 1950s carbonara had already established a firm foothold. Its biggest fans were foreigners, especially Americans and the British: not surprisingly, since the bacon-and-egg pairing seemed natural to them.

Gossip columnists caught all the celebrities of the day digging into bowls of carbonara, which was seen as the most appetising, satisfying, quintessentially Italian – or rather, Roman – thing one could possibly order. Its fans included Gregory Peck, Linda Darnell, Pearl Bailey, Mamie Van Doren, Victor Mature and even the very Italian Sophia Loren.[16] As for Oliver Hardy, they say that 'in Rome, while on a publicity trip in 1950, he ate five dishes of spaghetti alla carbonara in one sitting'.[17]

It was an utterly new and up-to-the-minute dish. Above all, one that stuck to your ribs: just what people wanted in the postwar period of rebirth, when they were eager to forget the hunger, hardship and breadlines that were still so vividly impressed on every mind. Rome, in particular, was all abustle with the activity at Cinecittà studios and the constant to and fro of Hollywood stars, as Federico Fellini depicts so well in *La Dolce Vita*.

The portrait of carbonara that emerges is of a dish explicitly aimed at the other side of the Atlantic. And the courtship was successful. This can be seen from the vast number of recipes printed in the US up to 1960 (at least as many as in Italy) and the ample evidence of its popularity overseas.

If carbonara suddenly began to rise in the ranks of Italy's favourite pasta dishes, it was in part because it embodied the kind of postwar reconstruction that every-one wanted: rich, calorific and English-speaking.

But in carbonara's spread through the international star system, a key role was played by a few food-loving actors who served as its early ambassadors, and even got their own hands dirty making the dish.

Roman actress Marisa Merlini – famous for *Pane, amore e fantasia* (*Bread, Love and Dreams*), where she starred alongside Vittorio De Sica and Gina Lollobrigida – was, for instance, particularly proud of her version. We learn this from a *Corriere della Sera* article that came out in 1955 during the Punta del Este festival in Uruguay, the biggest cinematic event in Latin America, which drew actors, directors and producers from around the world, including Italy.

It was actress Marisa Merlini, the midwife in *Pane e amore*, who made the spaghetti, or rather the bucatini alla carbonara, with prosciutto, pepper, eggs and cheese, on a rudimentary cooker fuelled with cones from the pine grove. A fine evening, that warmed all hearts; spaghetti is the food of fellowship.[18]

The carbonara that Merlini so prided herself on was made with prosciutto. Some might think she was forced to use what was available on the other side of the globe. But actually, the choice was completely deliberate. The proof comes from another article, three years later, that tells of a dinner organised at her house in Rome with singer Domenico Modugno and a few other friends, while shooting the film *Io, mammeta e tu*.

Meanwhile, we sat down at the table and applauded the spaghetti 'alla carbonara' that Marisa is as proud of as her most celebrated performances: she herself measured out the various ingredients, egg yolks, San Daniele prosciutto, pepper and parmesan, which must be mixed and kept ready in a pan, so that as soon as the pasta is cooked, it can be steeped in a sauce that would raise the dead. This is a Roman speciality that can also be made with other ingredients, and should be paired with a dry white wine [. . .].[19]

Another famous apostle of the dish was Ugo Tognazzi, who was not only a great actor, but a sophisticated gourmet. He once said: 'When I look back over my acting career twenty years from now, I may have one regret: that I didn't quit halfway through to become the greatest chef in America, and maybe the world.'

He himself tells the story of the 1964 press launch of *Marcia nuziale* (*The Wedding March*). The Italian producer came up with the idea of having Tognazzi make pasta for everyone at the party, which was held in a huge suite on the 48th floor of the New York Hilton. There were 350 guests in all. Once the hotel kitchens had been commandeered, the big dilemma: what should he make for this horde of Americans?

> I immediately ruled out spaghetti with tomato sauce and basil because they might mistake it for pizza. I didn't have time to make a meat sauce, which wouldn't have been new to them anyway. Amatriciana was crossed off the list because I had my legitimate doubts about the flavour of American tinned tomatoes. By exclusion, I settled on carbonara.[20]

Four kilos of bacon, 250 whole eggs and 100 yolks, 2 kilos of cream, 5 of parmesan and 10 shots of cognac, for 30 kilos of spaghetti. All prepared with a stopwatch in hand: it took the elevator exactly 57 seconds to get from the kitchens to the suite, and there was the risk of overcooking the pasta. The American guests went wild over the dish – though they struggled with its name, pronouncing it along the lines of 'kerboonarow' – and forced Tognazzi to cook it again and again in the homes of wealthy hosts on every leg of the tour. His feat never made it into the Guinness book of world records, but is probably still the biggest carbonara ever served.

Here's the recipe:

My Kerboonarow (carbonara)

'Ingredients' (for six):
half a kilo of spaghettini,
a cup of cream,
six eggs (less the whites of three),
150 g bacon,
100 g prosciutto, both fat and lean,
50 g butter,
100 g parmesan,
30 g pecorino,
black pepper,
cognac (or other brandy).

Beat the six egg yolks and three whites in a bowl, add the cheese, cream, salt and pepper, and mix well. Fry the bacon, and after a while add the prosciutto: both of them diced. After draining the spaghetti al dente, stir in the butter, then add the egg sauce, and finally the meat. As a final touch, the cognac. If it seems too liquid, toss it in the pan over the heat for ten seconds.[21]

Guanciale (and cream)

The 1960s opened with the definitive triumph of carbonara, which for the first time was included in two major cookbooks: Luigi Carnacina's *La grande cucina* (1960), and *Il piccolo talismano della felicità* (1964),[22] a new edition of Ada Boni's classic.

There are two basic innovations in Carnacina's recipe.

To start with, he is the first to specify guanciale, offering no other options. Although the version with pancetta took a while to die off – and may not yet be extinct – this can be seen as the first true step towards formulating what is now considered the canonical recipe.

The second is the addition of cream in order to make the sauce more velvety and clinging. The inclusion of this often deprecated ingredient, which came into vogue on Italian tables in the 1960s and peaked in the 1980s[23] – the dark era that carbonara purists would love to erase – is not really a surprise. Although it may seem illogical at first, from a historical perspective it was actually the addition of cream that definitively established the texture of the dish: the visual experience, consistency and mouthfeel, as opposed to the taste. In earlier recipes, as we have repeatedly seen, the eggs were allowed to firm up in the pan, which made the carbonara too dry; butter or pancetta grease could only compensate to some extent. The cream introduced by Carnacina adds softness, envelops the pasta and blends with the other ingredients to achieve the smoothness that has come to be considered fundamental to a good carbonara. Now that cream has fallen from grace, it takes more effort to recreate the same effect, but we'll get back to that later. For now, here's Carnacina's version:

Spaghetti alla carbonara

[for six people] 600 gr. spaghetti. 50 gr. guanciale (pork cheek) cut in pieces. A spoonful of olive oil. 50 gr. butter. 6 whole eggs. 50 gr. of grated parmesan. A few spoonfuls of very fresh, rich liquid cream.

Cook the spaghetti in plenty of boiling, lightly salted water, and drain when al dente. Meanwhile, sauté the guanciale in a small pan with the oil; beat the eggs in a bowl, mixing in the cheese, a pinch of salt, a little freshly ground pepper and the cream. In a large pan, melt the butter; when it begins to brown, pour in the eggs, let them set a little, add the spaghetti and guan-ciale; mix rapidly and dish out the portions straight away. It is important for the cooked spaghetti to be ready just as the eggs begin to set.[24]

The 1964 edition of Ada Boni's *Piccolo talismano della felicità* includes a recipe not only for spaghetti alla carbonara, but for 'Spaghetti alla carbonara di magro'[25] (i.e. a meatless version), with eggs, oil, milk, parmesan and Gruyère – making a comeback after that early appearance in *Cucina Italiana* – and 'Spaghetti con pancetta affumicata',[26] practically identical to a classic carbonara, but with pancetta that is smoked rather than simply salt-cured or fresh.

Spaghetti alla carbonara

For six: Spaghetti, 600 grams – Eggs, three – Pancetta, 200 grams – Butter, 30 grams – Parmesan, 50 grams – Onion – Parsley – Pepper – Dry white wine.

Slice the onion thinly and dice the pancetta, putting both in a small pan to brown in the butter. As soon as the onion and pancetta have taken on a little colour, pour half a glass of white wine into the pan and let it burn off slowly.

In a bowl, beat the eggs as if for an omelette and add the grated parmesan, the finely chopped parsley and the pepper. Put the pasta to boil in unsalted water and as soon as it is cooked, drain it and add to the bowl with the eggs. Mix well, add the hot pancetta to the pasta and serve immediately.[27]

By 1960, carbonara had reached a level of fame comparable to that of its 'older' cousin, amatriciana. If we take the section on Rome in the Italian/French guidebook *Guida gastronomica e turistica d'Italia* as a sample,[28] we find eight restaurant entries in all (out of forty-two) that mention carbonara and amatriciana, neatly split between four for carbonara and four for amatriciana, with a single restaurant offering both. The amusing thing is that these two dishes are completely overshadowed by the eighteen references to cannelloni, which were unquestionably more fashionable at the time yet have now almost vanished from menus. A sign of the times: gourmets visiting the Eternal City must have shown a clear preference for baked pasta as opposed to mere spaghetti. (And maybe they had good reason.)

The golden age

In the forty years that followed, carbonara gained full traction even in more sophisticated culinary circles and was picked up by major names in Italian and international cooking. Versions were proposed by Henri-Paul Pellaprat,[29] Anna Gosetti della Salda,[30] Gualtiero Marchesi,[31] Alain Senderens[32] and Antonia Monti Tedeschi,[33] among others. Although by this point it had reached maturity, the recipe was still very instable and subject, like any dish, to the personal interpretation of the authors describing it. In general, however, one can trace an evolution in which some characteristics gradually won out over others.

First of all, ingredients beyond the triad of eggs, pancetta (or guanciale) and cheese began to disappear, albeit slowly. Wine, onion and parsley, a herb we have just seen in Boni's recipe, still turned up in a few formulations from the 1990s. The fats stood their ground for a while, particularly the oil and butter used to brown the pancetta or guanciale. The cream came and went, with a few peaks in the late 80s, and could still be found on the eve of the new millennium. One of the most celebrated chefs to have tried his hand at carbonara, offering a cross between haute cuisine and the popular recipe, is the legendary Gualtiero Marchesi. With 250ml for 320g of spaghetti, the amount of cream in his version is one of the highest ever ventured – outdone only by the French cook Alain Senderens's from 1981,[34] which uses almost as much cream, by weight, as pasta! Here is Marchesi's recipe from 1989, as a historical curiosity or for a dinner party with an 80s theme.

Spaghetti alla carbonara

Ingredients for 4

320 g spaghetti. 80 g guanciale. 250 ml fresh cream. 2 egg yolks, 20 g grated pecorino. 10 g butter. Salt and pepper.

In a bowl, beat the egg yolks with the cream, pecorino and freshly ground pepper.

Cut the guanciale in strips and brown it well in a frying pan with the butter.

Cook the spaghetti in salted boiling water, drain it al dente, pour it into the pan and mix. Remove from heat, add the cream and egg mixture, stir until all ingredients are well blended. Portion the spaghetti on to plates and place the crisped guanciale on top.[35]

The definitive victory of guanciale over pancetta came in the 1990s or thereabouts, after three decades of vacillation.

The stable adoption of pecorino as the sole cheese was even slower. Starting in the mid-1960s, it became increasingly rare for parmesan to be used on its own – except in cookbooks outside of Italy, which preserved a preference for it – but a blend of parmesan and pecorino remained a viable option until the turn of the millennium (and in many cases still is).*

It is almost comical to note that until the 2000s, the only recipe that strictly adhered to the trio of guanciale, pecorino and eggs, admitting no variations – the same recipe now presented on all sides as the 'original' carbonara – is one that appeared in Santi–Brera in 1966.

> For 4 people: 500 grams spaghetti – 100 grams guanciale – 50 grams butter – 4 egg yolks – Salt – Pepper – 50 grams of grated pecorino. Fry the diced guanciale in butter until it is crisp. Boil the spaghetti in plenty of salted water, drain it al dente, put it in a bowl and add the butter and guanciale, mixing carefully. Serve out the pasta into 4 dishes, sprinkle it with plenty of pepper and drop an egg yolk into each one. Give it a quick stir and top with grated pecorino.[36]

As regards the ratio of other ingredients relative to the pasta, there seems to have been no steady progression over the past forty years. The two recipes that suggest the highest and lowest amounts of pancetta or guanciale come just five years apart: Luigi Carnacina in 1960, with just over 8g of guanciale per 100g of pasta, and the American *Fannie Farmer Cookbook* of 1965, which calls for as much bacon by weight as spaghetti. In Italy, no one

---

* Even today, many of the Roman restaurants famous for their carbonara continue to use a blend of the two cheeses – with less parmesan than pecorino – for a taste that is milder and less salty.

has ever broken the historical record of 50g of pancetta per 100g of pasta set by Felix Dessì in 1955.

Lastly, the pepper. Almost every recipe recommends it, but few bother to specify how much, simply advising that it be used 'generously'.

If we line up every version of carbonara from the first five decades of its existence, there is no one ingredient – parmesan, pecorino, pancetta or guanciale – that appears in all of them, except for the eggs.

In short, the recipe for carbonara seems less like a script and more like a *canovaccio* from the commedia dell'arte, where everyone can improvise and experiment at whim.

Good to eat and good to think

And nowadays? In this new millennium, carbonara has reached a level of fame that places it in the pantheon of great Italian recipes, or rather, great international recipes, even surpassing amatriciana.

The most interesting change – even more than the shift in ingredients from early recipes to contemporary ones – can be seen in the narrative surrounding it. Because, as Claude Lévi-Strauss would put it, in order to be 'good to eat', a dish must first of all be 'good to think'.

From the outset, carbonara has lacked a backstory. A long, noble pedigree, for instance: there was no ancient tradition or medieval manuscript to cite. Moreover, the degree to which the ingredients varied over its first half-century of existence didn't help with the task of giving it a firm identity.

The one thing clear to all eyes was its regional nature, since it was definitely linked to Rome. Everything else was open to 'invention'.

So storytelling made a significant contribution to reshaping this recipe, turning it from a popular, international dish into a traditional, local one. Any ingredients that didn't seem to fit that description were purged from it (remember the garlic and onions in amatriciana?). Out went the pancetta, which was too common and had no regional associations – and perish the thought of foreign bacon. Out went the parmesan, although it was by far the cheese most widely used on pasta for over half a millennium. Better to opt for a local pecorino, the kind that generations of Romans had been raised on.

Out went all the additional ingredients that had been in its orbit from the very start, but which encouraged too much variation for a recipe in search of a strong identity. No to garlic, onion, wine and cream; yes to just three basic ingredients: eggs, guanciale and pecorino (plus black pepper). So that's the 'true' carbonara.

'Good to think', but very recent from a historical standpoint.

Since there are no real sources backing up this reconstruction (which would actually be contradicted by them), it once again has to rely on legend. The legend of humble, hard-working shepherds – or charcoal burners, it's all the same – who used to set off from home with a lunch tin of spaghetti, seasoned with a few cheap but wholesome ingredients such as cheese from their herd, eggs fresh from the henhouse and the pork they put up in December.

Now, don't get me wrong: peasant life was indeed based on a subsistence economy. But it was totally different from this picture.

The vision of carbonara as an autarchic recipe, which can't include parmesan or pancetta because those weren't traditional products in the area of Rome, is just a naive fantasy influenced by the locavore approach, a modern concept that is admirable to be sure, but never really existed even in the Middle Ages. The point is that carbonara, like many other traditional specialities, has had to *construct* its own identity – real or invented – and then defend it at all costs.

At the time of writing, I feel it's safe to say this process is coming to an end. Of course, at the popular level protective feelings about the 'canonical' recipe still run very high. Social networks are filled with zealous guardians of traditional cuisine who will attack anyone suggesting the slightest modification. Anything that ventures outside the guanciale-pecorino-egg troika is pilloried to the cry of 'Don't call that carbonara!'

But let's take a look at what is now considered the quintessential heresy: cream.* What if I told you that this very ingredient introduced a hallmark quality into the 'idea' of the dish?

---

* For that matter, any Italian over forty has definitely eaten carbonara with cream by the cartload, in addition to farfalle with prosciutto, peas and cream; tagliolini with smoked salmon and cream; and pennette with vodka and cream – all of which were very fashionable in the 1980s.

Adding a spoonful of science

The ousting of cream from the ingredient list after more than thirty years of honourable service has had a rather interesting side effect: making carbonara much more complicated to pull off. If you use only eggs and cheese, it's anything but easy to achieve the velvety smoothness that should envelop the spaghetti, punctuated by crisp bursts of flavour from the strips of guanciale. All it takes is a few extra degrees of heat or a few extra seconds of stirring, and you'll end up with a slimy soup of raw egg, or a pasta omelette.

The technical difficulty of this dish has sparked a debate engaging everyone from ordinary fans to great chefs, while the popularity of cooking blogs and the proliferation of food porn on social networks has done the rest. Giving just the right texture to the sauce has become such a key problem that people have turned to chemistry and other technical fields to solve it, applying principles already used in other realms of cooking, especially pastry.

Of course, some may apply them instinctively, relying on innate culinary skills and a well-trained eye to make sure the pasta gets just the right amount of heat as they stir, and never once getting it wrong. With all due respect to these talented cooks, other people have gone to the trouble of analysing the chemical reactions involved in the process of cooking the egg, to guarantee perfect results every time.

The first to lay the groundwork for this 'scientific carbonara' was the chemist Dario Bressanini in 2008, in his
'Scienza in cucina' column for the magazine *L'Espresso*.[37]
Like all his articles, this one is both interesting and simple
to understand, well within the grasp of anyone with a
basic knowledge of cooking and a food thermometer. I'll
try to summarise it just as clearly.

For the egg in carbonara to come out right, Bressanini
explains, you must keep its chemical composition in
mind, and the fact that it is composed of various proteins that coagulate at temperatures below 100°C. The
yolk and white contain different percentages of water, fat
(only in the yolk) and proteins.

The latter play a pivotal role, because when heated, they
break down and form a web that can trap and hold water
molecules. But if the heat is too high, this web 'contracts'
and expels the water molecules, becoming completely
solid and dry. The yolk, which is the part of the egg that
interests us most for carbonara, starts to thicken at 65°C
and becomes completely solidified at 70°C. The white
instead contains various proteins, including ovotransfer-
rin – which makes up 12 per cent of the yolk and starts
to coagulate at 62°C, becoming solid at 65°C – and oval-
bumin, which makes up 54 per cent of the protein in the
white and coagulates at 85°C. If you are making the sauce
with yolks alone or with a low percentage of whites, then
to obtain that coveted creaminess, you should stay under
65°C. Otherwise, you will end up with scrambled eggs on
your pasta, the effect now considered most execrable.

With these basic principles in mind, various food
writers and cooks have come up with strategies to

guarantee perfect results every time.

Laying aside the method that calls for adding the raw eggs to the freshly drained spaghetti, which is the most traditional but also has the outcome most difficult to control, there are at least two other options.

The first is to make a savoury zabaione to add to the spaghetti.

This is done by combining the yolks and whole eggs (a possible ratio is one whole egg and two yolks to 160–180g of spaghetti, but one could also use just the three yolks) with the grated cheese (black rind pecorino romano or parmesan, or a blend of the two, totalling about 80–100g), 3 or 4 tablespoons of water, and an equal amount of the rendered fat left over from frying the guanciale. This mixture should be poured into the top of a double boiler set over simmering water, whisking constantly. The mechanical action of the whisk and the rising temperature will make the proteins in the yolk start to break down, trapping the water and air inside, until it completely coagulates at around 70°C. To ensure just the right texture for your carbonara, it's best never to go over 63–64°C. Why? Because slightly varying proportions of yolks, whites, water and cheese could affect the outcome, so a keen, watchful eye is still necessary. Once the desired temperature is reached, you should immediately remove it from the heat, while still mixing to continue incorporating air. If necessary, this operation can be repeated more than once, putting the top of the double boiler back over the simmering pot until the sauce reaches the desired consistency. If the mixture is a little too thick, you can add a small amount of cooking water while stirring in the spaghetti (off the heat) to obtain the perfect density. When your savoury zabaione is ready, it can be added to the drained spaghetti along with the fried guanciale and the pepper; just make sure that the pasta temperature is not much over 70°C, otherwise all your efforts could be wasted.[38]

The second option involves using a device that keeps the water in a vessel at a constant, controlled temperature, for the 'sous vide' method of cooking.

In this case, all the ingredients listed above should be put in a heat-safe plastic pouch, and immersed in a water bath at 63°C for about an hour. Once the time is up, pour the mixture into a bowl, whisking vigorously, and pour it over the cooked pasta.

With the aid of a simple kitchen thermometer or a sous-vide machine, these two techniques will give your carbonara that perfect, velvety texture every time.

The forerunners of carbonara

Now that we've seen how the dish really did evolve, from the earliest recipes to the latest cutting-edge methods, it's safe to say that the legend of simple peasants or great-grandmothers who always made carbonara with guanciale and pecorino because those were the local ingredients is simplistic and ahistorical. We've also seen the important role that American tastes played in the origin of this dish. But it would be a mistake to think that the combination of foods in carbonara is totally foreign to the Italian tradition. Looking at old cookbooks, we can find recipes that laid the cultural groundwork for it to be invented.

In the Middle Ages the most common way of flavouring pasta, and sometimes the only one, was with grated cheese – sometimes along with spices, and with the addition of butter starting in the mid-fifteenth century.[39]

The pairing of eggs and grated cheese found in the twentieth-century carbonara is also an ancient one, at least when it comes to soups.

An early example shows up in the fifteenth-century recipes attributed to Maestro Martino: in one of them, meat broth and grated bread are boiled together, allowed to cool, and then beaten eggs are added along with cheese and saffron.[40]

Over the centuries this kind of soup led to various broth-based dishes such as stracciatella (Italian egg-drop soup), millefanti, and finally, in the late eighteenth century, passatelli.

The first reference to using eggs and cheese on pasta instead came along in 1773, in Vincenzo Corrado's famous Neapolitan cookbook *Il cuoco galante*: 'Thin Pasta can be cooked in light Capon broth, or even dark Beef broth, or milk; and once cooked, it can be served with egg yolks as a thickener or without them.'[41] In this case, we are talking about very small pasta, and the egg yolk is used both to bind and to flavour the broth or milk it is cooked in. The same approach can also be found in rice soups.

Another Neapolitan cookbook, the first edition of Ippolito Cavalcanti's *Cucina teorico-pratica* in 1837, included a recipe for 'Ordura di tagliolini':[42] little balls of thin noodles mixed with egg and a cheese similar to caciocavallo, filled with meat sauce, then dipped in egg and breadcrumbs and fried. Sort of like arancini made out of pasta: an idea that opened the door to what was then a new alliance of pastasciutta, egg and cheese.

The second edition of the same cookbook, from 1839, contains the same recipe, but also adds a 'Timpano di maccheroni di magro senza pasta' ('Crustless fast-day pie of macaroni').[43] This variation on the classic pasta 'timpano' (a baked dish that Italians would now call 'timballo') has no meat or sauce, only butter, parmesan, beaten egg, slices of mozzarella, and hard-boiled eggs cut in quarters. All of this is baked, then allowed to firm up in the pan before serving.

The combination of eggs and cheese becomes more explicit in a recipe titled 'Maccarune de tutte manere' ('Macaroni in every fashion'), where Cavalcanti notes that pasta can be topped 'with cheese and beaten eggs'.[44] This suggestion is developed on by another cook from Naples, Francesco Palma, who describes his own 'Maccheroni con cacio ed uova'[45] in 1881:

Macaroni with cheese and eggs

Three kilograms of macaroni, one hundred and sixty-seven grams of parmesan, two hundred and fifty grams of lard, seven eggs, salt and pepper. Take the macaroni off when halfway done, then drain it so that a little water remains, and put back in the pot with the lard, beaten eggs, and the rest, and let everything boil for a while. Then put it into a bowl and serve.

Reading closely, you'll note that along with the eggs and cheese, the ingredients include melted lard. From there, the idea of directly adding fried pancetta or guanciale required no great leap of the imagination – yet it took over seventy years for that to happen. This is not quite a carbonara *avant la lettre*, yet it shows that the combination of eggs, cheese and pork fat was one that had already been conceived of, in Italy, as a possible pasta sauce. In short, even a century before the 'birth' of carbonara, it seems that Neapolitans already had a certain propensity to combine its hallmark ingredients, bringing them into the same culinary picture. For that matter, the South of Italy, especially Naples, has historically been a wellspring of innovations in cooking that have then spread to the rest of the country. Mind you, this doesn't mean that Naples should be credited with inventing carbonara, just that the basis – that first step – for its creation can be traced to the area.

As for the pancetta or guanciale, while amatriciana was the most obvious trailblazer,[46] at least two other recipes set a noteworthy precedent when it came to pasta sauce. The first is the 'Pasta condita col lardo rosso' in Giulia Lazzari-Turco's *Piccolo focolare* of 1947:

Pasta with lardo rosso

Finely dice a piece of lardo rosso, that is, smoked fatty

pork (about 50–60 gr) with both fat and meat. Fry it in a pan until the fat becomes transparent, add a walnut-sized piece of butter, and when it is melted and steaming, pour in a kilo of cooked, well-drained pasta. Serve with cheese on the side.[47]

The second is the previously mentioned 'Spaghetti al guanciale' that Ada Boni included in the 1950 edition of *Piccolo talismano della felicità*. You can't help but notice that this recipe is really just an amatriciana without the tomatoes: for all intents and purposes, a gricia, although it would only acquire that name years later.

Spaghetti with guanciale

For six people: 600 grams spaghetti – A spoonful of lard – 100 grams guanciale – Pepper – Pecorino.

Cook the spaghetti, and while it is cooking prepare this very simple sauce.

Put a spoonful of lard in a small pan, and slowly fry the guanciale, cut into small slices. When the spaghetti is done, drain it and pour over this sauce, adding grated pecorino and a very generous pinch of pepper. Mix and serve immediately.[48]

To sum up this brief dive into the prehistory of carbonara: the association between cheese, eggs and pasta has existed at least since the late nineteenth century, while pasta sauces with pancetta/guanciale and cheese (and no tomatoes) appeared in the late 1940s, preceding carbonara itself by just a few years. Everything was ready for that one little spark.

The puzzle of the name 'carbonara'

Much of the speculation about this recipe's origins is inspired by a perplexing problem: to this day, no one has been able to convincingly explain where the name 'carbonara' comes from. The theories most often encountered revolve around three possible derivations: the Carbonari, charcoal burners or the colour of the dish.

Let's start with the first hypothesis, that it could be linked to the Carbonari. This secret society was initially formed in the early nineteenth century to oppose Napoleonic rule in Italy, and its activities came to a definitive end in the mid-1800s. Although in this very period a number of cookbooks were printed in and around Naples – where the underground network got its start, and where, as we have seen, the first cheese-and-egg pastas were also invented – none of them use the term 'alla carbonara' in any recipe title. Unless the Carbonari were also masters at covering their culinary tracks and diligently hiding the secret of carbonara, it would be odd for the name to exist yet never be recorded, in an era when food writing was in full flower.

Then there's the second theory, centred on charcoal burners: labourers from the lowest rungs of society who were forced to go up into the mountains for months at a stretch, often with their families in tow, to gather wood and transform it into charcoal.

This ancient, gruelling job began to disappear in the twentieth century with the advent of modern fuels. Little or nothing is known about the eating habits of these workers, and we can be certain that by the 1950s, when carbonara made its first appearance, the profession was well on its way to extinction. The idea of a centuries-long culinary tradition, handed down by generations of charcoal burners in Umbria or Lazio, is romantic but implausible. Sadly, it is very difficult to imagine nineteenth-century charcoal burners consuming anything but a monotonous diet of bread and polenta – and certainly not spaghetti: pasta, contrary to what one might think today, only recently took on the connotation of a cheap, popular food.

The fact remains that none of the early sources describing carbonara show a connection to coal or charcoal. Poetic as it is to theorise that the name came from the coal-mining father of Pietro Lencioni (one of the owners of Armando's, the Chicago restaurant mentioned earlier as the indirect source of the first carbonara recipe), the two things are truly difficult to fit together, geographically or chronologically. The most we can do is suspend judgement in the hope that more clues will turn up.

Finally, there is the idea that the name comes from the colour of the pasta, black as 'a charcoal burner's face'. The first to venture this imaginative comparison was Carlo Scorza, who suggested in 1958 that one of the original ingredients might have been squid ink, quickly replaced by egg yolk.[49] 'Imaginative', as I said. There are obviously no recipes or descriptions out there to back this up.

Another chromatic explanation is based on the amount of pepper employed, the notion being that the spaghetti is literally black with the stuff. But none of the early recipes emphasises any such abundance of pepper, which sometimes isn't even listed among the ingredients. It's clearly a stretch to associate the colour of carbonara – which is mainly yellow from the eggs – with the blackness of coal, no matter how much pepper is added.

There are other, less common theories. Sometimes they mention an unidentified Roman trattoria where 'carbonai' (in this case, door-to-door coal peddlers) used to gather, and where, according to legend, this unusual dish could be sampled. If the place really existed, maybe even with a name referring to coal, the mystery would be solved. But as we saw before with 'spaghetti al Moro' or 'fettuccine Alfredo', these names don't tend to escape the notice of cooks, historians and foodies. Alas, there seems to be no trace of any such restaurant.

Another less frequent hypothesis is that it came from 'carbonata', a term often encountered in recipe books, from the 1400s all the way to the mid-twentieth century. This was a method of cooking meat that got its name from the glowing embers on which the pan or grill was placed. It was most commonly used in reference to mutton, beef, or veal; pork, too, at times, but not with anything approaching the same frequency. So although the influence of this word cannot be ruled out, it seems improbable.

There are at least two other theories, even less well known, but more plausible. The first is based on a previous use of the term 'alla carbonara' to describe a polenta recipe in Giulia Lazzari-Turco's *Manuale pratico di cucina* from 1904. Her 'Polenta alla carbonara'[50] called for adding a range of ingredients to the mixture of water and ground maize: butter, beans and parmesan, or cheese and cubes of salami or ham. There is unquestionably a similarity in the combination of cheese and cured meat, and Alberto Capatti may be right to say that 'the reference to charcoal burners probably suggests a mishmash of affordable ingredients, varying in kind and proportion, but also the plain, natural tastes of people used to eating outdoors'.[51] Still, the idea that this affinity between the two recipes meant that the name of the polenta dish was extended to the new spaghetti sauce as well remains rather unlikely.

Except for this first appearance, the vague name 'alla carbonara' was so uncommon that the recipe cited above is the only known precedent in print.

Another theory is based on the idea that the dish was invented in Rome at the end of World War II, using eggs and bacon from US army rations. These two products, fresh or tinned, were obviously not easy for Italians to come by, given the rationing then in force and the extreme difficulty of procuring even the bare minimum for survival. The troops that liberated the city were instead well supplied, so as always happens in such situations, these foods began to circulate on the *borsa nera*, the black market. The same sense of humour that led Romans to call illegal traders 'borsari neri' (a pun on Emilio Salgari's *Corsaro Nero* series of adventure novels) could have led to this name for carbonara, since the ingredients were secretly procured on a market as black as coal.

The hypotheses listed above are obviously just that – hypotheses, plausible or not – and given the total absence of solid facts they are also hard to prove wrong. Until more evidence emerges about the origin of this mysterious name, we're all free to let our imaginations run wild.

Who invented carbonara, anyway?

We have one last myth to bust, since it pops up too frequently to be ignored. Despite all the uncertainties surrounding the origins of carbonara, there is one personal account from an authoritative chef who claims to have invented and cooked it for the first time on 22 September 1944.

The occasion was the meeting of the British Eighth Army and the US Fifth Army in Riccione, which had just been liberated. The high command was made up of Field Marshal Harold Alexander (supreme Allied commander in the Mediterranean) and Lieutenant-General Sir Oliver Leese (who succeeded Montgomery as commander of the Eighth) accompanied by Harold Macmillan (high commissioner of the Allied military government in Italy and future prime minister of the United Kingdom). The banquet was to be prepared by Renato Gualandi, a young cook from Bologna who was then head chef at the Hotel Vienna, headquarters of the British command. Gualandi, in an interview with the *Corriere di Bologna*, explains how it went:

> The Americans had fabulous bacon, very good cream, some cheese and powdered egg yolks. I mixed it all together and served this pasta to the generals and other officers for dinner. At the last minute I decided to add black pepper, which brought out the flavour beautifully. The pasta was almost swimming in sauce, and it was a big hit.[52]

The same interview in the *Corriere della Sera* includes Gualandi's recipe:

> 150 grams of julienned bacon, crisped in 50 grams of butter, bathed in 250 ml of cream, 150 grams of cheese (Gruyère or another tender cheese). Add powdered eggs and, off the heat, an egg yolk. Drain the pasta al dente, but not too dry, and stir in this mixture. When the dish is ready, dust with a sprinkling of black pepper.

Everything about the story seems convincing at first glance. And here and there on the web one can still find interviews where Gualandi, by then over ninety years old, explains or shows how to make carbonara. Six years went by between 1944 and the first mention of the dish in 1950: not a long span of time to be sure, but enough for the dish to have caught on. The ingredients listed by Gualandi also are perfectly in keeping with later versions of carbonara and would confirm the connection to Allied army rations. Lastly, the rapid success of the dish in the United States and in Britain could be linked to the fact that Anglo-American troops were there at its very debut (during a prestigious banquet, no less).

But there are almost as many reasons to think that this story doesn't add up.

First, all the early Italian references to carbonara are tied to Rome, which at any rate is the city where it put down roots. But in the postwar era, Gualandi almost never budged from the region of Bologna, where he opened 3G, the restaurant that made him famous. Second, in his interviews he never explained the reason for the name 'carbonara' – which, as we have seen, is the subject of much debate – even though he was the supposed inventor of the dish. Claiming authorship of something without knowing how it got such an unusual name is no minor incongruity.

But there's a more serious one.

Gualandi's own biography, written in 2006 with Adolfo Fabbri, contains a rather detailed account of that famous reception:

> We served 3000 petits-fours, various pastries, raw cru-dités, assorted canapés with cheeses and meats. Then a soup of lettuce hearts and a classic Irish stew with lamb, mutton and vegetables. After that, a bone-in roast of beef covered in kidney fat, to be cut on the diagonal like salmon, with a savoury pudding and gravy. Last, a

111

cake a metre and a half tall, shaped like the two towers of Bologna. And then at the end of the dinner came a Welsh rarebit: cheddar cheese on toast with egg yolks, rum, salt and sugar, broiled in the oven and washed down with plenty of beer.[53]

In short, anything but a frugal meal patched together out of troop rations; rather, a gala dinner with specialities from the British Isles. But above all, no mention of carbonara. Even though it was a universally famous dish by the time the book was written, and the circumstances surrounding its invention would have been one of the most interesting anecdotes from the multifaceted career of a great Bolognese chef.

There's one other discrepancy: the powdered eggs mentioned by Gualandi don't seem to have been among the foods supplied to the Allied army. There was a breakfast tin of eggs and bacon[54] that could indeed have been added to pasta, but that is not the form the chef described.

So what was the real story? We don't know and perhaps never will. The most likely theory is still that carbonara originated upon the arrival of the Allies in 1944, when some cook in a Roman restaurant made a virtue of necessity and a new pasta sauce out of army rations, by combining them with local ingredients.

What we do know is that carbonara definitively enshrined the encounter of two worlds by merging two different, complementary culinary concepts in one recipe.

The eggs and bacon brought to Italy as rations by US soldiers, combined with the classic Italian dish of pasta with cheese, created a very special hybrid: midway between the two countries' tastes, a bridge across the Atlantic. Or, to put it differently, it was an American dish born in Italy: no common flag could have been more compelling, no statesman could have done better.

I realise that some people, reading this reconstruction, may be disappointed by the lack of noble or ancient precedents for carbonara in Italian cuisine. But it doesn't diminish the dish. Far from it. I think the circumstances surrounding its invention are uniquely fascinating, as something good that came out of the darkest chapter in the twentieth century, when the ravages of war and hunger seemed inescapable. Carbonara brilliantly embodies the talent for improvisation that Italians have always been known for: even in the most difficult times, they somehow manage to create masterpieces.

4

Gnocchi

My grandmother always knew which potatoes to use for gnocchi. Floury, low in moisture, on the old side if possible and never, never new. The best and easiest to recognise are russets, with plenty of starch.

I remember how in the winter, when I was little, my nonna would boil potatoes for gnocchi; the steam filled the kitchen and fogged the windows for me to doodle on. We would peel them together while they were still piping hot, then mash them with the same ricer we used to make passatelli. It was fun to knead flour into that soft, warm substance till the dough no longer stuck to your hands: a sign not to add any more, that it was enough.

We ended up with a large ball, which then had to be divided into many smaller pieces and rolled on the big cutting board to make long, thin snakes, as even as possible. This was the most eagerly awaited moment by far. With quick strokes of a knife, we sliced the dough into short cylinders, pressed them against the back of a grater or with the floured tines of a fork and voilà: we had gnocchi. Quick and easy, topped with butter and parmesan, tomato or meat sauce, they were always delicious.

It certainly wasn't a dish for the most important occasions – holidays called for stuffed pasta or lasagne – but it always felt festive nonetheless.

When you learn certain methods and handle certain ingredients from an early age, you come to think of them as somehow being timeless. But like many of the other dishes discussed here, the potato gnocchi I grew up with are just the latest chapter in a very long history.

These knobbly lumps of pasta have gone through dozens of variations over the years, some of which have continued to evolve, while others have inevitably vanished. The common denominator of the recipes is that they tend to be humble ones, almost always prepared at home using everyday ingredients, since gnocchi haven't reached a stage of industrial production comparable to dried pasta. Yet despite their lowly origins, their extreme versatility as a base has often inspired great chefs in the course of their long history, yielding highly sophisticated dishes for aristocratic banquets.

The fact is, gnocchi are really much more than a dish: they're a whole branch of pasta, with its own array of shapes, categories and recipes.

Gnocchi simply means dumplings, so even today, traditional Italian cuisine still includes at least three very common types in addition to the one with potatoes: 'gnocchi alla romana', made from coarse semolina; canederli from South Tyrol, made with stale bread, eggs, onion and speck (but there are many possible variants); and Sardinian malloreddus, which are made from semolina flour and can be considered their own pasta shape. There are also other specialities that share the same name and roots, but have crossed over into the vast world of fritters: savoury, like the Emilian 'gnocco fritto', or sweet, like the dozens of variations on struffoli and castagnole.

Even this brief overview offers some idea of how diverse the family is, with no one ingredient that turns up in every recipe. Paging through old cookbooks, we come across a staggering range of gnocchi: many have left only faint traces on contemporary cuisine, and some are true forgotten treasures, waiting to be rediscovered.

Potatoless gnocchi

Let's start with one important point: gnocchi were a well-established Italian speciality long before the first potato was brought to Europe from the Americas.

The story of gnocchi began in the Middle Ages. Although we don't know the exact circumstances surrounding their invention, the fundamental insight – as with other kinds of pasta – was that morsels of dough, made from flour and other ingredients, could be boiled rather than baked or fried.

One of the first actual recipes to have survived can be found in a fourteenth-century manuscript now in the library of the University of Bologna, almost the only such record from that era.* The list of ingredients is short and simple: fresh cheese, egg yolks and flour. Like most

* One may suppose that even back then, there were many other kinds of gnocchi that were never recorded in writing. This chronic time lag

recipes of the time, it says nothing about the quantities to be used or even the type of cheese, which might just be curds, or perhaps some soft, fresh variety similar to robiola, caprino or quartirolo. One step in the instructions turns up in many later recipes as well: spooning the mixture into the pot of boiling water. This suggests a dough much softer than we are used to seeing, which must have remained quite tender even after boiling. The only condiment was grated cheese, as was usual in the Middle Ages (a characteristic that, as we have seen, was shared by all kinds of pasta).

If you want gnocchi

Take fresh cheese and mash it, then take flour and mix it with egg yolks as if making migliacci,[1] and put a pot of water on the fire, and when it boils put the mixture on a board and spoon it off into the pot, and when it is cooked put it in trenchers and sprinkle over plenty of grated cheese.[2]

In short, the original dough for gnocchi was soft and not easy to mould into elaborate shapes, so it was spooned out directly into the boiling water and finished off with cheese, which here plays the double role of both main ingredient and topping. The dish certainly sounds like a keeper. And indeed, it turns up almost unchanged in different parts of Italy, as 'gnocchi alla fioretta' (or 'fioreta', a very liquid ricotta) in the area north-west of Vicenza,

between the actual spread of a recipe and its entry into cookbooks should always be kept in mind when looking at ancient sources.

or as 'fiocchi di neve' ('snowflakes') in Maremma, or as 'n'dueri' on the Amalfi Coast: flawless artefacts from the archaeological layers of Italian cuisine.

But it was only in the Renaissance that gnocchi began to enjoy a degree of popularity, when great Italian cooks brought them to court.

They are discussed in a cookbook published in 1570 by Bartolomeo Scappi, the celebrity chef of his age. He got his start working at the courts of nobles and cardinals in various Italian cities, including Venice, Ravenna and Bologna, but reached the height of his career as the 'secret' (meaning 'personal') cook to Pope Pius IV, and then to his successor, Pius V.[3] While in the service of the latter, he published a wonderful illustrated treatise on every aspect of his craft, from raw ingredients to the right equipment for mixing, cutting and cooking, along with almost a thousand recipes. Two are devoted to gnocchi, with one version for 'feast days' and one for 'fast days'.

The title of the first recipe might seem a bit confusing: 'To make a dish of macaroni, called gnocchi'. This wording shouldn't surprise us, however, because at the time, 'macaroni' was a category that included every kind of pasta, including long shapes resembling spaghetti or tagliatelle. Even the macaroni rolling down the hill of grated parmesan in the imaginary land of Bengodi, described two centuries before by Giovanni Boccaccio (as we saw in the chapter on fettuccine Alfredo), could well have been gnocchi.[4]

Unlike medieval gnocchi, Bartolomeo Scappi's no longer contain fresh cheese. The only ingredients are flour, breadcrumbs, water or broth, and egg yolks: 'Take two pounds[5] of flour and a pound of grated and sifted white bread, temper these together with rich boiling broth or with water, adding four beaten egg yolks while mixing the dough.'[6]

This dough is firmer, and pieces of it can be pressed against the back of a grater to give them the right shape, just as we still do with potato gnocchi. 'And when this dough has been made so that it is neither too dry, nor too wet, but has reached its perfect form, take a piece like a walnut and dust the back of a cheese grater with white flour, and put the dough on this grater, and make gnocchi.' There we have it, the very first description of an ancient ritual still performed in Italian homes. The result must have been almost identical to the gnocchi of today: a piece of dough a few centimetres long, slightly curved, with little bumps on the back. The author gets even more specific, suggesting that if you have no grater, you can press them on a board with three fingers. Even then, the dough was not supposed to be too firm, or it would become rubbery when cooked, so readers are advised to add as little flour as possible 'so that they remain more tender'. And in those days, pasta simply drained and topped in the dish was not as popular as it is now, so most recipes called for a little time in the oven, or at any rate a second round of low-temperature cooking.

Scappi, too, adopts this approach: after the gnocchi are boiled in water or broth, they are arranged in a pan in three layers, alternated with grated cheese, mozzarella or small chunks of provolone. As the finishing touch, he of course adds the flavourings that characterised so many Renaissance dishes: the signature trio of butter, cinnamon and sugar. And finally, after a quick toasting over hot ashes, the gnocchi are ready to be served: 'when they are cooked, put them in dishes with cheese, and grated provatura that is not too salty, and sugar, and cinnamon, and morsels of fresh butter [. . .] and let them cook again between dishes over the warm ashes'.

WWWWWWWWW

As for Scappi's 'fast-day' gnocchi,[7] they were made of water, flour, breadcrumbs and oil with just a touch of saffron, and served with an 'agliata' sauce of crushed walnuts, garlic, soaked bread, pepper and cinnamon. He notes that the same dough could be used to 'make macaroni rolled out with a rod'[8] (that is, with a rolling pin), yielding a sheet of pasta to be served with green sauce, which was very common at the time in Lenten dishes and has come down to us in various forms – the best known being pesto alla genovese.[9]

An almost identical recipe for 'maccheroni'* was described by Cristoforo di Messisbugo about twenty years earlier in his treatise *Banchetti, composizioni di vivande, et apparecchio generale*. Not much is known about this prominent Renaissance cook. We do know that he spent much of his life serving the House of Este in Ferrara, the town where he is buried. As one of the

* The ingredients are the same – flour, breadcrumbs, water and eggs – as is the method of forming them on the back of a grater, but Messisbugo does not call them gnocchi either; they are simply 'maccheroni'. Cristoforo di Messisbugo, *Banchetti, composizioni di vivande, et apparecchio generale*, Ferrara, Giovanni di Buglhat et Antonio Hucher Compagni, 1549, c. 11 v., 12 r.

richest and most influential courts in Italy, it drew some of the peninsula's most famous artists, scientists and men of letters – for instance, Ludovico Ariosto, the author of *Orlando Furioso*, who must have attended the banquets that Messisbugo prepared.

In the mid-seventeenth century, an even simpler version of potatoless gnocchi was described by the Bolognese nobleman Vincenzo Tanara in *L'economia del cittadino in villa* (1644). This was a compendium of advice on how to properly manage country estates, in accordance with the seasons and the zodiac. It covered animal husbandry, agriculture, leisure activities, and – what matters most here – cooking. Tanara's gnocchi are made only of breadcrumbs, water and a little flour; they too are shaped on the back of a grater, and are once again topped with butter and cheese, or with agliata for fast days. Then as now, the innumerable shapes of handmade pasta had deep local ties and their names would often change just a few kilometres away; Tanara takes care to point out that depending on the town, 'they call them strozzapreti, macaroni, or as we do, gnochi [sic]'.[10]

He also describes two other kinds, one of them sweet, made with 'crumbled biscuits, milk and eggs'[11] and the second made from stale millet bread, crumbled and mixed with water and butter. (The latter were apparently so tasty that Tanara warns: 'if you want some left over for the evening, hide a portion, because I assure you that the dish you clear from the table will be empty, but these you have hidden for the evening can be heated again, in a pot or pan, so that they form a crispy and delectable crust'.)[12]

Towards the end of the century, especially in southern Italy, great chefs began to notice that this extremely versatile food could also serve as an excellent base for sophisticated dishes. So in just a few decades, gnocchi became all the rage, growing in popularity until they reached the tables of princes.

They owed their debut within fine cuisine to Neapolitan chef Antonio Latini, who included a recipe for 'gnocchetti' in his cookbook *Lo scalco alla moderna* (1693).[13] This was no longer a simple breadcrumb dough, but a rich mixture that included hard-boiled egg yolks, spices, sponge cake, marzipan and sugar. The result was a sweet, cinnamon-scented delicacy, perfectly reflective of the exuberant cuisine then in vogue in that city.

But it was another Neapolitan, the brilliant Vincenzo Corrado, who brought gnocchi to the true pinnacle of sophistication exactly eighty years later. As chief cook overseeing the kitchens of Don Michele Imperiali, prince of Francavilla, he had the opportunity to experiment with all kinds of sophisticated dishes, at banquets that drew titled guests from Naples and elsewhere to dine at Palazzo Cellamare.

The various versions of gnocchi presented in his cookbook *Il cuoco galante* (1773) include wildly imaginative ingredients ranging from calf brains to capon breast and from hard-boiled egg yolks to spinach; the only constant is the binder holding the mixture together: eggs and breadcrumbs, or more rarely, flour.

Building on earlier Neapolitan recipes, one of the simplest, humblest dishes imaginable had by this point been turned into a work of culinary art that could please the most demanding palate. It sometimes even achieved considerable technical complexity, as we can see in these 'Gnocchi alla panna' stuffed with capon breast, which are first boiled, then used to fill an elegant pie:

For timbales of Gnocchi with cream

Cook white flour with milk, so that it becomes a firm dough, and before removing it from the fire put in egg yolks and a few whites, and let it cool on a board. Once it is cool, roll it out, and make gnocchi half a finger long, filling their hollows with a stuffing of Capon breast mixed with parmesan, egg yolk, or cream, and let them boil for a short time in Capon broth. Then arrange them inside a crust with parmesan, butter, cream, and slices of truffle, cover them up, and let the Timbale bake.[14]

Corrado had not forgotten the previous tradition of breadcrumb gnocchi, but they too lost their original simplicity and were transformed into 'gnocchi alla regina':[15] morsels of a dough made with butter, eggs, milk and cinnamon, cooked in capon broth and served in a timbale with a coulis of veal and parmesan. Having started out as a simple way to reuse stale bread, gnocchi had travelled through a long series of reincarnations and reinventions to officially become a dish worthy of even the most aristocratic repast.

The gnocchi lost along the way

At this point, there's a fork in the road. While potato gnocchi, as we are about to see, were starting to get off the ground, 'traditional' gnocchi continued to be popular. It is hard to keep track of the dozens of variants that sprang up and intertwined in the eighteenth and nineteenth centuries. Cookbooks from the time are full of gnocchi 'alla reale', 'alla trevico', 'alla tedesca', 'al riso', 'verdi', 'bruschi', 'alla sidoine', 'al buon amico', 'ai ceci', and many, many more.

The ones with the most widespread success were definitely gnocchi 'alla veneziana', an eighteenth-century recipe that has survived into the present, while changing its ingredients, methods and name over the years.

By the end of the eighteenth century, gnocchi alla veneziana had already spread far beyond the boundaries of Venice. They show up in Naples in 1773, where Vincenzo Corrado includes them in a list of courses,[16] and an actual recipe appears eight years later in *Il cuoco maceratese* by Antonio Nebbia, a chef from Macerata.[17]

They were made from a cooked dough of milk, butter and flour, with grated parmesan added at the end. After being spread out to cool, this mush firmed up enough that it could be shaped into dumplings and plunged into boiling water.[18]

In 1790, Francesco Leonardi offered two variations:

one where the eggs are cooked along with the other ingredients, and another, called 'gnocchi all'acqua' (water gnocchi),[19] where the raw eggs are added only after the dough has cooled, yielding a basic beignet dough. And that is precisely the name that Vincenzo Agnoletti uses for them just a few years later, 'gnocchi bignè'.

Beignet gnocchi

[. . .] set milk, or water, etc., to boil in a pot with enough flour to make a dough that can be handled, stir it constantly with a wooden spoon, cook as if making a dough for water Beignets, then let it cool. When it is cool, put in two whole eggs for every pound of flour, and beat them in well. Spread this dough out on a pot lid, and with salted boiling water on the fire, push in the gnocchi a few at a time with the handle of an iron spoon: when they are cooked and well puffed up, put them in a plate or dish, dress them with butter, grated parmesan, and powdered cinnamon, and serve them immediately.[20]

For decades this dish was practically the definition of gnocchi.[21] Yet despite its enormous success, it literally disappeared from recipe books somewhere in the mid-1800s, reappearing only half a century later. It turned up again in 1908 in *100 specialità di cucina italiane ed estere*, in the section on Veneto, under its old moniker 'macaroni alla veneziana'.[22] But this was to be its last appearance: after that, no further authors included it in their cookbooks, at least not with a name referring to Venice. Thirty years later, the French chef Henri-Paul Pellaprat did bring it back for an encore as 'gnocchi alla parigina' ('Parisian gnocchi') in *Arte nella cucina, l'eleganza della mensa*,[23] a book bridging the gap between the cuisines of France and of Italy, which would soon shake off the heavy influence of its neighbour. But the real reason for the disappearance of this recipe and of so many others was above all the parallel rise – slow at first, then more and more irresistible – of potato gnocchi.

Potatoes, from famine fare to fine cuisine

So let's go back a step. At the end of the eighteenth century, there was still no trace of potato gnocchi. Why not?

The reason is that potatoes began to make their first shy appearance in European kitchens only in the seventeenth century, and like other plants imported from the Americas,[24] they took quite a while to gain a stable foothold there. Compared to other products such as tomatoes, they are rarely mentioned until the seventeenth century, perhaps due to an initial lack of interest in bland vegetables that grow underground. All in all, they didn't seem to deserve much attention.

Judging by the scientific literature of the time, potatoes were seen more as a curiosity for botanical gardens than a potential food. They were probably already being grown by peasant families in their own plots for private use, but not yet in the open fields, let alone for an established market.[25]

The idea that they could be found in small family

gardens by the first decades of the seventeenth century is suggested by Ugo Benzo, author of a huge tome titled *Regole della sanità e natura de' cibi* (Rules of Health and the Nature of Foods, 1620):

> From France to Piedmont they have brought an herb, which [. . .] has large, tender, tuberous roots, in great number, which are white [. . .] Some say that they are the roots of Clusius's Battatas,[26] whose roots are quite nourishing, both cooked and raw, and when cooked in hot ashes they lose some of their tendency to cause flatulence, and nowadays many of these roots can be found in kitchen gardens.[27]

These were the first inroads of a vegetable that would soon become omnipresent across Europe, but it took a new political climate, along with a serious food crisis, to make it the cornerstone of a new culinary scene.

Between the seventeenth and eighteenth centuries, the American tuber began to draw new interest as a possible response to the new demands of an agricultural revolution in full swing,* which called for an increase in crop productivity so that the surplus could be sent to market and bring higher returns.

---

* The Agricultural Revolution got under way in England in the mid-seventeenth century and reached the rest of Europe in the century that followed. It was a profound transformation that served as a prelude to the Industrial Revolution that followed.

One of the many innovations accompanying this process was the large-scale introduction of potatoes – along with another successful crop from the Americas, maize – to help solve the problem of feeding the people who laboured in the fields, while setting aside a bigger surplus of more desirable and costly products (such as wheat) that landowners could sell for a bigger profit margin.[28]

In short, the interest in the lower-class diet that one sees in the literature of the time was solely concerned with cheaply nourishing those who actually worked the land, in order to keep expenses to a minimum. Especially since in the meantime, due to the new agricultural system, many small landowners or tenant farmers had been slipping into the ranks of salaried workers or day labourers, which implied a dramatic decline in general living conditions.[29] Potatoes seemed like an excellent solution to this problem.

But there were other factors.

Potato production also got a huge boost from the catastrophic famine that wracked south-central Italy, the Balkans and North Africa from 1760 to 1770, with one of the worst grain shortages in the modern era. The erratic climate of those years was to blame: very hot summers, sudden downpours, and above all freezing winters with abundant snowfall and frost until late spring. This weather favoured the spread of certain grain diseases, with devastating results.

This series of bad yields came to a head with a terrible harvest in 1763 and a resulting famine in the years that followed, lasting until 1767. As if the general impoverishment of the average diet weren't enough, an epidemic broke out, probably of typhoid fever, which made conditions even more difficult for the vulnerable sectors of society.

On the heels of these tragic events, a series of studies appeared that examined the problem of weather-sensitive crops, especially wheat, suggesting various solutions. The first and most obvious was to find hardier, more resilient grains capable of surviving severe conditions and warding off future famines.[30] Other agronomists began to discuss the cultivation and possible dietary uses of potatoes, and a chorus of expert voices soon rose up around Europe, all echoing the same advice: grow potatoes as a major crop.[31]

While proclaiming the noble goal of preventing the catastrophic effects of famine, the initiatives that followed hid the deeper aim of protecting landowner profits. This can be clearly seen, for instance, in the words of the Bolognese agronomist Pietro Maria Bignami, in a small pamphlet of 1773 that exhorted the local gentry: 'Landowners should in no way be dismayed, but should rather oblige their Tenants to grow the aforesaid potatoes' because 'our Region, though well cultivated, is not capable of maintaining such a large Population with its current produce'; he was certain that if they followed his advice, 'our Province could become one of the richest and happiest in Italy'.[32]

But although there were clear advantages to growing potatoes, it was still necessary to figure out how and in what forms they could replace grains.

Potato gnocchi

Despite the enthusiasm of eighteenth-century agronomists, it soon became clear that potatoes on their own were no good for making bread, and even mixing them with flour did not give promising results. New approaches thus had to be sought.

One of the first to suggest using potatoes for gnocchi and other kinds of pasta was Antonio Zanon, an agronomist in Friuli; in *Della coltivazione e dell'uso delle patate e d'altre piante commestibili* (On the Cultivation and Use of Potatoes and Other Edible Plants, 1767) he writes: 'said dough works very well for making macaroni; but it should be prepared without leavening, and with only as much wheat flour as will render the dough easy to handle, insofar as necessary'.[33] Our old acquaintance Bignami gives similar advice with his 'tagliatelle di patate',[34] as does Nicolò delle Piane, who describes using a potato-based dough 'for the purpose of making tagliolini or lasagne'.[35] We do not know if these pasta recipes made solely with potatoes and flour were popular at the time, but it seems likelier that they weren't, since over a century went by before any recipe of the kind was set down in a cookbook.

Just a few years later, some cooks began to experiment with incorporating potatoes into tried-and-true gnocchi recipes. The first to attempt this was a figure we've encountered before, Vincenzo Corrado. In 1798, twenty-five years after his main work *Il cuoco galante*, he published another book whose very title shows a clear interest in the tuber that had been a focus of debate for almost forty years by then: *Trattato delle patate ad uso di cibo* (Treatise on Potatoes as Food).

Among his various proposals, the ancestors of our ordinary potato gnocchi finally make their appearance. This recipe obviously caters to late eighteenth-century tastes, however, so the main ingredients are hard-boiled egg yolks, veal fat, ricotta, beaten eggs and spices, and the potatoes are only there to bind the mixture and give it a softer texture:

> *Potatoes in gnocchi*
>
> After potatoes have been baked in the oven, their peeled flesh is mashed with a fourth part of hard egg yolks, an equal amount of veal fat, and another of ricotta. This is then combined, and bound together, with a few beaten eggs, seasoned with spices, and divided into many morsels the length and breadth of half a finger, which are floured and put in boiling broth, and boiled for a short time, and dished out and dusted with cheese, and served with gravy.[36]

We're getting closer.

In the nineteenth century, potatoes gradually began to take centre stage, but in recipes that were still quite rich, incorporating ingredients such as milk, cheese, flour and eggs (in Antonio Odescalchi's version) but also parsley, fried garlic, butter and spices (in Giovanni Vialardi's).[37] At the time it would probably have been hard for anyone to imagine that gnocchi made of just potatoes and flour would become so successful as to outlive almost every other kind.

Their first official appearance in this 'pure' form can be traced to two nineteenth-century Genoese cookbooks with almost identical titles, Giovanni Battista Ratto's *La cuciniera genovese*, from 1863 ('Gnocchi con patate' with meat gravy)[38] and *La vera cuciniera genovese* ('Gnocchi al sugo', 'Gnocchi col pesto' and 'Gnocchi al burro').[39]

This time the boiled potatoes are kneaded with an equal amount of flour, and the gnocchi are shaped by pressing and dragging small pieces of dough against a wooden surface. The shape is slightly different from what one might expect, and is described by Ratto as 'a little shaving from a lathe', hence something more similar to trofie (also from Genoa) than to the gnocchi we know.

The agronomists' basic recipe from a century earlier, with its dough of just potatoes and flour, had finally made its way into a cookbook. It is abundantly clear that this was not due to any recollection of what eighteenth-century scholars had suggested, but was instead the result of a natural evolution in the dish, which gradually led to the elimination of all non-essential ingredients.

So are potato gnocchi really from Genoa? Well, the picture that emerges from those decades makes it hard to attribute them to any one region.

In *Il cuoco sapiente* (1871)[40] they reappear, for no apparent reason, as 'Gnocchi alla marchigiana' ('in the style of Marche'). This becomes 'Gnocchi alla lombarda' ('in the style of Lombardy')[41] in *Il vero re dei cucinieri* (1890), but 'Gnocchi di patate'[42] also show up in the section on Bologna in *100 specialità di cucina italiane ed estere* (1908).

At this point, gnocchi couldn't help but be listed among the specialities of Rome as well: first in *La nuova cucina delle specialità regionali* (1909)[43] and then in *Il talismano della felicità* (1927), where Ada Boni sings their praises as 'the traditional Thursday dish of small Roman trattorias, and the dish chosen by many good Romans for their family get-togethers'[44] (which shows that the modern Italian saying *giovedì gnocchi!* – 'Thursday means gnocchi!' – is based on an actual tradition of the past).

After humble beginnings and then a dazzling debut in Neapolitan high society, gnocchi thus became the dish that everyone began to consider part of their local heritage: from Marche to Lombardy, from Genoa to Bologna, and all the way down to Rome.

Pellegrino Artusi, who is always the real watershed marking modern Italian cuisine, included a recipe for potato gnocchi[45] in the very first edition of *La scienza in cucina e l'arte di mangiar bene* (1891). His version basically copies the one from *Il cuoco sapiente* that we saw earlier; the only thing that changes is the amount of flour – reduced to 150g for 400g of potatoes – and the fact that the dough is shaped on the back of a grater (like gnocchi in the Renaissance). The author is well aware that 'The gnocchi family is a large one', but only includes the kinds most common in his era: 'gnocchi alla romana', 'with semolino', 'with maize flour', 'with milk' (a sweet version) and 'in broth' (with chicken breast).

A few years later, Giulia Lazzari-Turco instead takes the opposite approach: in her huge *Manuale pratico di cucina, pasticceria, credenza* of 1904, she includes some twenty-six recipes under the heading 'Various gnocchetti for soups' and just as many under 'Gnocchi (to serve dry)' – and that's not even counting the fried and sweet versions.[46] I think that these numbers alone give a sense of how, at the dawn of the twentieth century, potato gnocchi were still a tiny minority within the avalanche of dumplings pouring out of Italian kitchens.

It was the period between the two wars, when cost, simplicity and versatility became the key factors guiding the process of 'natural selection' in middle-class family cuisine, that led to the definitive triumph of potato gnocchi.

But nowadays, to be honest, gnocchi are not exactly flourishing. Unlike fresh egg pasta – for which the industrial market seems to steadily grow, with good products easily found both on the shelf and in the refrigerated section – gnocchi are extremely delicate and poorly suited to large-scale distribution. In restaurants, the situation is not much better, and fewer and fewer professional cooks choose to put them on the menu.

And yet, when made properly, gnocchi are still a stellar dish. So what's to be done? Well, put some potatoes on to boil, gather some grandkids to help with the dough, and turn it into a family affair.

5

Tortellini alla bolognese

In the Italian culinary universe, filled pasta is a world — or maybe galaxy — unto itself.

Let's take a little tour: we can start off with the agnolotti of Piedmont and head across to the casunziei of Lombardy and Veneto; these, in turn, become tortelli in the area around Cremona, along with marubini, and then anolini in Parma and Piacenza. Travelling further down the ancient Via Emilia, we'll come across variations on tortelli, tortelloni and tortellini that peacefully coexist with the agnolini of Mantua and the cappelletti of Reggio Emilia; around Ferrara, they become cappellacci, then cappelletti throughout Romagna and beyond, into Marche. There are also the pansoti of Liguria that give way, as soon as we cross the Tuscan border, to tordelli; we could finish up with the various ravioli found in Marche, Umbria and further south, but we shouldn't forget the culurgiones of Sardinia, the schlutzkrapfen of Alto Adige and the cjarsons of Friuli. Even though this map isn't exhaustive, it's already somewhat dizzying, and there's no way to avoid leaving something out. The variants number into the hundreds.

This world could be seen as an intricate mosaic where every piece declares its uniqueness, with an interplay of shapes, ingredients and sauces that blend into each other, blurring boundaries that are often proclaimed, but almost never real.

Sometimes the differences are so minimal that even experts lose their way amid the details of closing techniques, fillings and cuts of meat for the broth; these are foodways deeply rooted in the habits of individual families.

Every stuffed pasta, in short, has its own story to tell. And out of all of them, there is one shrouded in legend whose origin myth even drags in the gods of Olympus: Bologna's tortellini, aka 'navels of Venus', the world's most famous and oft-imitated filled pasta.

By tradition, each one is small and elegant, sealed by wrapping it around your little finger. The dough is made from eggs and flour alone, with a very pungent filling: mortadella, prosciutto, pork loin and parmesan, bound with egg and flavoured with nutmeg. These tortellini are plunged into capon broth, in which they are both cooked and served. The essence of Emilian artistry. Pure magic.

Anyone who, like myself, has spent many hours around the pasta board sealing tortellini before the holidays, knows that it is a collective ritual, the epitome of cooking, in which the meal that will be shared is only the last step in a long process. It's a shame to miss out on that or delegate it to others. Even today, in Bolognese homes, making tortellini is a ceremonial act, especially in the days leading up to Christmas. In recent years I've made it a habit to get together with old friends and their children, to repeat the same gestures I watched my grandmother and mother perform when I was little. The pasta is always rolled out with a pin, cut into squares and closed around the fragrant filling. Hundreds of tortellini take shape. Sealing them is the trickiest step: children are watched carefully, with more practised cooks making sure they do their part and don't wolf down too many raw ones. Some of the tortellini are cooked that same evening, always in broth (well, okay: it's no crime to sauté a few with cream and parmesan – but we'll get back to that), while the rest are set aside for the holiday table. Every so often, a whole peppercorn is slipped into the filling – an innocent prank on whoever eats the most bowlfuls at Christmas.

But in Bologna, they *really* tend to serve tortellini on every possible occasion. A perfect anecdote about this was told by Guido Piovene, a journalist that the RAI (the public broadcasting company) sent out to travel around the country in the 1950s for a radio show about Italian customs. In the episode of 21 March 1955, he describes encountering a legendary figure in Bolognese cuisine: Cesarina Masi, founder of the city's famous Ristorante Cesarina.

Cesarina, a renowned Bolognese *ostessa* – if that classic word *ostessa* [innkeeper] isn't an insult to such a cook – says, 'While you're waiting for the first course, let me give you some broth.' She brings me a starter of tortellini. I say I wanted broth. 'In Bologna, broth is what's sitting in front of you,' Cesarina replies. 'You can't call those tortellini, there are thirty at most.'[1]

Even a simple broth, around these parts, can't come without its chubby gold pasta parcels – which should give some inkling why, over the centuries, the city has come to be called 'La Grassa', i.e. Bologna the Fat.[2]

The egg pasta, meat filling and capon broth seem to summarise the spirit of a whole region: the skill in curing pork for which the Po Valley and Bologna are world-famous; the dairylands ruled by that king of cheeses, parmesan; and the bounteous farmyards symbolised by the eggs and poultry.

In short, it seems natural that tortellini should come from Bologna and nowhere else, since they pack all the riches of this area into a little treasure chest of pasta. But all too often, this means that the real story of its long, multiform evolution gets buried under fanciful legends.

The legends of tortellini

A product as perfect as tortellini could only be inspired by Venus, goddess of beauty.

It all started with Alessandro Tassoni's *La secchia rapita* (The Rape of the Bucket, 1630),[3] a classic of Italian mock-heroic verse that tells the story of a war between Modena and Bologna over the boundaries set by Emperor Frederick II.[4]

But of course, Tassoni makes no actual reference to Bolognese tortellini (which, as we will see, did not yet exist in their current form). The legend was created almost three centuries later by an engineer, Giuseppe Ceri,[5] in a long poem of 1908 inspired by Tassoni's *La secchia*, where he invents a whole new episode (nowadays we might call it fanfic) about the 'origin of tortellini'.[6]

The miracle, according to Ceri, took place 'In the ancient inn of Castelfranco'. This establishment was visited by none other than Mars, Venus and Bacchus, who had come down from Olympus in pure Homeric style to aid the warring armies. The location is no coincidence. Since the poet wanted to place the invention of tortellini in the territory of Bologna, his choice naturally fell on the first town across the border from Modena, its rival in this claim (although ironically, ever since the boundaries were redrawn in 1929, Castelfranco Emiliano has been in the province of Modena).

Here's the story: when Venus wakes up in her room to find her companions gone, she summons the innkeeper for an explanation. Then she jumps out of bed with total insouciance, lifting her nightgown up over her navel.

> Then to the great amazement
> Of the innkeep at the door,
> She shrugged off the bedclothes
> As if she were quite alone,
> And flung them to the floor;
> Stretching out a lovely leg,
> She rose from the ample bed
> With a leap so indiscreet
> That her gown happened to slip
> Just a bit above the hip,

> And that happiest of hosts
> (Shall I be coy or honest?)
> Espied the sacred navel of the goddess!

This vision sends the 'squinter from Bologna' into a creative frenzy. Rushing to the kitchen, he seizes a piece of pasta and twists it around his finger to recreate the shape of the 'holy navel':

> He ran quickly down the stairs;
> Seizing the pasta freshly made
> By his ancient kitchen maid
> Who had rolled it on a board,
> He took a tiny round,
> Which he twisted all around
> In a hundred different ways,
> Trying hard to imitate
> The holy navel's special shape.
> And so that squinter from Bologna,
> Eyeing Venus's bellybutton,
> Learned the art of tortellini
> To gladden every glutton!

Ceri remained a fairly obscure poet, but these verses became wildly popular[7] – or at any rate, the story did, and has even acquired variants like an oft-cited one where the innkeeper actually peers through the keyhole to spy on the naked Venus (a detail completely lacking from the original poem, and probably an apocryphal addendum).

This legend had the advantage of placing the invention of tortellini in a town midway between Bologna and Modena, two cities divided by centuries of rivalry but gastronomically connected by tortellini. So for some people, Castelfranco Emilia has become the link uniting two territories under the banner of the 'holy navel', while for others it remains an outpost of Bolognese supremacy and pride. But as they say, when two parties fight the third wins, because in the meantime Castelfranco has risen to fame as the birthplace of tortellini.

VVVVVVVVVVVVV

There is at least one other legend – or rather, fiction – related to the date of their invention. It is an erudite Latin phrase from the twelfth century which seems to be quoted everywhere nowadays: 'tortellorum ad Natale ed ovorum a Pascha'. For at least half a century now, people have erroneously associated it with the Bolognese custom of presenting local prelates with tortellini at Christmas and eggs at Easter. It was made famous by Bolognese historian Alessandro Cervellati, who, in a collection of local legends and stories, pointed to it as a demonstration of the city's ancient ties to this pasta.[8]

But the full phrase is actually 'Consuetudinem Tortellorum ad Natale, et ovorum ad Pascha reddent hospites S. Juliani',[9] and it has no connection to Italy, let alone Bologna. In fact, it comes from one of the many letters written by Maurice de Sully, Bishop of Paris from 1160 to 1196. Taken out of context, the phrase was later quoted in a famous collection of late antique and medieval Latin texts, which may be what led to this gigantic blunder. A blunder made all the worse by the fact that

that 'tortellorum' didn't even refer to any ancient form of stuffed pasta: rather, these were the much more common medieval pies that were often given as gifts or used to pay tithes.* But the mix-up was due in part to the fact that, as we are about to see, 'torte' and 'tortelli' are close relations.

With the legends out of the way, we can move on to the facts.

From torte to tortelli: the medieval roots

Thinking about tortellini, it's impossible not to wonder how anyone came up with the idea of packing so many ingredients and flavours into such a small space. The answer is very simple. Filled pasta was invented in the Middle Ages as a *miniaturisation* of meat, cheese and vegetable pies and pasties, in which a filling was sealed between two layers of dough and then baked. The words 'tortello', 'tortelletto' and 'tortellino'[10] – which all come from adding diminutives to the root word 'torta', meaning cake or pie – clearly show this common origin.

But before moving into the realm of pasta that they inhabit today, these miniature 'torte' belonged to a much larger family that included all doughs made with water and flour: the difference in classification is really more semantic than culinary. After all, a meat filling wrapped in a thin piece of dough is the same basic concept whether it is then boiled or fried; yet the modern observer will see stuffed pasta in the first case and a fritter in the second.

---

* This is made clear by other texts of the time.

At least until the Renaissance, this distinction was much less important, and there was just one category for all 'dishes with dough', no matter how they were cooked.[11]

In medieval cooking treatises, we often find identical recipes that can be cooked in different ways without the status of the dish changing in the least. In some cases a trace of this has survived in modern names, such as Bologna's 'raviole' – which change their grammatical gender, becoming female, to indicate the sweet, baked version – or 'tortelli', a sweet, fried variant that exists with many other names in different parts of Italy.

As always, to retrace the earliest roots of this culinary tradition, we must start by heading to the archives.

The first examples of tortelli meant to be served in broth can be found in two medieval treatises probably composed between the thirteenth and fourteenth centuries. The first is Codex 255 at the Biblioteca Casanatense in Rome, also known – since it is by an unidentified author who wrote in Venetian dialect – as *Anonimo Veneziano*; the second is Manuscript 158 at the Biblioteca Universitaria in Bologna.

The former contains one of the most famous recipes of the Middle Ages, which is always cited as the ancestor of today's filled pastas: 'Torteleti de enula' – *enula* being elecampane, a broad-leaved plant that when cooked has a delicate flavour resembling wild nettles.

Little tortelli of elecampane, etc.

If you want to make little tortelli of elecampane in broth, take capons or beef for XII people, take III pounds of pork loin and take three ounces of mixed fine spices, sweet and strong and quite yellow; take two derate of elecampane and XX eggs, and take the pork loin and put it to boil with the elecampane cleaned of its stems, and when it is well cooked, mince the loin and elecampane, but do not put in all the elecampane. Take the cheese that you have and pound it in a mortar with the loin, and put in enough spices and eggs so that it does not taste too much of elecampane; and put all these things together and make a mince, and then make little tortelli with sheets of yellow pasta. These tortelli should be very yellow and powerfully spiced.[12]

As you can see, the ingredients of the pasta are not specified, only that it should be yellow. Given that eggs were not commonly used in dough at the time, it must have been made with only soft wheat flour, water and some colouring agent, probably saffron. The filling is made of pork loin and elecampane, boiled, finely chopped, and mixed with cheese and eggs; capon or beef is instead used for the broth. The spices called 'sweet and strong' in the recipe are described earlier in the same manuscript, and are pepper, cinnamon, ginger and cloves.[13] With a few calculations, one can see that the weight of the spices is about one-twelfth the weight of the meat in this recipe, hence a truly massive amount. There is instead a total vagueness about the quantity of elecampane, which is indicated only as two 'derate' – two 'denari's' worth, the 'denaro' being a medieval coin – and as if that weren't enough, we are advised not to use all of it, so there is no way to make even an approximate estimation. The shape of these tortelli also remains a mystery, since we are only told that they should be small.

In Manuscript 158 from the Biblioteca Universitaria in Bologna, however, we find not one but three (very brief) recipes for tortelli. Though they are much more concise, one can easily see that they have many points in common with the recipe described just above.

If you want tortelli with elecampane and pork loin

Take the loin and boil it and mince it and take fresh cheese and a few eggs and strong spices and make a stuffing of these things and fill the tortelli and cook them in broth of capon or of anything else and cheese and peppered sauce in bowls.

If you want tortelli in broth

Take well-cooked pork loin and fresh or aged cheese and sweet spices and minced dates and raisins and with these things make tortelli.

If you want tortelli for invalids

Take a chicken wing to make a soup and cook it well and mince it and pound it, and put in sweet spices and orange juice and make very thin wrappings and take

} almonds and temper them in the broth of the chicken
} and cook this milk well and then cook the tortelli in it.[14]

In the first two recipes the main ingredient is once again pork loin that has been boiled, finely chopped and flavoured with cheese and spices. In the first elecampane turns up again (under a different name, 'ella', which appears in the title but not in the text), while the second takes on a much sweeter note with the addition of dates and raisins – a pairing of sweet and savoury that remained very popular until the late seventeenth century, and can still be found in some traditional Italian dishes.* The third and last is the most unusual: a dish intended for invalids, nourishing yet light – or at least so people must have thought at the time. The main ingredient is chicken, which is mixed with orange juice and spices, while almond milk is added to the broth. Using poultry in pasta fillings now seems very strange to Italians, but historically, chicken and capon meat was often employed due to its softness and delicate flavour. As we shall see, this is just the first of many examples.

Moving along, to the middle of the fifteenth century, Maestro Martino offers a more complex and sophisticated recipe for 'Raviuoli in tempo di carne', with a filling that seems inspired by the fried dumplings of an earlier tradition.

---

* The famous tortelli of Mantua have a filling made from pumpkin, apple mostarda, amaretti, parmesan and nutmeg. There are also the cjarsons of Friuli, which have a sweet version with ricotta, jam, crumbled biscuits, raisins and other ingredients, and the tortelli of Cremona, with raisins, candied citron, mostaccioli, amaretti and mints, finely chopped.

To make raviuoli for feast days

To make ten dishes take half a pound of aged cheese and a little of another rich cheese and a pound of fatty pork belly or a cow udder and boil it until it falls apart. Then mince it well and take good herbs, well minced, and pepper, cloves and ginger, and adding the ground breast of a capon will make it better, and mix all these things together. Then cut the pasta very thin and seal this substance in the pasta so that these ravioli are no bigger than half a chestnut, and put them to cook in capon broth and let them boil for the span of two Our Fathers. Then dish them out and put on grated cheese and sweet spices mixed together, and similar ravioli can be made with breast of pheasant and partridge and other fowl.[15]

To summarise: two kinds of cheese (fresh and aged), pork belly (or alternatively, cow udder) that has been boiled, finely chopped and seasoned with spices (pepper, cloves, and ginger) and unspecified herbs (later recipes suggest these could be narrowed down to mint, marjoram and thyme). An optional but recommended addition is capon breast, which can be replaced with pheasant, partridge, etc.

But unfortunately, not even Maestro Martino describes what shape these ravioli should have, saying only that the pasta should be rolled out thin. What's more, compared to the scientific precision we are used to seeing nowadays in recipes, his units of measurement may seem a bit primitive: the ravioli are to be no bigger than 'half a chestnut', and they are cooked in capon broth for the time it takes to say 'two Our Fathers'.

Fried at first

What about in Bologna? What were the filled pasta specialities? The very first recipe for 'Tortelli bolognesi' turns up in a cookbook manuscript (which was never printed) from Veneto, dating to 1501 or 1502. This document is of extraordinary historical importance, since it helps to bridge the geographic and chronological gap between Maestro Martino in the fifteenth century and later cooks in the Renaissance.

The text presents two versions of tortelli bolognesi: the first, with cheese, eggs and spices, could be fried in oil (and was thus suitable for fast days), while the second had a filling of capon or other fowl, flavoured with cheese, eggs, raisins and spices (specifically: cinnamon, cloves, ginger, grains of paradise,[16] mace and pepper).

Bolognese Tortelli

Take 1 ½ pounds fresh cheese & grate it & mix with 5 eggs and half an ounce of fine spices & saffron and make a crust with saffroned sheep's milk and fry in lard or oil.

Tortelli with capon, cockerel or other fowl in the manner of Bologna

Take 1½ pounds of well-ground meat & 6 eggs & blend together with 6 pounds of good cheese and a few raisins & 2½ ounces of spices, to wit, half of cinnamon, eighth of cloves, eighth of white ginger, eighth of grains of paradise, eighth of mace & two *denari*'s worth of pepper & make the crust as said before & fry & put sugar on top.[17]

As for the pasta that encloses the filling ('make the crust as said before'), it was a simple dough of flour and sheep's milk tinted with saffron. The instruction to sprinkle the tortelli with sugar after frying – along with the raisins in the filling – offers an early example of the sweet flavours that would be fashionable for the next two centuries. The only cooking method indicated for these tortelli, like all the others in the manuscript, is frying, and the author never suggests boiling them as an alternative. Looking at these two recipes, we can pick out a few themes that would become recurrent in later versions of tortellini, starting in the second half of the seventeenth century. First, the double options for feast days and fast days, which are characteristic of many traditional dishes: this can still be seen today in the meatless twin of tortellini alla bolognese that is served on Christmas Eve, 'tortelloni della Vigilia' (with ricotta). Second, the capon filling, which we've already seen in the earlier recipe by Maestro Martino, and which played a truly pivotal role in the evolution of tortellini alla bolognese up to the early twentieth century.

151

It is still hard to say just why these two recipes, and none of the others, were considered 'Bolognese'. In the sixteenth century, Bologna was already associated with certain culinary specialities – like its famous 'salsiccioni' (large sausages that were the ancestors of today's mortadella) or its 'torta verde', similar to the 'erbazzone' still made in Reggio Emilia – but was still far from being famous for stuffed pasta.

What we do know is that this first reference to 'tortelli bolognesi' remained the only one for over a century, during which the evolution of tortelli is much easier to trace in other Renaissance cities and courts.

Renaissance tortelli and their names

As the Renaissance moved into full swing, the habit of serving pasta as a side dish to meat – a practice that had ancient precedents[18] and continued to be common in Italy until the late nineteenth century[19] – became firmly established, and then reached its peak.

One example is the recipe for 'Feast-day tortelletti, excellent to serve on their own, or to top duck, pigeon, or other fowl'[20] by Cristoforo di Messisbugo. Whether served in broth, or arranged in layers over capon, duck, pigeon or other fowl and sprinkled with grated cheese, cinnamon and sugar, they were filled only with beef or veal fat, aged cheese, eggs, cinnamon, raisins and sugar (optional).

Another new development in the world of tortelli came from Bartolomeo Scappi; his *Opera* describes two different types that may have influenced the evolution of tortellini alla bolognese.

The first, 'Tortelletti with capon meat',[21] calls for a very rich filling of boiled capon breast and cow udder, bone marrow, chicken fat, cheese, sugar, cinnamon, pepper, saffron, cloves, nutmeg, mint, marjoram and eggs. But the most interesting aspect is the pasta, which is made from flour, rosewater, salt, butter, sugar and warm water: there are still no eggs, which means this dough is particularly soft and sticky.

The same pasta is also used in the second recipe, 'To make tortelletti with pork belly and other ingredients, commonly called annolini'.[22] In this case, the filling resembles the one seen in Maestro Martino's recipe, with pork belly and cow udder, to which one adds cheeses, spices, raisins and elecampane root (the plant appears here for the last time before definitively disappearing from Italian cookbooks). What's truly important about this second recipe is not the choice of ingredients, however, but the fact that it contains the earliest references to the appearance, size, and method of sealing the pasta. 'Make the anolini as small as beans or chickpeas, with the two bits joined together so that they come out looking like little hats [*cappelletti*].' However brief these instructions may be, they allude to what is now a centuries-old practice: pinching together the corners of a tiny dumpling.

At this point, we should make a slight linguistic digression to look at the names that are used for different filled pastas by the various authors cited here. While texts from the Middle Ages employ only the words 'tortelli', 'tortelletti' or 'ravioli', in the Renaissance such terms begin to

153

multiply. In addition to the oldest and most generic name, 'tortelli', we start to find the term 'annolini' – which gradually ushers in the variants 'agnolini' and 'agnellotti' – and finally 'cappelletti'. Judging by the way that the earliest cookbook authors use them, it is clear that these terms were initially thought of as synonyms.[23]

Today, the nomenclature has crystallised into different names for clearly defined forms that have to be kept straight. In Mantua, if you ask for pumpkin cappellacci instead of tortelli, people may point you down the road to Ferrara; the same goes for those who confuse Romagna's cappelletti with Bologna's tortellini. But any reconstruction of the history of filled pasta, whatever the kind, must take this previous interchangeability of the terms into account, because they were being constantly swapped until the twentieth century. Much as it may annoy the more intransigent pasta fans of today, old recipe books contain references to both 'cappelletti alla bolognese'[24] and 'tortellini alla romagnola'[25] at least up to the 1940s. Likewise, there was nothing strange about saying that 'tortellini alla bolognese' should be twisted into the form of 'cappelletti',[26] because the first term was referring to the type of filled pasta, and the second to the final hat-like shape.

Anolini bolognesi

In 1631, Antonio Frugoli, a *scalco* (chief steward or master of ceremonies) from Lucca, published the book *Pratica e scalcaria*, describing various aspects of his job:

from organising banquets for foreign guests to recognising the qualities of different foods, including how to best cook and serve them in keeping with the fashions of the day.

In the chapter devoted to ways of serving duck – a meat that, as we have seen, was often accompanied by filled pasta – Frugoli mentions a dish called 'annolini alla bolognese'. One hundred and thirty years after the first appearance of fried tortelli alla bolognese, we finally come across a boiled version, to be eaten either as an accompaniment to duck or in broth.[27]

> Domestic duck, like wild duck, can be boiled, and should be served hot, covered in various layers of various pastas [. . .] with Annolini alla Bolognese, filled with finely minced veal *rognonata*, or else with bone marrow, with syruped quinces inside, and the right amount of sweet spices, to be served hot with grated cheese, sugar and cinnamon on top.[28]

Although Frugoli offers no further details about the shape or recipe, he provides a basic list of ingredients. And as was customary in the Renaissance, the tortellini are dusted with a blend of grated cheese, spices and sugar. Once again, the description is not quite what we would expect for a stuffed pasta from Bologna. The bone marrow actually made an earlier appearance in Bartolomeo Scappi's fillings, and would become very popular in later recipes as well, but 'rognonata' is mentioned here for the first time. The author is probably using this term to refer to the fat surrounding veal kidneys,* an unusual ingredient found in two other recipes a century apart. It turns up again in the early nineteenth century in a cookbook manuscript by Alberto Alvisi,[29] a cook from Imola, who combines it with bone marrow, parmesan, eggs and nutmeg, and it reappears in exactly the same way in the *Manuale pratico di cucina* of 1904, in a particularly frugal recipe for 'cappelletti alla bolognese'.[30] These versions of the Bolognese speciality show a branch of its evolutionary tree – one of many – that made it to the dawn of the twentieth century before disappearing for good.

Several years after the publication of Frugoli's book, but still in the seventeenth century, two other illlustrious Bolognese authors began to discuss tortellini: Vincenzo Tanara and Bartolomeo Stefani.

We ran into Tanara in the previous chapter.[31] Though his description of tortellini does not yet refer to this pasta as a speciality of Bologna, he was born in the shadow of that city's ancient towers, so it's worth looking at what he had to say on the subject.

Aside from telling us, as other authors do, that 'you can also cover any kind of boiled meat with annolini, or as some say tortellini',[32] he suggests an alternative to cooking them in broth: when describing the courses in a 'Dinner of dairy, and eggs' (that is, without meat or fish) he mentions a dish of 'Anolini, or as some say tortellini,

---

* This hypothesis is based on the fact that it is listed as an alternative to beef marrow, so it must have had somewhat similar characteristics.

cooked in butter, coated in grated Lodi cheese, and served with powdered cinnamon'.[33] This idea of cooking them in butter sounds very odd and has prompted many different interpretations; the most plausible theory is that Tanara did not mean to fry the tortellini in butter, but rather to boil them in a mixture of water and butter, an expedient used to add flavour to 'fast-day' tortellini that could not be cooked in meat broth. The first to mention this trick was Cristoforo di Messisbugo, whose recipe for 'Tortelletti in the style of Lombardy, for meat days, and for fast days' advises cooking them 'in good broth for feast days, and for fast days in water with butter':[34] a method that has been completely forgotten in modern Italian cuisine, but which remained in vogue for several centuries.

The second person to write about tortellini in the seventeenth century was Bartolomeo Stefani, a Bolognese cook who spent most of his career at the court of the Gonzagas in Mantua, where he published his famous treatise *L'arte di ben cucinare* (1662). Like Frugoli, he suggests serving duck topped 'with agiolini, that is, tortelletti filled with marrow and various spices';[35] and in a later passage, he describes 'Domestic duck topped with Genoese crocetti, and around the edge of the plate, Bolognese aiolini,[36] all of this served with Parmesan cheese, and cinnamon . . . ' An actual recipe for agnolini only appeared in the second edition of 1685, where Stefani presents a selection of more budget-conscious, everyday dishes geared to ordinary readers (not just the nobles at court). His agnolini – which, here again, one can deduce are Bolognese due to the author's provenance, but not because they are called that – are made from boiled capon meat and beef marrow mixed with parmesan, eggs, and breadcrumbs quickly cooked in broth, seasoned with cinnamon, cloves, pepper and nutmeg. The pasta dough, which is equally rich, calls for flour, butter, egg yolks and saffron.[37]

Round tortellini

While Bartolomeo Stefani could be considered the last great Italian cook to carry on the traditions of the Italian Renaissance, in the seventeenth century the map of food was about to be redrawn: for the next hundred years or so, it was France that would set the culinary rules for Europe. There was a break here, a sort of hiatus. Many Italian recipes that had begun to emerge at the time either vanished altogether, or at least were put on pause.

And that is exactly what happened with tortellini alla bolognese.

For another recipe to turn up, we have to wait more than a century. More specifically, until 1790, when tortellini reappear in Francesco Leonardi's masterpiece *L'Apicio moderno*, the book that did more than any other to pull the compass needle of modern gastronomy back towards the Italian peninsula.[38]

This time, the name of the dish, 'Zuppa di Tortellini alla Bolognese', leaves no room for doubt that we're nearing our goal. Give or take a few details.

Soup of Tortellini in the Style of Bologna

Make pasta as in the previous recipe. In a mortar, pound some roast chicken breast, add cleaned beef marrow, grated parmesan, a piece of butter, salt, nutmeg, finely powdered cinnamon and two raw egg yolks. Cut the above pasta with a small round stamp, put a bit of filling on each of these rounds, wet all the edge with beaten egg and cover with the other round. You will cook them like tagliolini, but they need to be cooked a little longer. The two egg yolks will depend on the preferences of the person making them, since they can be omitted. This recipe can also be used to make Ravioletti, or Cappelletti. For the former, cut the rounds a little larger, and fold them like ravioli. For the latter, once you have folded the ravioli, join the two corners together to make cappelletti; I will talk about these and the others later, since they are served with various Entrées, Entremets, Baked Dishes, Soups, etc.[39]

Though this is a simpler recipe than Stefani's, it is not much different. The pasta is now made only with eggs and flour, and with rare exceptions (like the sporadic inclusion of a varying amount of water), this will remain the general rule in later eras. The filling is still a mixture of marrow and poultry (in this case, chicken replaces capon); the bread cooked in broth has completely disappeared and even the eggs have become optional. A preference for parmesan over other cheeses has begun to take root, while only cinnamon and nutmeg linger on as spices, foreshadowing a gradual disappearance that will leave only the latter in the modern-day recipe.

At long last, this recipe also describes how these famous tortellini should be closed: after cutting out a round disc of pasta, one daubs on a little filling and tops it with a second disc, carefully wetting the edges with beaten egg to help seal them. Now, this description makes one thing clear: tortellini alla bolognese had *not* yet acquired their current shape; instead, they were perfectly round dumplings made from two circular pieces of pasta, like the anolini one now finds in Parma. Leonardi goes on to describe two other ways of closing them: if the discs with filling in the centre are folded into a half-moon shape, they are called ravioli, whereas if the corners of a raviolo are joined together, it becomes a cappelletto. Given this first description of the shape of tortellini alla bolognese, we can see why they were still being called anolini in the seventeenth century.[40] Although a more specific vocabulary for filled pastas had begun to emerge after the free-for-all of the Renaissance, it was still evolving. Vincenzo Agnoletti, for instance, in *La nuova cucina economica*, published only thirteen years later, has a completely different take on the matter: cappelletti have a filling sealed between two discs to form 'the dome of a hat' (what Leonardi calls a tortellino), while tortellini are made by joining the points of half-moon-shaped ravioli.[41] In this description, Agnoletti finally identifies the modern shape of tortellini, the one still used today, although the piece cut from the pasta was still round and thus lacked the characteristic upward point we are used to seeing. The square shape caught on only in the 1930s, above all in homemade versions.*

This recipe calls for serving tortellini alla bolognese in broth, but further on in Leonardi's book we also find two other options: in a 'terrine' (what we would now call a baking dish)[42] – and in a pastry crust.[43] In the first case, after being drained of broth and tossed with parmesan, butter, a ham coulis and truffles, the tortellini are topped with parmesan and butter and given a quick turn in the oven; the 'en croute' version instead calls for the tortellini to be mixed with a béchamel sauce of cream, butter and flour seasoned with parmesan, truffles and cinnamon, then sealed in shortcrust and baked. These variations are far from insignificant: rather, they are bound to come as a shock to all the purists who now clutch their pearls at baked versions of tortellini, since they prove that from the very beginning, anolini and tortellini 'alla bolognese' were never *only* served in broth.

* As proof of this fact – which many Italians would find astonishing – all early illustrations of tortellini alla bolognese still depict them as round. One example among many is a famous magazine cover illustration by Augusto Majani for *Bologna la Grassa* (1907), where a buxom woman flaunts a hat that is actually a (very round) piece of filled pasta. See *Bologna la Grassa*, 6 January 1907.

Nineteenth-century trends and Artusi's doffed hat

Throughout the 1800s, though a number of variations are recorded, the basic range of ingredients remained fairly loyal to the version set down in the late 1700s by *L'Apicio moderno*.

To briefly summarise the trends of the nineteenth century: the main meat in the filling is chicken, or sometimes capon, with beef marrow almost always added to bind and soften the mixture; in just a few cases, veal or brains (usually from a cow) are used. Parmesan, with very rare exceptions, turns up in every recipe, often along with ricotta. Bread cooked in broth or milk comes back into vogue in a series of recipes between the 1830s and the 1860s, but then completely disappears. A mixture of spices continues to be mentioned, with a prevalence of nutmeg, which by the end of the century was starting to be the primary seasoning employed.

And the key ingredient in modern recipes, pork? The first to mention it, indirectly, is the *Codice gastrologico economico*, from 1841, which in a recipe for tortellini alla bolognese advises using, as an alternative to marrow, 'cervellato di Milano'.[44] This unusual sausage, primarily used to flavour fillings, bases and soups, was made from a blend of pork belly, brains, parmesan, salt and spices.[45]

Prosciutto, on the other hand, was first introduced in *La cuciniera moderna* in 1845, but in a somewhat roundabout manner. The recipe in which it appears, 'Zuppa composta con carne',[46] describes pastaless dumplings similar to the Tuscan gnudi of today, but made from boiled or stewed meat, prosciutto, bread soaked in broth, egg yolks, parmesan, parsley, cinnamon and nutmeg. All of this is mixed and moulded into small meatballs, rolled in flour and cooked in broth. Only at the end of the recipe do we find this note, as an afterthought: 'this mixture can also be used to make cappelletti alla bolognese'.[47]

Pork loin, which is now one of the fundamental ingredients in the filling, appears for the first time in the recipe for 'Cappelletti alla bolognese'[48] in *Il cuoco sapiente* of 1871, along with chicken, parmesan, ricotta and eggs. It is used again in two other cookbooks published shortly thereafter[49] and then abandoned, reappearing only in the 1930s, as an element that still came and went.

As regards the various names for filled pasta from Bologna, until the very end of the nineteenth century there was still no general consensus about what it should be called. The recipes are almost evenly split: about half already use the term 'tortellini alla bolognese' (with the variants 'tortelli' and 'tortelletti'), while others refer to 'cappelletti alla bolognese'. The first to draw a clear boundary between tortellini bolognesi and cappelletti romagnoli – as authoritative as ever – was the father of modern Italian cooking: Pellegrino Artusi.

'When anyone mentions Bolognese food you should doff your hat, for respect is due.' This is the famous opening sentence of Artusi's chapter on 'tortellini alla bolognese', which was destined to change the contours of this recipe for good.

La scienza in cucina e l'arte di mangiar bene (Science in the Kitchen and the Art of Eating Well)[50] was first published in 1891, a century after Leonardi's recipe and the two versions in Stefani's second edition. Just as they had, it marked a clear turning point in the evolution of the Bolognese speciality, but in this case the leap was so modern in taste that it still reverberates in the recipe used today.

By Artusi's era, certain features of tortellini alla bolognese had already become well established: the pasta made only from eggs and flour, the round disc and the way it was folded. To show how the pasta should be cut, Artusi even includes a drawing with the exact width: 37 millimetres.* This standard had already been noted by *Il cuoco sapiente* in 1871,[51] which calculated it based on the diameter of a 'five-lire silver coin', and this become the rule for most later authors until the advent of the square shape.

The most substantial innovation has to do with the filling, though. The previously canonical beef marrow and parmesan are still there, but the rest of the meat is replaced by two cured pork products whose long reign has

---

* One should note that a tortellino made from a 37mm disc is really quite small, as is the amount of filling that can fit inside. Given the proportions, each of the 300 tortellini that Artusi promises the recipe will yield must contain less than a gram of filling.

continued without interruption up to the present: prosciutto and mortadella. All of this is mixed with a whole egg and spiced with nutmeg alone. The capon breast and egg yolk are demoted to optional ingredients that can be used to make the filling 'milder'. But here's the full recipe, since it's worth a look.

Tortellini alla bolognese

When anyone mentions Bolognese food you should doff your hat, for respect is due. The city's style of cooking is a bit heavy, perhaps, because the climate demands it; yet it is succulent, flavourful and so healthy that lifespans of eighty or ninety years are more common there than elsewhere. The tortellini below, though simpler and less costly than the ones described above, are no inferior in taste, and if you try them you will see.

Prosciutto, both fat and lean, 30 grams.
Bolognese mortadella, 20 grams.
Beef marrow, 60 grams.
Grated parmesan, 60 grams.
Egg, 1.
Grated nutmeg.
Salt and pepper, none.

Mince the prosciutto and mortadella well with a mezzaluna; mince the marrow likewise without melting it over the heat, add it to the other ingredients and blend them all with the egg, mixing well. Seal the filling in egg pasta as in the other recipes, cutting it with the small no. 8 stamp. These tortellini will keep for days or even a few weeks without spoiling, and if you would like them to preserve their fine yellow colour, put them above the oven to dry as soon as they are made. This recipe will make just under 300, and is for three eggs' worth of pasta. [. . .] If you want tortellini that are even milder in flavour, add half a capon breast cooked in butter, an egg yolk, and the proper amount of all the other ingredients.

This recipe marks a definitive turning point in the literature and almost all later authors will be forced to work in relation to it, whether they are among Artusi's innumerable imitators, or the very few who attempt to move away from his model.

The registered recipe

The most revolutionary aspect of Artusi's filling, which set the recipe sailing on its current course, is the way it foregrounds the cured meats – to which another cut of pork, usually cooked, chopped loin, will soon be added, gradually edging out the chicken and capon.

The first example of tortellini alla bolognese made only with pork loin, mortadella, prosciutto, parmesan, egg, nutmeg and a small amount of beef marrow appeared in 1934, in a brief recipe published by the magazine *La Cucina Italiana*.

Tortellini alla bolognese

Make a filling with: 250 gr. pork loin; 100 gr. mortadella; 100 gr. prosciutto; 200 gr. grated parmesan; 25 gr. beef marrow; salt to taste (not too much), grated nutmeg.

Make a sheet of pasta using 6 eggs and 700 gr. flour, and immediately, before it becomes too stiff, cut it into rounds or squares. Put a little filling into the centre of each round; fold them over into a half-moon shape. Lastly, close the tortellini by pressing the two corners together. Cook in broth.[52]

This recipe is also the first to offer the option of cutting the pasta either into the former rounds or into the one shape still used today: a square. This coexistence of these two shapes would linger on for a few decades, but as Giuseppe Oberosler points out in his 1954 cookbook: 'The classic way to make tortellini is with a round disc, but at home the pasta is often more quickly cut into small squares, which are handled in the same way as the rounds.'[53] In other words, a more practical but less elegant approach, which was fine for family use, but not in restaurants or for a sophisticated dinner.

It may come as a surprise to some that an iconic aspect of the 'traditional recipe' which is now thought of as set in stone – cutting the pasta in squares – is so recent. And it may come as an even bigger surprise that this 'traditional recipe' has a specific date of birth (which is anything but remote): 7 December 1974.

On that day, the Dotta Confraternita del Tortellino ('Learned Brotherhood of the Tortellino'), in collaboration with the Accademia Italiana della Cucina, registered the notarised recipe 'Filling for the True Tortellino of Bologna' with the Bologna Chamber of Commerce. Yet this proclamation of the most authentic way of making tortellini was not arrived at, as one might imagine, through in-depth historical research, but rather through a competition in the newspaper *Il Resto del Carlino*, which invited families and homemakers throughout Bologna to send in their recipes.[54] The winning entry came from Signora Maria Lanzoni Grimaldi. Here it is:

[. . .] the Recipe for the Filling of the True Tortellino of Bologna, whose fame is not only universal, but centuries old, lost in History and blurring into legend, is as follows:
300 g pork loin browned in butter
300 g prosciutto
300 g authentic Bolognese mortadella
450 g Parmigiano-Reggiano cheese
3 eggs
1 nutmeg

Directions for properly preparing approximately 1000 tortellini. The Bologna Delegation of the Accademia Italiana della Cucina decrees this recipe to be the most reflective of a formulation which will ensure the classic, traditional flavour of the True Tortellino of Bologna, the one that has been prepared, cooked, served and enjoyed in the Families, Trattorias and Restaurants of the Fat and Erudite City of Bologna for centuries. This recipe was developed and submitted by Signora Maria Lanzoni Grimaldi, whose long experience and culinary skill deserve to be honoured by present and future generations.[55]

Compared to the previous tradition, a few things are clearly missing. For instance, there is no sign of the beef marrow, which as we have seen was one of the most frequent ingredients in the history of tortellini alla bolognese (although it had already begun its decline in the 1940s, sometimes replaced by beef brains). The only meat now employed is pork, with no interference from chicken or capon – which are not mentioned even as a possible alternative, as many cookbooks did at the time. The proportion of cured meats and parmesan in the filling thus increases to over three times the weight of the fresh meat, making this filling much drier, leaner and denser than older versions.

At this point, one has to wonder: why on earth was this specific kind of recipe singled out, when it does not remotely resemble even the most authoritative historic examples (Artusi, for starters)?

As always, the answer may come as a let-down to zealous champions of authenticity: I suspect that the recipe was influenced by the fillings used by artisanal and industrial pasta makers. For mass-produced tortellini, the main goal in formulating the filling was to make the product flavourful, but above all, make it keep well, despite the meat it contained. The high proportion of cured meats and parmesan, ingredients with quite a bit of salt, had the advantage of creating the ideal conditions for the filling to dry without deterioration, while also imparting a stronger, more aromatic flavour than home-made tortellini made with beef marrow, white meat and small amounts of pork.

By the 1970s, when the registered recipe was published, the industrial production of tortellini was anything but new. One need only look at success stories such as Bertagni, a company that in the late nineteenth century had already come up with a way to dry and package tortellini for export; they were a hit at fairs around the world, starting with the famous Exposition Universelle of 1889 in Paris, where the firm was awarded a bronze medal for its products.[56] The Italian market responded by welcoming the invasion of mass-produced tortellini with open arms, to the point that by the early twentieth century, some cookbooks merely provided tips on cooking times, as Giulia Ferraris Tamburini does in *Come posso mangiar bene?* (1913):

> The tortellini known as Bolognese are usually eaten in broth, and since they can be found ready made in shops, I will explain how to cook them. To make them in broth, put them in the liquid when it is still just slightly warm, and once the boil has made them rise to the top, which takes about half an hour, serve them nice and hot.[57]

You may have noticed that the recipe registered in 1974 contains no instructions about the shape of the tortellini or other details. This text, which has not been widely reprinted, has been replaced by a second 'official document' that can instead easily be found online.[58] It contains additional information, from the shape of the tortellini – which are to be made from a three-centimetre-square piece of pasta – to the fact that they are cooked in broth; the latter is emphasised even in the title, which clearly states that the 'true recipe' is for tortellini *in brodo*. This is an important distinction, given that the dish also came in many sauced or baked versions. More specifically, the most common alternative to broth in the nineteenth century was meat gravy, or coulis, and a lavish sprinkling of cheese, whereas in the twentieth, the most frequently recorded was butter and parmesan. There were also versions baked in pastry with béchamel, or drained and served with an array of sauces: prosciutto and chicken livers, tomato sauce, ragù alla bolognese, the liquid from beef stew or finanziera, and the most infamous of all – cream.

Just a word in defence of this last version, which is now unquestionably the one most frowned upon. Because once again, history contradicts the purists: tortellini with cream were actually invented at one of Bologna's finest restaurants, and that's easy to prove.

They were the brainchild of none other than Cesarina Masi, the famous chef that Piovene encountered at the beginning of this chapter. And don't make the mistake of assuming that her trattoria, La Cesarina, must have been a glorified greasy spoon: it was listed in the Michelin guide, starting with the very first French edition of 1956. We're talking about a pillar of traditional Bolognese cooking. Tortellini with cream began to appear on Cesarina's menu in the early 1940s at the Via degli Albari location that she ran with her mother, and she brought them along to the restaurant in Piazza Santo Stefano that opened in 1947 (and is still there today). Cesarina gradually became one of the most famous figures in Bologna, and when she opened Il Transatlantico in Rome, her reputation followed. Located at 209 Via Sicilia, this establishment was close to Via Veneto, the street of VIPs and of Fellini's *Dolce Vita*: on any given day, politicians, actors and filmmakers could be found at its tables. As with fettuccine Alfredo, this star factor contributed quite a bit to the spread and popularity of tortellini with cream.[59] So much so that – like carbonara, too – the recipe for it first appeared in print outside of Italy, in the British cookbook *Italian Food* by Elizabeth David, published in 1954.[60]

〰〰〰〰〰〰〰〰

The story we have retraced here, from the earliest days of fresh filled pasta all the way to the tortellino, is one of the longest in Italian food history. And the lesson we can draw from it is that no one ingredient, or shape, or other feature can be pointed to as the common denominator of all the tortellini seen so far. Although there is, perhaps, one thing that the majority of authors agree upon: tortellini are supposed to be small.[61]

As in other cases, when the registered recipe obtained the seal of authority, it acquired a status that seems to elevate it above the rest, for better or for worse; it has become a touchstone establishing what is 'traditional' and what is not, even though its formulation may be more reflective of industrial constraints than of any real historical continuity. But registering a recipe can only slow down experimentation for a while, not stop it. It's true enough that almost half a century later, most tinkering is still focused on the proportions of the ingredients. Yet in recent years we have begun to see small tectonic tremors in the bedrock of tortellini, and some cooks are daring to go further – leaving out the prosciutto, for example, to make the filling more delicate. These gradual inroads may allow the recipe to start evolving again. Even the dry version with cream, so harshly and so wrongly criticised, has begun to be transformed: some are adding a bit of broth, some are blending in parmesan, some are trying to achieve the same rich silkiness with completely different ingredients, such as a tempting savoury zabaione.[62]

In short, it seems that once again, however slowly, new frontiers are opening up.

6

Ragù alla napoletana

If I asked a sample of Italians to list the ten most important pasta dishes, I'm not sure how many would mention
ragù alla napoletana, the meat sauce of Naples. But in
this chapter, which forms a sort of diptych with the next
one (on ragù alla bolognese) we will see just how pivotal
its role in food history has been.

Let's start at the end this time: here's the most 'official'
recipe for Neapolitan ragù that can currently be found on
the web.

Ragù napoletano

Various cuts of meat can be used, even from different
species: the most common are beef 'locena' (from the
clod/chuck region, in any case, a fatty, sinewy cut from
the shoulder of an adult cow), in fairly large pieces
(five to six centimetres), and pork 'tracchie' (a cut of
ribs with little meat and lots of fat); some also add
pork sausages, with a hand-chopped filling or with

offal (like 'nnoglia' or 'pezzente', with pork liver or lung), or meatballs made from stale bread, eggs, grated pecorino and minced beef and pork. There must always be 'braciole': a fairly thick slice of locena, spread with a mixture of finely chopped pecorino, garlic, parsley, pine nuts and raisins, salt and pepper, rolled up and tied with twine or secured with toothpicks or metal skewers. In place of the beef one can also use pork rind, with some of the fat removed first by boiling. Whatever meat is used, it is cooked first, adding it to an abundant amount of 'old' (plaited) white or yellow onions, celery and carrots, diced and cooked in lard or in extra-virgin olive oil over very low heat; the meat may be wrapped in pancetta or prosciutto. In any case, it should be cooked at very low heat to keep it from drying out, adding red wine several times and letting it boil off. Once it has browned in the pot, one should raise the heat slightly and add tomato paste (in the past, one would have used 'conserva': tomato purée dried on plates in the sun) and then, after it has cooked for quite a while, tomato purée, a little salt and fresh basil leaves; some people also add a spoonful of white wine vinegar and a very small amount of sugar.[1]

As you can see, this is an opulent, elaborate recipe, which calls for stewing various cuts of meat with a vast array of flavourings and vegetables. And the pasta? Well, unlike its cousin from Bologna, the Neapolitan version of ragù tops it only with the sauce derived from cooking the meat in tomato purée.* Upon its first appearance, this approach set the stage for an entirely new way of serving pasta, and all other modern sauces are to some degree indebted to it.

But now let's take a look at how it all began.

Dangerous delicacies

As one might guess from the name, ragù – or rather, 'ragoût' – got its start in France.

For at least two centuries after its invention, the purpose of ragoût/ragù/ragout was to flavour other dishes, especially meat and fish, adding verve to foods that would otherwise be perceived as a bit monotonous. But what was meant, at the time, by ragout? It was really a whole universe of sauces, all different but all designed to accompany roasts and boiled meats and give them a completely new, sometimes unexpected flavour. Sometimes these delectable concoctions even carved out a place of their own on the table and were served as an independent dish; this fashion, launched by the French in the early 1600s and quickly adopted by all other European cuisines, vanished for good only at the turn of the twentieth century. In the meantime, however, the sauce had been wedded to pasta – luckily enough, since otherwise it might have disappeared from menus long ago. But the pairing of pasta and ragù was neither obvious nor 'natural'; like any radical innovation, it moved by skips and hops over the years to arrive at its current form.

---

* In the most recent versions, an increasing portion of the meat also winds up in the pasta.

As with all new ideas, especially the appetising kind, the appearance of ragù at first raised many concerns about its effect on the body. Sauce, after all, was an extra indulgence; an artifice for gluttons who were tired of always eating the same boiled or roasted viands; an invention of sybaritic cooks who thought only of the palate and cared little for health.

That, at least, was the view expressed by the anonymous author of the cookbook *La cuciniera piemontese*, in discussing the new fad imported from France:

> *Ragout:*
>
> a delicacy, or rather, sauce, dressing, condiment meant to reawaken the appetite of those who have lost it. [. . .] [Foods] dressed up in a hundred different ways, with a profusion of spices and condiments to enhance their flavour, are harmful to the health, since they provoke violent fermentations, which corrupt our humours, and make the firm parts of the body lose their elastic virtues; and in the end, they destroy the principles of life.[2]

It is hard to say what physical reactions might actually correspond to these 'violent fermentations' or impairments to the 'elastic virtues' of the 'firm parts of the body' – not to mention the destruction of the 'principles of life' – but this all sounds truly catastrophic. In short, if the doctors of today tell you to avoid saturated fats and excess salt, in the eighteenth century they definitely would have vetoed ragù.

Almost a century earlier, the famous French cook François Massialot must have thought much the same, but in loyalty to his profession felt obliged to venture a token defence: 'And even if all these ragouts should contribute to the corruption of the body, is it not also true that they help sustain it, by warding off both lack of appetite and lassitude [. . .]?'[3]

Despite such dietetic qualms, in the seventeenth century ragouts became all the rage. Any recipe book worthy of the name included them among the cornerstone dishes of fine dining, yet as is often the case, literature had noticed the fad long before it made its way into cookbooks.

To find what is probably the first reference to ragout, we must peer into a French comic novel of 1623 that describes the amorous adventures of a character named Francion. At one point the narrator lists the dishes served at a luncheon, and upon reaching the third course, mentions a round of ragouts (in this context, a standalone dish).[4] Other allusions would follow in a range of publications, but they are always vague, with no indication of the ingredients or method adopted.

By the time chefs finally bothered to describe it, more than fifty years later, it was already a well-developed concept with several variants. Actually, at this point, ragout was still a cooking method rather than a specific recipe (manuals of the time often referred to dishes as 'cooked in ragout', just as we would now say 'braised').

One of the first to offer an exhaustive explanation of ragout was François Massialot himself, in *Le cuisinier roïal e bourgeois* (1691). This court chef reached the pinnacle of his career serving Philippe d'Orléans, the younger brother of Louis XIV, and was an authority on French cooking at its very peak. His ragout recipes are often scattered within descriptions of other dishes, but some are specific enough to give us an idea of what the term meant in the late seventeenth century, as in this recipe for 'Bisque de Pigeons':

> To make the ragout, you must take well-blanched Veal sweetbreads cut in half, diced mushrooms, sliced truffles, quartered artichoke bottoms [. . .] You will brown this ragout with a little lard & flour & an onion piqué [with a bay leaf and cloves], & let it become just golden. When it is thus browned, add a small amount of good broth and let it cook with a slice of lemon.[5]

This sauce is served over pigeons that have been stewed in another dense broth of cockscombs. In short, this is a complex dish and the ragout is only one part of it. But the structure of this recipe, however concise, reveals the basic steps: meat and vegetables, cut into chunks, are first browned in fat – usually lard or butter – and then braised in broth, thickened at the end with a little flour.

The ingredients in this early recipe often turn up again over the centuries that follow. Veal sweetbreads, mushrooms, truffles and artichoke hearts are used in the most common versions, but seventeenth-century ragouts could also be perked up with cockscombs, morels, garlic cloves, poultry livers, ham, chestnuts and unlaid eggs (found inside laying hens). The recipe very often incorporated some aromatic, acidic note like lemon (slices or juice), vinegar or verjuice (a condiment inherited from medieval cuisine: the juice of unripe grapes or other sour fruit).

Ragù comes to Italy

Around the time that Massialot was writing his treatise, the ragout craze swept across Europe, and this new word began to ricochet though all kinds of publications. A French–English dictionary from 1677 offers this definition: 'RAGOUT (m) ragoo, a dish of meat dressed in a curious sauce.'[6] The anglicisation and the 'curious sauce' seem to indicate that the fashion had already arrived, but was still far from being to everyone's taste.

Though Italy was still clinging to its solid Renaissance tradition, French customs began to make ever deeper inroads, and would shape the evolution of food for at least two centuries.

This influence was also felt by the Bolognese chef Bartolomeo Stefani. His handbook *L'arte di ben cucinare* (1662) contains one of the first references to 'ragù' by an Italian cook: 'Four Turkeys larded between flesh and skin, wrapped in caul fat, dusted with ground mostaccioli biscuits, nutmeg and cloves, baked under embers, and served with a Ragù made from egg yolks, mastic, lemon juice and veal kidney fat.'[7]

This succinct reference to the French speciality confirms that, by this point, the concept of ragout/ragù was spreading even within Italy, and that the recipes probably resembled those across the Alps.

More than a century would have to go by, however, for a cookbook to provide real instructions on how to make one. It was Vincenzo Corrado[8] who finally did so in *Il cuoco galante* (1773),[9] which contains a series of brief recipes for ragù, like these three examples:

> *Breast of Veal – In Ragù with prugnolo mushroom sauce*
>
> Having barded the Veal in well seasoned and herbed strips of lard and prosciutto, one puts it to stew with the usual things, bathing it in white wine; and upon serving it is covered in a sauce of prugnoli [St George's mushrooms].
>
> *Sturgeon – In Ragù with oil*
>
> The Sturgeon is fried in olive oil, with parsley, thyme, onions, minced mushrooms, and truffles; and once it is well seasoned, it is bathed in the broth of other fish, and white wine to cook it. Upon serving, it is covered in a Coulis of Prawns.
>
> *Ragù of eggs*
>
> The Eggs are cooked in ragù; after being hard-boiled and cut in half, they are put in a pot, containing a ragù

⁓ of mushrooms, truffles, spring onions and parsley,
⁓ flavoured with butter and spices.*

As in the French tradition, a ragù could be used to add zest to other dishes, or be served as a dish unto itself, but was not yet associated with pasta. The two foods would soon be wedded, however, with the help of another delicacy that was also brought into vogue by the brilliant Corrado.

The era of timbales

As we've noted more than once, in the Middles Ages pasta was traditionally topped with cheese, and almost always cheese alone; then, in the mid-fifteenth century, butter began to be added. Other ingredients, such as spices and sugar, came along to liven up this base and remained in use until the end of the Renaissance. But filled varieties aside, there were really very few recipes that paired pasta with meat or vegetables until the eighteenth century at the earliest. Rare, famous examples include the medieval 'torta di lasagne'[10] or a recipe for hare with pappardelle[11] by Renaissance cook Domenico Romoli.

The earliest link to our modern approach was the timballo: an Italian take on what was originally a French speciality, the timbale. And the first treatise to bring this dish to the attention of Italian cooks was *Il cuoco*

---

* As one may note, ragùs could be made from many different foods; the author describes other recipes with kidneys, veal ears, lobster, grouper and so on.

piemontese perfezionato a Parigi ('The Piedmontese Cook Perfected in Paris', 1766),[12] which borrows heavily from a French cookbook published shortly before it, *La cuisinière bourgeoise*.[13] In addition to a pigeon timbale copied from the French book, it presented a primordial form of baked pasta in which meat is mixed in with the macaroni.

This was something of a revolution.

> One can also cook Macaroni in broth, along with a pullet, and when the macaroni is ready, the pullet too will be ready; remove the pullet, and cut it into pieces; place a layer of macaroni in the dish, sprinkling grated cheese over it, and a quantity of pepper, and salt if needed; put in some pieces of pullet, with cheese over it, and then another layer of macaroni with cheese, and then the rest of the pullet, and macaroni, with a quantity of pepper, a few pieces of fresh butter, and abundant cheese. Let it take on a golden colour in the oven.[14]

As this example shows, the pairing of pasta with chicken meat, which is now almost unheard of in Italy, was enjoyed there for many years. But the main point is that this recipe opens up new vistas that Vincenzo Corrado will fully explore seven years later, when the pasta timballo becomes a more structured dish. In *Il cuoco galante*, baked pasta holds such pride of place that ordinary pasta, dished up and dressed with cheese, almost disappears from the list of foods.[15] It was probably the demand for theatricality at the great banquets of Neapolitan nobles that led pasta to take on a more opulent, elegant guise – a glitzier one. And macaroni sealed in a crisp coffer of pastry became the star of the show.

Let's take a look at one recipe:

Timballo of Macaroni with sauce

The crust to use for timballi is puff pastry, or a light shortcrust, but without sugar. After cooking the macaroni in Beef broth, and letting it dry and cool, put it into the dough, well covered in cheese, with quantities of thick Beef gravy, with Pork sausages, mushrooms, truffles and ham, all minced and cooked in the same sauce. Cover all of this with another sheet of pastry, bake it in the oven, and serve.[16]

The cheese is still there – the habit of 'cheesing' the macaroni as the first step remains unchanged – but has taken a back seat to the other ingredients. The timballo filling is truly characterised by an ingredient that would soon become essential in any good pasta dish: *sugo di carne*.[17]

This exquisite gravy is obtained by searing meat in a fat such as butter or lard (or, in Corrado's case, by putting it on a spit, although there are no other examples of this in the later literature), along with additional ingredients meant to add richness and fragrance. Once it takes on the classic brown crust (that is, once the flavours and colours have been enhanced by the Maillard reaction)* it is bathed in beef broth to finish cooking, letting

---

* The Maillard reaction is a complex chemical transformation that takes place when meat is cooked at high temperatures, and is what gives it that classic 'grilled' smell.

the aromatic drippings melt into the liquid.* When it is done, the ingredients are all mashed and filtered, their juices are squeezed out and the excess fat is skimmed off. Lemon juice is added off the heat, for an acidic note that cuts through the unctuousness of the sauce. This method extracts every ounce of flavour from the meat, vegetables and spices, distilling them into a fragrant, savoury liquid, its consistency varying between a dense broth and a thick *glace de viande*. The procedure for making it remained more or less unchanged for centuries.

When it reached the Italian peninsula, the traditional French timbale became the container for an entirely new kind of filling. A pasta base, mixed with something that was not the ragù we know today, but was beginning to resemble it. The new currents from France had helped to free pasta from the traditional framework (almost exclusively based on dairy products) that had encaged it for centuries, and had finally opened the door to experimentation with new pairings.

The path to modern pasta was now free and clear.

Francesco Leonardi's revolution

Naples was a major trade hub. It had its own rich culinary tradition long before the eighteenth century. And

---

* Although the procedure differs, this base still exists in Italian cooking as 'fondo bruno' and is used to add flavour, especially to meat dishes.

pasta was among its most traditional foods, going so far back that by the mid-sixteenth century there was already a version of 'maccheroni alla napoletana' for Cristoforo di Messisbugo to record.[18] But that early recipe reflects the canonical tastes of the time, presenting tagliatelle or thick spaghetti made from flour, egg, breadcrumbs and sugar, cooked in broth and served as a side dish to capon or duck.[19] Nothing could be further from the dish that goes by the same name today.

It is described in its fully developed form more than two centuries later by Francesco Leonardi,[20] in *L'Apicio moderno*. This massive work predated Pellegrino Artusi's *Scienza in cucina e l'arte di mangiar bene* (which we will examine in the next chapter) by a century, but can be considered just as much of a milestone in Italian culinary literature. In its multiple volumes, drawing on his vast knowledge of Italian and European cooking, Leonardi tries to revive the spirit of his native cuisine after the long interlude of French domination, presenting a compendium of culinary doctrine in his time and heralding the revolution that was on its way in the next century. A revolution that would spawn a vast number of books on food aimed at the growing middle class, which was trying to preserve the prestige of aristocratic customs, yet find a culinary sphere of its own.

Thanks to Leonardi, pasta began to have its own specific place even on the 'map' of the meal: it was in the nineteenth century that it put down definitive roots as part of the first course. In other words, it was with *L'Apicio moderno* that pasta embarked on the slow path of conquest that led it to the heart of Italian cuisine.

Although the book does not contain a huge number of pasta dishes,* it introduces a few pivotal innovations, pairing the food with new sauces – as Vincenzo Corrado had already begun to do – and firmly establishing the practice of boiling it in salted water rather than broth.

Out of the specialities it describes, the most interesting for our purposes is unquestionably 'Maccaroni alla Napolitana': the sauce here already bears a resemblance to modern-day ragù alla napoletana, albeit in embryonic form. Let's have a look at the recipe in the first edition (1790):

Macaroni in the style of Naples

Terrine [baked dish] = Cook macaroni with water and salt, and when it is three-quarters done, drain and mix it in an earthenware Terrine with grated parmesan, crushed pepper, and a Sauce of veal, or other beef, or a good broth from a stew, either plain or with cloves, strained through a sieve. To improve the dish some add fresh butter to the Sauce, or Coulis, but the true manner is the one described above. Cover the Terrine, put it over hot ashes, or at the mouth of the oven, so the macaroni absorbs all the flavour, and serve it while it is still quite full of sauce.[21]

The sauce is similar to the one in Vincenzo Corrado's timballo, but it is in the way the pasta is served that

---

* The relative space devoted to pasta is still quite limited in Leonardi's tome, which presents a total of 18 recipes for it (as opposed to 94 sauces not for pasta).

Francesco Leonardi takes a key step forward. In not even two decades, the macaroni has been freed of its pastry crust, so that the oven only serves to reheat the pasta and help it absorb the sauce. We thus have the first attempt at a pastasciutta with meat sauce, containing the seed of today's ragù alla napoletana. But the story is just getting started.

What were these sauces that the author suggests putting on the macaroni? They are very similar to the one discussed earlier by Vincenzo Corrado, and Leonardi describes them with great care, as we can see in the recipe for 'sugo di manzo'.

Beef Sauce

Depending on the sauce you want to make, put a piece of butter in the middle of the pot, and on top of it an onion or two split in half; cover the bottom in slices of lard, and over that put pieces of beef, adding a carrot, a parsnip, an onion with two cloves, a piece of ham; put the pot on a moderate fire with a ladleful of broth, letting it cook slowly until the meat gives up its juices; then put it on a higher flame and when it begins to brown, let it go back to cooking more gently, so that it forms a fine, rather dark glaze; then bathe it all over with *brodo generale*, and let it simmer over a slow fire with just a little salt. When the meat is cooked, strain the broth through a sieve or cloth into a bowl, taking care to make it clear. If you want to put a few pieces of this browned beef into your soups, then you should take them out before adding the broth.[22]

These sauces made with meat, vegetables and spices figured in a wide range of dishes and were a key element
in the cuisine of the time. A 'brodo generale' (standard
broth) of beef and vegetables (carrots, celery, parsnips,
turnips, leeks, onions and parsley root) was added to
deglaze the browned ingredients and extract all the concentrated flavour of the meat. Thanks to the Maillard
reaction, the resulting liquid was dark, glossy and highly
fragrant: a true delight (even for modern palates). It is no
coincidence that the second edition of *L'Apicio moderno*
starts off with the declaration that 'Broths are the foundation of fine cooking.'[23]

Francesco Leonardi's book also marks the broadest
use of ragùs up to that point, with a proliferation of different kinds – he presents 73 recipes, no less. These sauces
are now a culinary category unto themselves. I will quote
just one that is particularly classic and enduring, for
'Ragù Melè'.

Mixed Ragù

Take one or two *mongana*[24] sweetbreads blanched
in boiling water and cut in large pieces, or whole
sweetbreads of kid or lamb blanched in the same way,
and put them into a pot with sliced truffles, good
prugnolo mushrooms, a slice of prosciutto, a bouquet
of different herbs, a piece of butter; let them cook on
the fire, then bathe with a little meat coulis, half a glass
of Champagne, or another white wine, and when two
thirds of it has boiled off, season with salt and crushed
pepper; simmer it gently, then skim the fat, remove the

prosciutto and bouquet, add chicken livers, combs and
testicles, unlaid eggs, prawn tails, artichoke bottoms,
all of them cooked and properly prepared; let it boil
again for a short while, and the eggs should be added
last to the ragù. Serve with some small Chenefs [delicate
meatballs], and lemon juice, or in a Terrine [a baked
dish], or for an Entremet, garnishing the dish with fried
croutons; or over an Entrée of poultry, game &c. If
you want to use this Ragù to fill a Grenade [a moulded
dish], a Timbale &c., you must make it without too
much Sauce, and without Chenefs. See in the section
on special Ragùs how to prepare the chicken livers,
coxcombs, testicles, &c.[25]

Among many possible applications, *L'Apicio moderno*
recommends using 'a good reduced Ragù of kid sweetbreads with truffles, and prugnolo mushrooms'[26] to
flavour a traditional baked pasta dish, 'Maccaroni alla
Riscelieù' (à la Richelieu): the pasta is mixed with cream,
parmesan, pepper and nutmeg, with a space left in the
middle of the composition for the ragù, which is then
covered with a second layer of macaroni. This is the first
time that pasta directly encounters a ragù from the French
tradition.

Naples and tomatoes

Rarely does one get the chance to watch a recipe evolve
step by step, and most of the time we must make do with
comparing similar ones by different authors.

But Leonardi's 'Maccaroni alla Napolitana' is a unique case.

Eighteen years after the first version of this recipe was published, the author updated it for the second edition of *L'Apicio moderno* (1807–8) by adding one significant detail.

Macaroni in the Style of Naples

Terrine = Cook macaroni with water and salt, then when it is three-quarters done, drain and mix it in a Terrine dish with grated parmesan, crushed pepper, and a Sauce of veal, or beef, or a good broth from a stew, either plain or with cloves, *made with tomato sauce* and strained through a sieve[. . .].[27]

This is where tomatoes make their debut in the recipe. What is here just a slight variation noted by Leonardi's keen, quick eye would in time become an indispensable ingredient.[28]

Another cookbook published in Naples in the early nineteenth century was *La cucina casareccia*, whose unknown author signed it only with the initials M. F.; it was not unusual for recipe collections to be published anonymously, and from this era on such cases became increasingly common. They tended to be slim publications with titles that evoked healthy, frugal, modern cooking, or referred to a particular geographic area. A new type of cookbook was emerging, no longer penned by a great professional chef, but by a nameless compiler. And its intended audience was also new: a vaster, more varied readership, well educated, but from the middle class, and interested in eating well without spending too much (although the recipes may still seem overly elaborate to today's readers).

While up to this point the meat sauce used on macaroni had been called 'sugo di carne', *La cucina casareccia*[29] finally uses the term 'ragù' in association with pasta, rather than as a dish unto itself. It is no longer a French ragout made from various diced ingredients, but a large cut of meat wrapped in prosciutto, with cloves inserted in small, deep incisions. The tomatoes are added raw, or as a concentrated purée, depending on availability. The procedure has also been considerably simplified and suggests a more casual, everyday approach to cooking. In keeping with tradition, the meat itself is eaten separately and only the sauce from braising it is used on the pasta.

Ragù of Beef, or Veal

Bard the meat with strips of prosciutto and stud it with cloves, and put it to cook in the same pot where you have browned the onion, with prosciutto, herbs, salt, pepper and lard, putting in water, or better yet broth; take care to add more broth when necessary until it is fully cooked, because otherwise, if you let it dry out, it may easily take on an unpleasant odour; and if needed, you can also add fat. The sauce will be even better if you add some tomatoes in season along with the onion, but cleaned of their peel; and is also excellent to add, when almost done, a glass of good wine, and some rosemary.[30]

The recipe that follows, on the other hand, can be considered the first true prototype of modern maccheroni alla napoletana, and was handed down with very few changes until the 1960s. One should note that the directions now include the option of serving the pasta immediately, without any extra time in the oven, which definitively ushers in the era of sauced pasta as we know it.

Macaroni in the style of Naples

Boil Macaroni of any kind, taking it off the fire when it is not too done, drain it well, coat it with aged cheese and grated caciocavallo, and dress it in a good broth of ragù, in which you have cooked tomatoes, either fresh in season or preserved; and it can be eaten immediately. It can also be left to simmer for fifteen minutes over a low fire, and will be equally delicious.[31]

As in previous examples, starting with Francesco Leonardi, the ragù is always added after the grated cheese and not the other way around as we do today. It is almost like a reminder that the original condiment was grated cheese alone: the sauce serves as a flavouring, but is not yet omnipresent, and above all, is not always necessary. Further proof of this comes from Francesco de Bouchard, who in *Usi e costumi di Napoli* (1858) paints a picturesque portrait of the 'macceronai' (macaroni vendors) of his time.

Neapolitans most often eat [macaroni] with white cheese alone. Next to the large, steaming *maccaronense*

vat is a platter, bowl or *scafarea* of snowy cheese, a
modern-day pyramid of Egypt, decorated from tip to
base with black stripes of pepper, and often topped
with a tomato, or lacking that, a red flower. [The
innkeeper] doles out the hot macaroni with the dish
in one hand, as the other reaches for the pyramid of
cheese, and that peaceable powder is sprinkled over the
macaroni [. . .] Sometimes then, after the cheese, the
macaroni is tinged with scarlet or vermilion, when the
innkeeper spoons on tomato sauce or *ragù* (a sort of
stew), like dew on a flower, over the sprinkling of cheese
and the snakelike twists of vermicelli or maccaroncelli.[32]

The definitive triumph of the dish came in 1837 with its
inclusion in one of the most famous Neapolitan cookbooks of the time: *La cucina teorico-pratica*, by Ippolito
Cavalcanti, duke of Buonvicino.[33] This book is a rather
unique one. While the first part contains various recipes
for timballo and sartù, classic examples of elaborate traditional cuisine, the second, written entirely in dialect,
shows a startlingly modern approach, in recipes that
clearly move away from the culinary framework seen up
to this point.

Maccarune

Macaroni is another sort of soup course; be sure
though to cook it till it is just barely done, tossing it
in the pot when it reaches a boil. [. . .] When it seems
cooked, take the pot off the fire straight away and put
in a ladle of cold water, then dish it out, draining it well

and mixing in ripe cheese, and provola, or any other
sort of cheese, then to make it even better, layer it all
in a bowl or in a dish with the red broth from stewed
meat, and then put it on the ashes to simmer till it turns
nice and red as can be.[34]

Just as in *La cucina casareccia*, we find instructions not
to cook the pasta too much (in dialect, he says to keep
it 'vierd vierd': very green, i.e. hard),[35] to toss the pasta
with cheese first, and then use heat to make it absorb the
fragrant liquid from the sauce. As for the exact composition of the latter, one must consult the stew recipes that
Cavalcanti includes a few pages later, where he gives precise instructions even about possible cuts of beef – which
are no longer barded and skewered – and the broth is
completely replaced by water.

Stew

Take a piece of ponta de nateca, or vacante, or lacierto
[cuts from the rump and round]. In a stewpan or pot
put half a quarter pound* of ground lard for a rotolo**
of meat, then put in a minced onion and then the meat;
sprinkle the salt, pepper and spices on top, and brown
it, and every so often add a bit of water, turning it all
the time: when the meat is good and red, put in tomatoes if they are in season, or else tomato paste, and
keep stirring, adding water. When the paste or tomatoes

---

* A pound was about 320g.
** The rotolo was an ancient measurement used in the area around
Naples, and here was the equivalent of 890g.

} have boiled down, put in enough water to make a broth
} [. . .].[36]

Innovation and conservatism

You could say that with Ippolito Cavalcanti's recipe, Neapolitan ragù had already arrived at its definitive formulation.

Over the course of the nineteenth century, a wide range of variations on 'maccheroni alla napoletana' existed side by side: most authors stuck with the old version of a tomatoless meat sauce,[37] and others were still using the term to mean cheese alone;[38] and then there was the version with tomatoes, which was picked up and passed on by Pellegrino Artusi as well.[39] In the twentieth century, the presence of tomatoes became so pervasive that it turned into the dominant note, elbowing out almost all other ingredients. In a few extreme cases, the term 'alla napoletana' even referred to plain tomato sauce, flavoured with herbs or spices and boosted with fat (butter and lard, more rarely olive oil).[40]

The classic, meat-based recipe lost ground to this new formulation for two reasons above all: the first was economic, and the second had to do with cooking time.

The turn of the twentieth century brought a boom in the popularity of pasta, which became firmly established as the national first course; it was helped along by the growing industrialisation of the sector, which made large quantities of dried pasta available at low prices.[41] Topping that pasta with Neapolitan meat ragù was no simple matter: it meant cooking a large piece of beef each time, for a very small yield in sauce. That's why macaroni with ragù came to be thought of as a dish for Sunday lunch or holiday meals, whereas the everyday sauce became tomato-based.

There had also been a change in the amount of time that could be devoted to cooking, and recipe books were no longer just addressed to cooks or housekeepers. They were read by wives and mothers who had to juggle household chores, childcare and other work, which increasingly took them outside the home. The need to save time had become a key factor in the selection of recipes, so innovative ideas sprang up around traditional dishes. Advances in the food industry now meant, for instance, that every household had a packet of meat extract on hand (Justus von Liebig had launched large-scale production of it in 1865): using it in place of the gravy from stew on macaroni with butter and parmesan was an obvious leap. This can be seen from the 'Macaroni with meat extract' that Ada Boni included in the 1931 edition of *Il talismano della felicità* of 1931: 'a handy little recipe that we trust will prove useful to many young mothers, who do not always have time for long and elaborate dishes'.[42]

Saturday, Sunday and Monday

As we have seen before,[43] when a pasta dish becomes iconic, it tends to ripple through the entertainment world. In the case of ragù alla napoletana – or rather, in dialect, 'o' raù' – it was Eduardo De Filippo who sang its praises.

The Neapolitan actor and playwright even put the sauce at the centre of a three-act comedy, with the tensions of an entire family revolving around it.

In *Saturday, Sunday and Monday*[44] the curtain lifts on the preparation of a ragù and the 'science' involved in the choice of ingredients, offering an indirect glimpse at the twentieth-century evolution of the recipe (whose current incarnation we saw at the beginning of this chapter). The main character is the *girello*, a five-kilo piece of *annecchia*: an impressive chunk of yearling that is tied with twine and set to brown with a mountain of onions. The procedure, which looks simple at first, actually requires great care to balance the cooking times of the various ingredients and achieve a perfect ragù. As the protagonist, Donna Rosa, explains:

> The more onions you put in, the more fragrant the sauce, and the more body it will have. The secret is to keep the heat low. When it cooks slowly, the onions all melt into a dark crust around the meat; then you add the white wine bit by bit and the crust dissolves, giving you this golden, caramelised substance that blends with the tomatoes; that's how you get a thick, dense sauce that will turn the colour of rosewood when the ragù is done just right.[45]

Another key passage follows, in which Donna Rosa waxes nostalgic about watching her mother make ragù:

> When the sauce had 'tightened up', as she put it, she would take the piece of *annecchia* out of the pot

and lay it on a platter just like you'd lay a baby in its *connola*, then prop the pot lid with a wooden spoon so it was slightly ajar, and go to bed, but only after the sauce had sputtered for four or five hours.[46]

While the version of ragù in De Filippo's play (which is from 1959) still has all the traditional characteristics we have seen in previous recipes, it's interesting to compare it with the one in the film adaptation from 1990 directed by Lina Wertmuller. The scene where Donna Rosa, played by Sophia Loren, orders the meat at the butcher's – a scene that does not appear in the original script, and was added for the film – lets one deduce that the ragù recipe in the stage version must have been out of date by then. The cuts of meat have multiplied, especially the pork, and ragù made with yearling alone is clearly no longer in style,* although there is some disagreement about what can be used and what can't.[47] The argument in the shop over the proper ingredients closely resembles the discussions we see all over social networks today:

Donna Rosa (*running into the butcher shop*): Donna Ceci, I love you to bits but I'm in a rush, give me a kilo of yearling, a kilo and a half of stew meat, *gammunciello*, ribs, shoulder, round, clod, and some tendons, flank and shank.
Butcher: Oh! That little basketful, nothing else?
Rosa: No, nothing else.
Butcher: Don't be stubborn, do yourself a favour: a

---

* A version with beef alone still survives in the Neapolitan sauce called *genovese* (see chapter 9).

couple sausages and that'll be some ragù!

Rosa: No, no.

Customer 1: Mother of God, sausages in ragù . . .

Customer 2: Well, why not? Sausages are perfect, and actually, if along with the yearling you add a cut of ham stuffed with a clove of garlic, a little parsley, raisins and pine nuts, it's heaven, you'll see!

Rosa: No, that's a matter of taste, some like it heavy, and some like it light and classic.

Customer 3: Uh-uh, you can't call it classic without pork ribs.

(*Laughter.*)

Aunt Memè: I'm no cook, but from what I hear you're supposed to use yearling and that's it.

Rosa (*scoffing*): Yearling and that's it . . .

Customer 5: No ma'am, it depends on the time of year: no pork in the summer, it just doesn't sit right.

Customer 6: Anyhow, the secret to ragù is the onions . . .

Rosa: That's the whole base, the foundation . . .[48]

Now more than ever, every family in Naples has its own carefully guarded recipe, and arguments about which version is 'traditional' are as heated as they are pointless. Ragù has been evolving for centuries, so there's no reason it shouldn't keep evolving today – with all due respect to those who know their own version is the best.

7

RAGÙ ALLA BOLOGNESE

For centuries now, Bologna has been a byword for rich, opulent, delicious food. Outside of Italy, perhaps even more than in it, the city's name is tied to its meat sauce,[1] universally known as 'Bolognese' – with the difference that in other countries, it isn't served with egg tagliatelle the way it is at home, but rather with spaghetti, a practice that ruffles more than a few traditionalist feathers. But we'll get back to that.

The oldest roots of ragù are sunk deep in French cuisine, as we saw in the last chapter. But unlike the related Neapolitan speciality, the early stages of ragù alla bolognese are hard to reconstruct, at least up to the appearance of Pellegrino Artusi's book. If we try to trace different versions through the sources, as we have for other dishes, we will soon note something curious: although recipe collections from the late eighteenth and early nineteenth centuries include various specialities from Bologna, no pasta dish was ever referred to as 'alla bolognese' except tortellini.

In other words, no ragù.

This absence from cookbooks is probably explained by the fact that the city had no great chefs in that era, unlike Naples, where there were plenty. But it could also be that ragù alla bolognese went through a long gestation where it existed only on family menus, escaping the attention of the observers and chroniclers who might otherwise have mentioned it.

Whatever the reason, our first written record of the recipe is not in a printed book, but a handwritten text.

The origins

Almost nothing is known about the life of Alberto Alvisi, the cook who compiled this recipe collection. All we can say is that he was employed, from 1785 to 1799, by Gregorio Barnaba Chiaramonti, Bishop of Imola, who later ascended the papal throne under the name Pius VII. We don't even know whether the manuscript was a draft meant for subsequent publication, or just for personal use, but from the opening dedication one can deduce it was written after Cardinal Chiaramonti's election to pope, and thus at the very beginning of the nineteenth century.*

Alberto Alvisi must have been well aware of the eighteenth-century recipes combining French-derived ragùs

---

* The date that this collection was compiled is uncertain. In addition to the recipe for ragù, it includes a number of other specialities that seem very modern compared to other cookbooks published around the same time.

with pasta, which for that matter were already showing up in Vincenzo Corrado's timbales and Francesco Leonardi's macaroni with meat sauce.[2] But up to then, no one had ever suggested serving pasta with a ragù of chopped meat, simply mixing the two and letting the dish rest in a warm place before serving.

The cook unfortunately does not go into the details of this sauce, and the list of ingredients is as vague as can be. Still, the dish is innovative enough that it can be considered the great-grandfather of the ragù alla bolognese that became famous almost a century later.

Ragù for sauced macaroni

Well-melted lard and an ounce of butter with crushed onion, and either veal or pork loin, or else chicken gizzards chopped fine. Put everything in the stewpot over a brisk fire to take on a fine dark colour, adding broth little by little, and an ounce of flour to give body to the ragù, making sure that this Ragù is neither too thin, nor too thick, but perfectly cooked, and properly seasoned with salt, pepper, cinnamon; or some other spice. The macaroni must then be perfectly boiled either in broth or water with a touch of salt before being served with said Ragù.

Taken from the water, it must be drained well and placed in a large bowl, pouring over said ragù, and mixing it in a little, which must be done at least an hour before the meal. But before being served to table while still good and warm, it must be dressed and sufficiently

blended. Note however that to make said Ragù heartier, one definitely ought to add salt, some finely minced
mushrooms, a bit of truffle.[3]

Aside from this manuscript, which was never printed,
there seem to be no recipes until the mid-nineteenth century that use minced meat in pasta sauce.

One of the first published examples, the 'Maccheroni
alla famigliare' from the 1844 edition of *Il cuciniere italiano moderno*, is very interesting for what it tells us about
the origins of this approach.

Family-style macaroni

Cook it in boiling water, dress it with a little sauce
from braciole, or braised meat, or stew you have made
for the meal, and with grated parmesan and cinnamon. To be more frugal, one can take some marrow,
prosciutto, and onions, all of them minced; butter and
herbs, a little pepper and cinnamon. Cook all of this
in a pot, then add tomato sauce, and enough butter
to dress the macaroni. After mixing it with this sauce,
dust it with grated parmesan and powdered cinnamon.
When putting the sauce on the fire, one can add leftover meat, letting it cook a quarter of an hour, then
take this meat out of the pot, pound it in a mortar,
and thin it either with broth or with the water from
cooking the pasta, to make a kind of gravy that should
then be put back into the pot of sauce, to boil for a
quarter of an hour.[4]

This is an everyday dish, conceived to save money while giving some extra substance to a dish – pasta – that would seem too spartan on its own. It starts with 'sauce from braciole, or braised meat, or stew': the same base used for pasta 'alla napoletana', except that here an extra portion of meat is added, to be mixed in with the macaroni.

One gets the sense that something is changing in the meals served at home. Up to this point, macaroni had basically been topped with cheese and a little of the gravy left over from cooking a large cut of beef or veal, whereas the success of this new approach to pasta lay in the reversed proportions. People now wanted plenty of sauce, even if this implied cooking an amount of meat that not everyone could afford, or at least, not very often. At the same time, macaroni was gradually becoming a more important part of the meal, although the meat dish still remained the main course.

The solution was to boost the flavour of a simple sauce by adding just a little meat, which would end up directly in the pasta. The author therefore suggests using 'marrow, prosciutto, onions, all of them minced; butter and herbs, a little pepper and cinnamon', with the option of also putting in some leftover meat, to be cooked with everything else and then ground in a mortar.

This is an era when timbales and other baked dishes with ragùs of sweetbreads, chicken giblets, meatballs and so forth were the most coveted item on any table, but could at most be a treat for the holidays. Middle-class households, though they did not want to forgo the dish of pasta which was becoming a fixture of everyday menus, had different needs and budgets. And so elaborate concoctions in pastry crusts inexorably began to drop out of cookbooks, giving way to ordinary pastasciutta.

To our eyes this may seem like an unremarkable, almost predictable development, but it is in recipes such as these that we find the first glimmers of pasta's emancipation from its secondary role in relation to meat. The idea of making the sauce heartier by adding minced meat yielded a single course that was more nutritious, doing away with the need for a costly main dish from which to use the gravy. This new trend laid the foundations not only for ragù alla bolognese, but for a whole new way of thinking about pasta.

From this point on, cookbooks began to include more and more recipes that took a similar approach to sauces.

It started with the Turinese cook Giovanni Vialardi in his *Trattato di cucina* of 1854,[5] which included a 'Maccheroni alla napoletana' involving small chicken roulades stuffed with meatballs and sweetbreads. Unlike the 'Maccheroni alla famigliare' described above, this is an unquestionably complex, sophisticated dish, combining actual macaroni with these little meat 'macaroni' cooked in sauce. But that's not all. The same book – which was based on Vialardi's years of experience as sous-chef and pastry chef to the House of Savoy – also contains a rather interesting recipe for 'Maccheroni alla sarda'. Here, a base of butter, Gruyère and jus from a roast is rounded out with finely chopped roast chicken. A different version of this recipe, using veal, was also presented by the same author nine years later in *La cucina borghese* (1863).

Sardinian soup of macaroni

Clean and dice an onion, put it in a stewpan on the fire with 60 gr of butter and when it has fried a little, add 2 hectograms of diced leg of veal and let it brown, adding 5 ripe tomatoes, peeled and seeded and with the tough parts removed; let all of this cook until tender and when it has reduced, add a little salt, pepper and spices. Cook half a kilogram of Genoa macaroni until tender, adding it to boiling salted water in a pot over the fire, drain it and mix it with 60 grams of butter, 60 grams of good cheese and half of the sauce you have made, then pour it into the serving bowl and spoon over the other half. You may also use other varieties of pasta. This sauce can be varied by adding poultry, mutton, or game, so long as it has a fine flavour.[6]

This shows a clear evolution. The aim is obviously to free the recipe of separately cooked elements that make it more complicated to prepare, starting with the meat gravy. The chopped veal is no longer an extra addition to the old kind of sauce, but rather the main ingredient. The aromatic base is replaced by a simple sauté of onions and tomatoes, while the meat is pre-diced and meant to stay in the sauce from the start. The first thing one notes is that although the preferred meat is the traditional beef/veal, there was already an openness to other kinds (although pork is still absent). The second is that Vialardi still suggests giving the pasta an initial coating of butter and parmesan, which continues to be the standard base, and only then adding the sauce one has prepared.[7]

Thanks to the precision of this recipe, we even know the weight of the pasta relative to the sauce (something that previous authors always left out), and it may come as a surprise to see that only 200g of veal are used for half a kilo of macaroni. This ratio can't help but seem scanty by modern standards, yet remained constant until the mid-twentieth century.

After these first few examples, the number of pasta sauces using small pieces of meat began to multiply. Cookbooks started to feature dishes like Francesco Palma's 'Maccheroni alla Siciliana con petronciane', which combines a 'little ragù of chicken giblets' with fried aubergines and parmesan;[8] or Valerio Busnelli's 'Maccheroni al sughillo', which tops the pasta with beef gravy, tomato sauce, finely chopped sausage and grated cheese.[9] But these are still baby steps in the direction of what would come to be a full-fledged revolution, culminating in the birth of modern sauces and of ragù alla bolognese.

It was a revolution that happened in stages.

The obstacles to this change were not just the rigid traditional culinary structures that hindered a freer approach, but the qualms of cookbook authors, who were often hesitant to pick up on the new ideas coming out of ordinary home kitchens. In other words, while Italian cuisine was slowly evolving, it needed a spokesperson who could shake off these strictures and invent, first and foremost, a new way of *writing* about food that would spread new ways of making it. What it needed, in short, was Pellegrino Artusi.

Pellegrino Artusi and 'maccheroni alla bolognese'

The title of his book is *La scienza in cucina e l'arte di mangiar bene* (Science in the Kitchen and the Art of Eating Well), but to most Italians it's simply 'Artusi': a word that Alfredo Panzini's *Dizionario moderno* even defines as 'by extension, a cookery book'.[10]

Perhaps no other cookbook is so deeply entrenched in the collective Italian memory, and though it was written at the very end of the nineteenth century, it still seems incredibly modern compared to everything that came before (and even much of what came after).

Artusi, who personally edited all the fourteen editions that appeared between 1891 and 1911, collected a total of 790 recipes that taught generations of Italian families to cook. At present, this is the only nineteenth-century cookbook that has never gone out of print and can still be found in any bookshop in Italy. Perhaps because, as one reads in the foreword to the 1902 edition, 'with this handy Manual, all you need to know is how to pick up a spoon, and you are sure to scrape something together'.[11]

The author was born in Forlimpopoli in 1820, into a well-to-do family that owned a grocery. In the early 1850s the Artusis moved to Florence, where they bought a silk and fabric shop. When Artusi turned fifty, he retired from business to devote time to his true passions – first and foremost, food.[12] Strange as it may seem, the biggest revolution in the history of Italian cuisine was not brought about by a chef. Artusi was a great expert on culinary matters, to be sure, but it was precisely his outsider status that allowed him to explore them with fresher eyes; with the help of his cook and housekeeper Marietta Sabatini, he collected, noted down and tested recipes from all over Italy. Although his main areas of interest were Tuscany and Emilia, *La scienza in cucina* is far from having a single regional focus. Artusi ranges across different traditions, guided by his tastes, but above all – and this was an utterly new concept – by his readers, who sent in suggestions and recipes that became an integral part of his tale of Italian cooking. Much has been written about the importance and success of this book.[13] But its key feature, from the standpoint of our story, is the extremely modern way that it captures a new approach to cooking and dressing pasta.

The category of 'minestre asciutte' ('dry soups', i.e. starchy boiled dishes without broth), for instance, which was given little attention in previous cookbooks, experiences a true boom here, both in the number of recipes and in the quality of the descriptions. Likewise, there is a definite leap forward in terms of pasta sauces that incorporate finely chopped vegetables, meat and fish, reflecting a trend that had already been under way for several decades in ordinary home kitchens.[14]

The recipe that interests us here is Artusi's 'Maccheroni alla bolognese', which paved the way to modern Bolognese sauce and to its tremendous success. Let's have a look.

Macaroni in the style of Bologna

For this dish, people in Bologna use a medium size of the pasta called 'denti di cavallo' ['horse teeth', rigatoni], and I, too, think that is the best shape when cooked this way; make sure, however, that the pasta is rather thick, so that it does not flatten out upon boiling; this is a flaw that tends to be overlooked in Tuscany, where due to the general preference for light foods, there are certain kinds of pasta known as 'gentili' ['delicate'], with large holes and such thin walls that they collapse completely when boiled, which is unappealing to look at as well as to eat.

As everyone knows, the best pastas are those made from hard durum wheat, which can be identified by their natural honey colour. Beware, however, of the yellow kind, which attempt to mask the fact that they come from ordinary wheat by using artificial dye, whereas at least this used to be done with innocuous colourants like saffron or crocus.

The following proportions are for about 500 grams or more of boiled pasta:
Lean veal (fillet is best), 150 gr.
Carnesecca, 50 gr.
Butter, 40 gr.
One-quarter of an ordinary onion.
Half a carrot.
Two hands' lengths of white celery, or the leaves from green celery.

A pinch of flour, but just a pinch.
A small pot of broth.
Little or no salt, given the saltiness of the cured meat
and the broth.
Pepper, and for those who like it, a grating of nutmeg.

Cut the meat in small pieces, mince the cured pork,
onion and herbs; then put everything on the fire, including the butter, and when the meat is brown sprinkle in a
pinch of flour, adding broth until completely cooked.

Drain the macaroni well and toss it with parmesan
and with this sauce, which can be made even tastier
by adding either bits of dried mushrooms or a few
shavings of truffle, or a chicken liver cooked in with
the meat and cut in pieces; when the sauce is done, if
you would like it even more delicate, add half a cup
of cream; in any case it is best for the macaroni not to
come to the table too dry, but rather swimming in a
little sauce. Since this is pastasciutta, I should take the
opportunity to note that this kind of dish is best cooked
until just done; everything within measure, of course. If
the pasta has a little bite to it, it will taste better and be
easier to digest.[15]

The key ingredients of the future ragù are all there: the
pork (called *carnesecca*, or 'salted pork belly', i.e. pancetta, as the author explains), beef, and 'aromatics':
celery, carrots and onions. There is no mention of adding
a separately made gravy, as with previous authors. The
meat is simply deglazed with broth after being browned,

so that all its flavouring potential is released right into the pot, through what is now known as the 'Maillard reaction'. A pinch of flour to bind it, and it's ready for the parmesan-coated macaroni.

The other additions suggested by Artusi – dried mushrooms, truffles, chopped chicken livers and cream – would come and go over the years in ragù alla bolognese. As you may have noticed, compared to today's version there is one conspicuous absence: tomato purée, which became a stable part of the sauce almost twenty years later.[16]

The recipe, in its simplicity, is something of a masterpiece. Replacing the elaborate meat gravy with broth simplifies the preparation quite a bit, while ensuring a fragrant concentration of flavours. Adding a carefully balanced vegetable component gives a fresher, more complex aroma, which became so essential to the sauce that in Bolognese dialect both the mirepoix – the mixture of finely diced carrots, celery and onions – and the ragù itself are simply called 'suffrét' (soffritto, in Italian). Lastly, we again find that step we've seen so many times: mixing the macaroni with plenty of parmesan before adding the sauce, for a spike of umami and to give the final dish a perfect texture.

As noted earlier about Vialardi's 'Zuppa di maccheroni alla sarda', the amount of sauce is rather scant in relation to the pasta: a total of 200g of meat for half a kilo (or more) of macaroni, without even any tomato purée to stretch it out.

It's worth looking for a moment at the fact that Artusi is careful to specify that this sauce, and this sauce alone, is 'alla bolognese'.

We have already seen his high opinion of that regional cuisine in his introduction to the recipe for tortellini: 'When anyone mentions Bolognese food you should doff your hat, for respect is due.' Bologna is unquestionably the best represented city in the cookbook, with a total of fourteen dishes,[17] three of them pasta-based (tortellini and strichetti – both in broth – and macaroni). To the modern Italian observer, however, the fact that Artusi presents this classic Bolognese dish with macaroni rather than tagliatelle, which was a speciality of the region even at the time, will seem rather strange.

This choice was surely influenced by the leading role that macaroni (in the generic sense of tube pasta) played in traditional recipes: from eighteenth-century baked pasticci, to Alvisi's 'Maccheroni appasticciati', all the way to more recent dishes. Artusi only mentions pairing this ragù with tagliatelle in his recipe for 'Tagliatelle verdi', which suggests topping them 'like spaghetti alla rustica, or like the macaroni or tagliatelle in recipes no. 58 [Maccheroni alla bolognese] and 44 [Tagliatelle col presciutto], or simply with butter and cheese'. There are two other sauces that he instead directly associates with tagliatelle: a fresh tomato sauce with butter, garlic and parsley in 'Tagliatelle all'uso di Romagna' (described in the recipe for 'Spaghetti alla rustica') and prosciutto with butter, tomatoes, celery and carrots in 'Tagliatelle col presciutto'.

Lastly, even the name 'ragù' remained elusive for many years. In *La scienza in cucina*, that word is never used in any context. Its definition kept evolving alongside the ragù recipes still reflective of French cuisine, where a ragout was a dish of meat in some kind of sauce. Curiously enough, this meaning of the term even turns up in the libretto for Puccini's *La Bohème*,[18] but it tended to vanish from recipe books starting in the early twentieth century. The last ones to use it this way are Katharina Prato's *Manuale di cucina per principianti* in 1893,[19] Jean Marie Parmentier's *Il re dei re dei cuochi* in 1897,[20] *Il cuciniere universale* in 1902,[21] and very few others. After that, a semantic shift left only the pasta-related meaning – although the complete transition took a few years, during which cookbooks continued to refer to the Bolognese speciality as an 'intingolo' or 'sugo', generic words for sauce.

Let a hundred ragùs bloom

While it is true that Artusi's example was followed by most later authors, ragù alla bolognese was still in an unstable phase in the early twentieth century; different versions overlapped, and food writers were still a long way from identifying any lowest common denominator for the recipe. But even at this indeterminate stage, one can single out three trends that eventually led to its current definition: the macaroni gave way to tagliatelle; tomatoes became an integral part of the recipe; and lastly, the proportion of pork gradually increased.

An initial turning point in the stabilisation of the ingredients came with Giulia Lazzari-Turco's *Il piccolo focolare* (1908), which includes a generic 'Pasta condita alla bolognese':

Pasta with Bolognese sauce

For a kilo of pasta, 80 gr. of veal or fillet (weighed without the bone), a spoonful of ground parsley, a small celery root, two carrots, two onions, 50 gr. of lard, 20 gr. of butter, a little broth or water, tomato purée, cheese, salt, pepper, and for those who like it a pinch of cinnamon. In a very wide, low pot or a large iron skillet, melt the lard until it smokes, add the butter, and when it too is smoking, the finely chopped vegetables. Let them brown a little and add the meat, cut into a very small dice. Stir the mixture with a spatula, and when the meat begins to darken, pour in a couple of ladles of broth and a little tomato purée and let it simmer for about thirty minutes. You will have added both salt and pepper, of course. At this point, if you like, you may also add the cinnamon. When the pasta is cooked and drained (this sauce goes best with tagliatelle, taglierini and smooth or ridged macaroni), add it to the pot, stir it in the sauce, dish it into a large serving bowl and sprinkle it with grated cheese.[22]

Macaroni and tagliatelle are listed here as equally good options; pork is still a no-show, and the meat is just a *fifth* of the already meagre amount suggested by Artusi. But the real innovation is the tomato purée: this would seem to be the first recipe to record the ingredient's debut in the sauce.

In that same year, 1908, and in the two years that followed, three cookbooks came out that played a fundamental role in shaping Italian regional dishes. A new approach to classifying the country's cuisine had emerged, driven by the sense that it was necessary, even urgent, to identify and record traditional specialities and where they came from. Yet many dishes, including ragù alla bolognese, were still taking shape. This can be seen from the range of versions that one finds, and it makes the lists of regional recipes drawn up in that era very different from those of today. Some of the most famous Italian specialities (to give just two examples: amatriciana and carbonara) simply didn't exist yet, while others were still in embryonic form and would go through radical changes.

The first of these three cookbooks is *100 specialità di cucina italiane ed estere*, an anonymously authored booklet, just 48 pages long, that was published in 1908 by Sonzogno. The hundred recipes it presents are organised by city and region, with dishes from Bologna, Genova, Milan, Naples, Rome, Piedmont, Sicily, Tuscany and Venice, as well as a few specialities from across the border. And it is here we finally find 'Tagliatelle alla Bolognese',[23] but it actually resembles Artusi's 'Tagliatelle col presciutto': nothing but diced prosciutto, butter and tomatoes, showing once again that in that era there was still no canonical version of a sauce by that name.

The second book is Vittorio Agnetti's *La nuova cucina delle specialità regionali*, where the specialities are also grouped by area of origin. Here, however, the author simply repeats Artusi for both 'Maccheroni all'uso di Bologna' and 'Tagliatelle all'uso di Romagna', so there's nothing new so far.

That changes with the third book in the trio, *L'arte cucinaria in Italia* by Alberto Cougnet, a journalist and author who in compiling his book (almost 5,000 recipes), drew on input from the greatest chefs of his time. Bologna is represented here by 'Cannelloni alla bolognese'[24] (which basically copies Artusi's 'Maccheroni alla bolognese') and 'Tagliatelle alla bolognese' (or in dialect, 'Tajadelle assôtte'),[25] where Cougnet rattles off a list of sauces that will complement this fresh ribbon pasta: 'Neapolitan style, Sicilian style, Genoese style with dried mushrooms. Some also use a purée of tomatoes finished off with melted butter, similar to the "pomarola" found in Naples.' Though Cougnet shows great precision when it comes to naming these noodles in Bolognese dialect, his notes on their actual preparation range all over the map: to him, anything involving tagliatelle is 'alla bolognese', no matter what the sauce.

But skimming through the same book, we find a recipe for 'Intingolo alla Bolognese' to be used on 'Green or mixed lasagne, for a Bolognese style of baked dish', and the version of ragù it presents is strikingly modern.

Bolognese sauce

2 kg of lean beef, 500 g of rather fatty prosciutto; 500 g total of onions, celery, carrots. Finely chop the prosciutto and the vegetables and brown them for a moment in the pot; add the chopped beef and let it swelter until half cooked, taking care not to let it burn. Add a cup of tomato purée with a little dark tomato paste; once it has dried out a bit, put in some good, light meat gravy, well flavoured with herbs, and let everything simmer steadily for 2 hours. This sauce can

be used, as a rule, to dress any baked pasta in the style of Bologna and Emilia.[26]

There you go. In this one we find practically all the main elements: pork (though only as prosciutto), beef, the traditional combination of aromatics in the soffritto (the standard mirepoix of celery, carrot and onion) and tomato purée rounded out with a light meat gravy, a holdover from classic nineteenth-century cooking.

The road to fame

Although Artusi's version was still very much alive and was a path that imitators would follow for years, it was Ada Boni's *Il talismano della felicità*, published in the late 1920s, that gave us a recipe for 'Tagliatelle verdi alla bolognese'[27] containing almost all the basic ingredients of ragù that are still used today.

Green tagliatelle in the style of Bologna

These tagliatelle, a jewel of Bologna's mouth-watering cuisine, are not well known outside its city walls. [. . .] Once you have made the tagliatelle, prepare the Bolognese sauce, which is also a little different from the usual stewed meat sauce. For the amount of pasta used here [three to four hundred grams of flour, three eggs, plus spinach], which should be enough for four or five people, take 150 grams of lean beef and chop it finely on the cutting board, or better yet, put it through the

221

mincer with 50 grams of salted pancetta (ventresca).
Put a pot on with 50 grams of butter, an onion, a yellow
carrot and a rib of celery, all of it finely chopped, add
the meat along with the pork fat, and a clove, and let
it brown until the meat and vegetables have taken on a
rather dark colour. Then pour in a little broth or water,
season with a bit of salt, add a teaspoon – no more –
of tomato paste, mix, cover the pot and let it simmer
very slowly on moderate heat. There is a more sophisticated Bolognese tradition that advises bathing the
mixture in milk rather than broth or water. That is a
question of taste . . . and budget. Of course, the addition of milk will make the sauce more delicate. When
it has simmered for half an hour, you may also add a
few chicken livers, a little diced prosciutto, a few dried
mushrooms soaked in cold water and a few shavings of
white truffle. But all of these additions are optional and
you can easily forgo them, obtaining excellent results
nonetheless. Once the sauce is done, boil the tagliatelle,
drain and dress with the sauce, adding a few pieces of
butter and grated parmesan. You can eat it right away,
or better yet, let it rest for a while in the pot, covered
and close to the fire so that it soaks up the flavour. If
you have a few spoonfuls of cream, you may add them
to the tagliatelle along with the sauce. In that case
no butter is needed. Some people, after browning the
aromatics and meat, and before pouring in the broth,
water or milk, add a spoonful of flour to the pot to help
bind the sauce. That's how to prepare green tagliatelle.
We see no need to say anything about ordinary tagliatelle alla bolognese, since the only difference is that

> the egg pasta contains no spinach, while everything else
> remains the same.

Aside from the possible additions that are mentioned
(milk, chicken livers, diced prosciutto, dried mushrooms,
white truffles, cream and flour), the recipe has the same
fundamental features as the ragù now considered classic:
the pork and beef, the standard aromatics (celery, carrot
and onion), the presence of tomato paste, however slight,
with no added meat gravy. It was a model that would be
replicated everywhere in the years that followed, although
there were still plenty of alternative versions.

Ragù in hard times

In the meantime, tagliatelle alla bolognese were having
their day in the sun.

In this period they're mentioned everywhere. One
curious example is an anecdote related to Umberto
Nobile's Arctic expedition in 1928. As the airship *Italia*
was bound for the North Pole, the *Corriere della Sera*,
which the funders had enlisted to give as much press cov-
erage as possible to the undertaking, recorded the crew's
culinary nostalgia: 'some went so far as to reminisce about
the merits of espresso machines or the absolute supremacy of tagliatelle alla bolognese over all other Italian
pasta dishes; I think this is like talking about cold beer
in the middle of the Sahara.'[28] The trip ended in tragedy,
with an accident during the flight that caused the deaths
of six expedition members. The radio operator Giuseppe

Biagi, from Bologna, was among the survivors, and the story of their return to Italy notes that 'his compatriots presented him with a singular tribute: a huge platter of pasta alla bolognese'.[29]

This anecdote prompts another reflection.

The history of these tagliatelle is unquestionably tied to the history of Italy: not only its tastes, but the ups and downs of the national economy. One of the most extreme versions of 'Tagliatelle alla bolognese' is the one in Emilia Zamara's cookbook *La cucina italiana della resistenza*, published in 1936. The sauce? Just butter, cheese and béchamel, with no trace of other ingredients.[30] A recipe that at first glance is Bolognese only in name.

But it says a lot about the era in which it was recorded.

The year of its appearance was the year in which the Society of Nations imposed heavy economic sanctions on Fascist Italy for having deliberately attacked Ethiopia. The reaction on the home front was immediate, and the adoption of autarkic policies encouraging extreme frugality had dramatic consequences even in the kitchen.

With respect to the publishing industry, one should note that even during the Second World War, and then in its gruelling aftermath, there was never any real pause in the production of cookbooks. On the contrary, there was something of an upswing, to help housewives cope with the difficult circumstances imposed by rationing.

Rich meat sauces were obviously not an option given the harsh limitations of this subsistence diet, although some interesting alternatives emerged, like the recipe for 'Pasta with blood sauce'[31] described in the 1944 booklet *Desinaretti per . . . questi tempi* ('Little Dinners for . . .

These Times') by Petronilla,* which begins: 'Does your grocer's counter still display a block of cooked, solidified blood? Then be sure to seize the opportunity, since pasta boiled in water can be served with a fine sauce made from this healthy, nourishing and tasty product, which in these times has the rare advantage of not requiring a ration card and costing practically . . . nothing.' Aside from the blood, all you needed was a little butter and oil, carrots, celery, a bit of flour and some tomato purée, to make a pasta dish that was 'good (and for these times, outstanding)'.

Towards the official recipe

The period just after the war saw the publication of *Il cucchiaio d'argento*, another famous cookbook that instantly earned a place in Italian homes. The first edition came out in 1950, and constant updates have made it a bestseller among food titles to this day. Its 'Tagliatelle verdi col ragù',[32] though they lack the adjective 'bolognese', are clearly a major leap forward. Actually, one might say that the very disappearance of this geographic specification – within Italy, at least – marked the dish's move into a newly global arena. The most important innovation is the minced pork loin, which continues the trend of increasing the pork relative to other ingredients.

---

* This was the pen name of Amalia Moretti Foggia della Rovere, one of the first women in Italy to earn a medical degree. Starting in the 1920s, she wrote several columns on health and food for *La Domenica del Corriere*. During the Second World War she became known for her pragmatic cooking manuals.

One can confidently say that at this point, the recipe has reached the end of its development stage and is nearing officialisation, just as we saw before with tortellini alla bolognese.

But the true final act of this story begins with the registration of a recipe for 'Ragù alla bolognese' with the Bologna Chamber of Commerce on 17 October 1982, by the Bologna delegation of the Accademia Italiana della Cucina.

[. . .] The Bolognese delegation of the Accademia Italiana della Cucina solemnly declares that the Recipe for 'Classic Bolognese Ragù', whose fame is not only universal but centuries old, lost in History and blurring into Legend, is as follows:

Ingredients and amounts
Skirt steak, 300 gr.
Pork belly, 150 gr.
Carrot, 50 gr.
Celery stalk, 50 gr.
Onion, 30 gr.
Tomato purée, 5 spoonfuls
or
Tomato paste, 20 gr.
Dry white wine, ½ cup
Full-fat milk, 1 cup

Necessary equipment
Terracotta pot, about 20 cm diam.
Wooden spoon

Mezzaluna

Instructions
Dice the pork belly, chop it finely with the mezzaluna, and soften it in the pot; add the vegetables, chopped fine with the mezzaluna, and let them sweat gently; add the ground meat and let it cook, stirring, until it sizzles; add ½ cup of wine and the tomato purée, thinned with a little broth; let it simmer for about two (2) hours, adding the milk bit by bit and seasoning with salt and black pepper to taste.

An optional but advisable addition, at the very end, is the skin formed by boiling (1) litre of full-fat milk.

The Bologna Delegation of the Accademia Italiana della Cucina decrees this recipe to be the most reflective of a formulation which will ensure the classic, traditional flavour of true Ragù Bolognese [. . .].[33]

This all sounds very familiar, right? The solemn tone, the invocation of 'History' blurring into 'Legend' to lend weight to a 'classic' version that, as we have seen just now, was actually no more than sixty years old.

Once again, the Accademia Italiana della Cucina's desire to set the recipe down in stone was guided by the idea of preserving the city's identity and culinary traditions, as part of the nation's intangible cultural heritage.

All well and good.

But any undertaking of this kind runs up against two major problems: the first is that one version of the dish must be singled out among the dozens of variants in circulation. This selection is always arbitrary, even when it is done by someone with the necessary skills to decide which recipe is most representative within this complex range.

Second, the notion of permanently pinning down the characteristics of a recipe implies that it has arrived at a stage where it cannot and *must not* keep changing, because it has reached the peak of its evolution.

But trying to keep a living, breathing recipe frozen in time is necessarily a wasted effort. It's much the same as when dealing with a language: a Latin dictionary can obviously do without constant updates; an Italian dictionary, by contrast, needs ongoing revision to reflect new patterns of speech and incorporate new terms that enter into use, otherwise it would soon become worthless.

The registered recipe is a touchstone for many people, but it's perfectly natural to treat it as what it is: one possible version among many, influenced by the era when it was written down.

It is no coincidence, for example, that its suggestion of adding milk or cream to the mixture, though it has famous precedents, is now considered heresy by many food purists – much to the dismay of the Accademia Italiana della Cucina and to everyone who sees this as the one, immutable recipe for traditional ragù (remember the carbonara of the 1980s?).[34] In short, what was inalterable and sacrosanct to the purists of the past is impugned by the purists of the present, due to their shared claim: that they and they alone are in possession of the *perfect* recipe.

Another spoonful of science

In recent years one has begun to hear views that are more moderate, though rigorous when it comes to research. I am referring in particular to a 'scientific' approach to cooking, which analyses recipes from the standpoint of food chemistry and of the transformations involved in various procedures. Its goal is to grasp the reasoning behind traditional cooking methods and come up with technical solutions to fine-tune them even more (we've seen one example with carbonara). These are known as 'science-based recipes': for instance, 'Quasi Bolognese Sauce', as Dario Bressanini[35] calls his version in an effort to avoid the ire of food purists.

Without being presented as dogma, the procedures that they recommend try to harness the characteristics of each ingredient, working to obtain the best possible flavour, fragrance and texture from the foods at our disposal.

A good ragù, for instance, should have a meaty aroma set off by the bouquet of vegetables, and a full-bodied consistency that envelops and sticks to the pasta. One must start off by deciding which ingredients will give perfect results while staying as close as possible to the canonical recipe. The blend of aromatics composed of celery, carrots and onion, which adds a characteristically fresh, herbal note, cannot be varied too much, except in the proportions of the individual ingredients, according to taste.

On the other hand, it is important to properly balance the pork and beef by putting some care into the choice of cuts. The pork is there to release a certain amount of fat, enough to give the final sauce the unctuousness that helps our taste buds perceive flavours. It would therefore be a good idea to use a portion of pork belly, and then another cut veined with fat, for instance from the neck muscle. The beef, on the other hand, needs to contain a fair amount of collagen, which will break down into gelatin with extended cooking. The best cuts for this are from the brisket or shank. A portion of skirt steak (the diaphragm, a lean cut from an area with high blood flow) suggested in previous recipes could help bring out the fragrance of red meat. Of course, all the meat must be ground or finely chopped with a knife. I happen to like slightly larger pieces, for instance, but this is a question of personal taste.

One of the key steps in cooking the ingredients is to be sure that the vegetables and above all the meat release their full flavour through the Maillard reaction. This is achieved by subjecting foods to temperatures between 140°C and 180°C, which triggers a reaction between the amino acids of the proteins and sugars. The simplest way is to brown the ingredients separately in a small amount of fat, which can be the fat naturally contained in the pork, or an added knob of butter. The 'secret' is to cook just a little meat at a time, so that it stays in contact with the heated bottom of the pot as evenly and for as long as possible. Alternatively, the chopped meat can be spread out in a pan and placed in the oven at a high temperature. Whatever the method, the objective is to develop that classic dark crust and roasted fragrance. The browned meat and vegetables can then be combined in the same pot; to bring out their aromas even more, one can add a generous amount of beef broth made from cartilage-rich cuts and bones, pouring in a little at a time until it has almost completely evaporated.

After all this, it is time to add the tomato paste diluted in water or broth, and then let the sauce simmer for several hours (at least three) to allow the collagen in the meat to dissolve all the way. If a more complex flavour is desired, the spices that will complement this ragù are cinnamon, cloves and nutmeg; but whether to use them, and how much, is up to the cook. Other additions such as milk (to give a rounder flavour), or wine, or a portion of sausage (which adds both fat and umami), are a question of personal taste: science, in the kitchen, can give everyone a degree of freedom.

Spaghetti Bolognese: a parallel history

Now that we have reconstructed the origins and development of ragù alla bolognese all the way to the latest innovations, we still need to look at the parallel history – a true success story – of the sauce outside of Italy. Once again, we must travel across the Atlantic and go back to the very start, when ragù didn't yet exist and 'Bolognese' meant recipes involving spinach.

Let's start at the beginning. In the mid-nineteenth century, about forty years before Pellegrino Artusi's 'Maccheroni alla bolognese' began to catch on, a recipe was published for 'Lasagne alla bolognese' in the Italian cookbook *Il cuciniere italiano moderno*. It called for the layers of egg pasta to be alternated with a filling of boiled, chopped spinach, sautéd either with meat sauce – in the 'feast day' version – or with butter, onions and herbs – in the 'fast day' version.[36]

Although one finds very few references to the dish in Italy, this variant must have had some degree of success, since it turns up again, unexpectedly, as 'Macaroni, Bolognese Style'[37] in the *Cook Book* (1896) by Oscar Tschirky, the famed maître d' of Delmonico's and later of the Waldorf-Astoria in Manhattan: a recipe for baked pasta – macaroni or lasagne – layered with spinach in meat sauce and parmesan. Years later, we find another confirmation of its popularity: a monthly magazine about Chicago hotels from 1908 includes 'Macaroni with spinach à la Bolognese' among its menu suggestions.[38]

In this same period, Pellegrino Artusi's recipe for tomatoless veal ragù was becoming so widespread in Italy that all previous recipes for 'pasta alla bolognese' were soon forgotten. The first record of ragù alla bolognese being served with spaghetti comes from Turin in 1898: more specifically, from a bill of fare that the Hotel Ville de Bologne advertised in the newspaper *La Stampa*, which includes 'Spaghetti di Napoli alla Bolognese' ('Neapolitan spaghetti, Bolognese style').[39] But the great success of this pairing only came when it caught on in the United States.

It was first popularised by Julia Lovejoy Cuniberti, through a book published in 1917 to raise funds for the families of Italian soldiers fighting in World War I. *Practical Italian Recipes for American Kitchens* brings together various traditional recipes, many of which, like 'Bolognese sauce of macaroni', were clearly borrowed from Artusi.[40] But in the original version of *La scienza in cucina*, this tomatoless ragù is explicitly associated, even in the title, with macaroni, and the pairing with tagliatelle is only suggested in passing elsewhere. Julia Cuniberti's English translation instead suggests using the sauce with 'macaroni or spaghetti'.

This was the first cookbook to green-light the idea of replacing tagliatelle with spaghetti, and it launched the fad of 'spaghetti alla bolognese' in America.

Setting aside the question of the pasta for a moment: the recipe for ragù that appeared in American publications early on was therefore just a literal translation of the one Artusi had published in Italy in 1891. In the US, this version remained practically unchanged up to the 1930s before incorporating, with an inevitable delay, the tomato sauce that had already been creeping into Italian recipes.

But then, over the next few decades, the American sauce underwent its own evolution, adapting to popular tastes and above all to the needs of the food industry, which was developing cheap, simple versions to be marketed as readymade sauces or directly as tinned pasta.

More and more, American society was cutting down the amount of time devoted to cooking, years before Europe began to do the same. Families had new needs that were being met by readymade foods, appliances and supermarkets: a dietary revolution that adapted recipes to industrial processes and standardised consumer tastes. With a few rare exceptions, many of the products labelled 'Bolognese' ended up having little or nothing left of the characteristics that had made the sauce famous.

Let's end this chapter by looking at the aspect that

some Italians find most painful about the American version, the choice of spaghetti. The reasons for this switch are actually quite understandable: compared to tagliatelle, durum wheat pasta was much easier to find. Of course, Bologna had a great tradition of homemade egg pasta rolled out by hand, but it would have been ludicrous to try to impose this custom in America, and the fragility of the product greatly limited its exportation. In the meantime, spaghetti had already spread through the American market via Italian communities, so substituting one form of long pasta for another was an obvious solution.[41]

In any case, spaghetti bolognese was an instant hit in the US. Before long it was on the menus of New York restaurants such as the Hotel Commodore, in 1920,[42] or Moneta's, in 1931.[43] So ever since, spaghetti bolognese has been connected in the popular imagination with the richest, tastiest kind of Italian cuisine, and even today is one of the most widespread and popular pasta specialities.

Although prewar chronicles suggest that this dish could be found even in Italy in military canteens, or in small trattorias (outside of Bologna and Emilia) that offered cheap, filling meals, spaghetti alla bolognese never caught on there, except as an attempt to please tourists from abroad who were used to the version back home. Even today, restaurant owners in Bologna have a hard time explaining to foreigners what the local tradition really is, despite the fact that interest in regional Italian cuisine has grown enormously of late. With a little effort, a good ragù can be made almost anywhere in the world, but handmade egg pasta is the true speciality unique to

Bologna and the surrounding area, and has remained so.

Italian culinary conservatives have always tried to defend ragù against heretical trends as much as possible. They recently made a strange and desperate last stand against those who dare to put it on dried pasta rather than tagliatelle; in 2018, the Accademia Italiana della Cucina registered a recipe with the Bologna Chamber of Commerce for 'Spaghetti alla Bolognese' made with . . . tuna.

Without getting into that recipe and whether it's actually representative of Bolognese tradition, one is forced to wonder: why did an institution like the Accademia Italiana della Cucina feel obliged to express its disapproval of spaghetti bolognese – the version which has been eaten around the world for at least a century – to the point of claiming the name traditionally means something else altogether?

Of course one can surmise that this was not a serious assertion, just a stunt meant to highlight a superlative dish (tagliatelle alla bolognese, of course) that doesn't get enough respect outside the borders of Italy. Yet whether Italians like it or not, spaghetti with meat sauce has been part of American cuisine for over a century, and though rooted in Italy, has taken its own path overseas. One thing is certain: if it weren't for this parallel history, Bologna would not be nearly as famous around the world.

8

LASAGNE

Now let's talk about one of the most sumptuous pasta dishes in Italy: lasagne. As a worthy heir to the timbales and other baked specialities that were a sine qua non on the aristocratic tables of yore, it is still associated with special occasions. Not only is it a celebratory treat, but the story behind it is one of the oldest – and most far-reaching – in Italian cuisine.

From north to south, it turns up all over the boot. Its most famous incarnations definitely include the version from Bologna, with green pasta, meat sauce, béchamel and parmesan; the 'carnival lasagne' of Naples, with ragù, salami, caciocavallo, ricotta and hard-boiled eggs; the vincisgrassi of Marche, stuffed with pork and chicken giblets; the timballo of Abruzzo, in both tomato-based and tomatoless versions; and last but not least, Genoese lasagne with pesto.

The most interesting aspect of this dish is perhaps not culinary, but cultural: nobody argues about lasagne. On the one hand, there are recipes that evolved over the years but now seem to undergo no major changes – at most, the age-old diatribe about the proper number of layers (seven, nine or twelve, like roses in a bouquet). On the other, in contrast to carbonara or amatriciana, 'lasagne' is a category that now includes hundreds of variants: a malleable dish, in other words, that allows one to experiment without getting into fierce disputes with food purists.

Yet even the baked version that seems to make everyone happy coexisted for many years – and upon closer examination, still does – with the unbaked branch of the family, which especially in southern Italy is often accompanied by pulses (like the 'sagne e fagioli' of Abruzzo). Less famous, or rather, less recognisable as lasagne, these fresh pasta dishes nearly vanished under a flood of new varieties in the last few centuries. As we are about to see, however, they are actually the oldest kind.

The only artefact of its kind in Italian food history, lasagne carries the genes of a food dating all the way back to the Romans: the *lagana* that are mentioned by many ancient authors, yet remain somewhat mysterious. The one thing which does seem certain is that this dish paved the way to the innumerable types of fresh and filled pasta that developed in the Middle Ages and, through a long process of evolution, have survived into the present.

So let's start there.

From lagana to lasagne

The most famous reference to lagana comes from the Latin poet Horace. In the first book of his *Satires* (1st century BCE) the poet addresses a Roman senator, comparing his own typical day to that of the illustrious man. Defending his frugal lifestyle, he claims he would never trade it for the riches and luxury of political office, which inevitably comes with its own headaches. He is happier to wander by himself at whim through the squares and marketplaces of the city, coming home to a humble meal of 'leeks, chickpeas and lagana':

> I live more comfortably than you, eminent senator,
> in this and in a thousand other ways. Wherever I please,
> I walk alone, asking the price of greens and grain,
> I stroll through the scam-filled Circus,
> and often in the evening through the Forum,
> lingering by the fortune-tellers, then back home I go
> to my bowlful of leeks, chickpeas and lagana.[1]

Although the poet does not go into the details of what he means by 'inde domum me ad porri et ciceris refero laganique catinum', this is clearly some simple dish, probably familiar to all his readers at the time. For us, on the other hand, it is anything but easy to figure out just what Horace's lagana were like. Were they part of the dish itself, a sort of pasta? Or, as others claim, were they flatbreads accompanying the stew of vegetables and pulses?[2]

The first theory, that lagana were a primordial form of pasta, is supported by several passages in the treatise *De Medicina*, written by Aulus Cornelius Celsus in the first century CE. Through these references, one can indirectly deduce the shape and above all the consistency of the dish.

In the first passage that interests us, the author begins by distinguishing between two kinds of foods based on flavour and texture: 'lenes' (mild) and 'acria' (acrid). Lagana belong to the first category, that of soft, gelatinous foods.

> Mild foods are broth, porridge, *laganum*, starch, barley gruel, meat that is fatty and glutinous, like almost any from domesticated animals, but above all the trotters and hocks of pigs, the trotters and heads of kids, calves and lambs, and the brains of all animals; also all the vegetables best referred to as bulbs; milk, *defrutum* [grape syrup], raisin wine and pine nuts. Acrid foods are everything too harshly flavoured, everything sour, everything salty, and even honey, and the better the honey the more acrid it is. Likewise garlic, onions, rocket, rue, cress, cucumbers, beets, cabbage, asparagus, mustard, radishes, endives, basil, lettuce and most greens.[3]

Lagana also turn up in the section on orthopaedics as a food that can be given to a patient with a broken jaw, who needs to gradually return to a normal diet after a liquid one:

> But regarding the jaw, one should add that the diet must be liquid for a long time. And even after some time has gone by, it must continue to be based on *laganum* and similar foods, until the formation of callus has completely strengthened the jawbone.[4]

240

Both passages suggest that the laganum mentioned by Celsus was a very soft, delicate food, not unlike the boiled dough of wheat and water that turned up over a thousand years later in the first medieval recipes for lasagne. Unfortunately, however, Latin literature provides no further support for the idea that this is what lagana were like, whereas there are many references to the existence of a paper-thin bread that was fried or baked.[5]

The most specific description of this kind comes from Athenaeus of Naucratis, a Greek Egyptian writer of the second century CE. In his work *Deipnosophistae* – a sort of philosophical dialogue modelled on Plato's *Symposium* – he gathers together many quotations on the theme of the banquet. The first passage to attract our attention refers to a kind of bread called 'artolaganon', made from a thin sheet of dough that other authors call 'tracta' (literally, 'pulled': much like the Italian verb 'tirare', which is used to describe the act of rolling out pasta).

> But in making the so-called *artolaganon* ('wheat-wafer'), a little wine, pepper, and milk are introduced, along with a small quantity of oil or fat. Similarly into *kapyria*, called by the Romans *tracta*, are put mixtures as into the wheat-wafer.[6]

It is in the second quotation, though, that Athenaeus supplies the first actual recipe (which is taken in turn from a treatise on bread-making by Chrysippus of Tyana, from the first century CE). Laganum, called here by the alternative name 'catillus ornatus', is made from flour, wine, lettuce juice, lard and pepper, then fried in oil.

There is another cake, which the Romans call *catillus ornatus*, and which is made thus: Wash some lettuces and scrape them; then put some wine into a mortar and pound the lettuces in it; then, squeezing out the juice, mix up some flour from spring wheat in it, and allowing it to settle, after a little while pound it again, adding a little pig's fat and pepper; then pound it again; draw it out into a cake; smooth it; trim it; cut it into small sections; put the pieces in a colander; and deep-fry them in olive oil that is as hot as possible.[7]

Lagana also appear several times in the Vulgate,[8] the version of the Bible translated into Latin by St Jerome. Here, too, they are described as a sort of thin unleavened bread that was sprinkled with oil. So around the time of this translation in the fourth century CE, the Latin term must have referred to bread, not pasta. Two centuries later, Isidore of Seville, in *Etymologiae*, explains that 'laganum is a broad, thin bread that is first boiled in water, then fried in oil',[9] combining two cooking methods that had probably coexisted for some time – boiling and frying – in one procedure.

The only recipes of any length that explicitly discuss lagana in the Roman world are from *De Re Coquinaria*, a treatise on cooking that is attributed to the cook Apicius, but which actually collects various texts from the first to the fourth century CE. The most interesting ones for our story are the recipes for 'patina apiciana' and 'patina cotidiana' (*patina* meaning 'cake' or 'pie'): two baked dishes made by alternating layers of dough with a filling of meat, fish, eggs, herbs and other ingredients.

The way that these two dishes are assembled and
baked closely resembles modern-day lasagne, with the
key difference that the layered sheets of dough are not
boiled first. As is often the case with old recipes, the text
is rather short on details and it is unclear whether these
thin wafers were supposed to be baked or fried first, or if
they were used raw. The one possible hint that the dough
was still soft is that we are instructed to top everything
with a final layer of laganum and then poke small holes in
it – a trick still used today for baked dishes with very wet
fillings, to let out the steam that would otherwise remain
trapped inside. The inner layers of pasta are thus boiled
by the liquid in the sauce, while the dry heat of the oven
turns the top one into a crust.*

Apician baked dish

Take small pieces of cooked sow's udder, fish, chicken,
cooked breasts of warblers or thrushes, and whatever you have that is best. Chop all of this carefully,
except the warbler meat. Mix raw eggs with oil. Grind
together pepper and lovage, pour in liquamen [fish
sauce], wine and raisin wine, put it in a pot, heat it
and bind it with starch. But first, put in all the chopped
meat and fish and bring it to a boil. When it is cooked,
take it off the fire with its sauce and ladle it into a pan,
alternating with whole pepper grains and pine nuts, so
that for each layer you put a layer of laganum above and

* Another kind of recipe is Cato's 'Placenta' (*De agricultura*, 76), which
uses sheets of bread (*tractae*) alternated with a filling of soft cheese and
honey, to make a sweet layered dish that is then baked.

below. However many sheets of laganum you put in, pour over the same number of ladlefuls. Pierce one last sheet with a reed and lay it over everything. Sprinkle with pepper. Before putting in the meat filling, however, bind it by adding the eggs. As for the kind of bronze pan to use, see below.

Everyday baked dish

Take a cooked sow's udder, cooked fish and cooked chicken. Chop them carefully. Take a bronze pan, break in eggs and beat them. In a mortar, grind together pepper and lovage; pour in liquamen, wine, raisin wine, a little oil. Transfer all of this into a pot, let it cook until it thickens. Add the meat and fish that you have chopped. Cover the bottom of the bronze pan with a layer of laganum, add a ladleful of filling, sprinkle with oil and do the same with another sheet. However many sheets of laganum you put in, add the same number of ladlefuls. Pierce one last sheet with a reed and lay it on top. Turn it out on to a platter, sprinkle with pepper and serve.[10]

To recap what we have seen so far, the historical references allow us to imagine that in Roman times there must have been two kinds of lagana: the soft variety described for the first time by Celsus, which was made by boiling the dough; and crisp flatbreads that were fried or baked, probably the most common type.

Which kind was meant by the poet Horace is a question still open to debate, although the phrase 'bowlful of leeks, chickpeas and lagana' suggests that all three ingredients were part of the same dish and that the dough may have been cooked with the pulses – just like the 'lagane e ceci' made even today in Calabria. If so, there is still the mystery of why no other sources mention this approach to using flour, which would place the invention of fresh pasta in Roman times. In any case it cannot have been widespread, and as the passage from Horace seems to suggest, may have been humble fare eaten by the lower classes: one of those foods that neither historians nor cookbooks paid much attention to. In any case, we are still worlds away from the medieval recipes that would turn lasagne, and fresh pasta in general, into an edible wrapping that could be filled and flavoured at whim.

A food for greedy friars

While Ancient Roman allusions to lagana suggest a dish that was definitely unassuming and even verged on 'hospital fare' (judging from the medical advice offered by Celsus), the first appearances of lasagne in medieval texts paint a very different picture: that of a heavenly indulgence. As a matter of fact, it often features in historical anecdotes or comic tales where it is a treat coveted by gluttonous peasants or friars.

A very early reference to the dish can be found in one of the richest sources of facts and stories from the thirteenth century, the *Cronica* by the Franciscan friar Salimbene di Adam. In his record of the year 1284, he tells of meeting another friar, a certain John of Ravenna, whose corpulence led Salimbene to note: 'I have never seen anyone more eager to devour lasagne with cheese.'[11]

We do not know exactly when this custom of serving lasagne with cheese came into fashion. The first known use of the word 'lasagne' in Italian seems to predate Salimbene's chronicle by just a couple of years, however. It appears in the legal records of the city of Bologna for 1282, where a popular rhyme in the vernacular[12] contains the verse 'de lasagne se fèn sette menestre' ('of lasagne they made seven dishes').[13]

In the two centuries after that, the dish shows up twice more in tales revolving around the comic figure of the greedy friar (a stock character in popular medieval literature), who is unable to resist temptation and resorts to all kinds of shrewd scheming in order to fill his belly.

The first of these stories, written by Giovanni Sercambi of Lucca in the early 1400s, tells of a friar who comes up with a ploy to coax a free dinner out of a peasant couple. The bargain is this: in addition to the meal they serve him, Brother Tomaso promises to eat, in atonement for his sins, twenty-five river pebbles. Eager to watch, the two gullible hayseeds go to gather the stones and prepare the rest of the dinner, happy to cook up anything he wants: 'The friar asked Ciaia if she had some flour: Ciaia said she did [. . .] Brother Tomaso had her get some cheese and grate it, telling her to make lasagne: and so she did. The pot was put on the fire, the lasagne was cooked, covered in plenty of cheese and set aside.'[14] After scrounging a fine meal, the monk naturally comes up with convoluted reasons to avoid swallowing the promised stones, much to the peasants' disappointment.

The second reference is in the *Novelle Porretane* (1478), a collection of stories modelled on Bocaccio's *Decameron*; its author, Sabadino degli Arienti of Bologna, claims to be gathering tales told by young visitors to the hot springs in Porretta. In the passage that concerns us, one reads of three friars who have their German cook whip up 'a good dish of lasagne with good grated cheese for their meal'. The fragrance alone makes their monastic temperance waver: 'when the smell of the lasagne reached the abbot's nose, it whetted his appetite so much that he immediately took a huge mouthful'.

But the lasagne has been dished out piping hot. So as not to be rude, the abbot tries to swallow it anyway, but tears start pouring from his eyes. Seeing his stricken expression, the other two ask why he is so pained, and the abbot replies that he is deeply moved by his memories of eating lasagne with many brothers in Christ who are no more. Touched by this explanation, the monks try to console their abbot. But once they bite into the same scorching pasta, it becomes clear that he was fibbing; so the insults start to fly, and in the end, so does the lasagne.[15]

Boiled but not baked

The key thing about these three sources, aside from the varying degrees of humour, is that although they cover a span of almost two centuries, they all seem to be describing a common (and apparently very popular) kind of pasta that could be cooked up on the spot. But the lasagne that tempted all those poor medieval monks into the sin of gluttony – how was it made, exactly?

The recipe manuscripts that describe it all come from one vast collection of treatises on cooking that was recopied and readapted up to the mid-fifteenth century, although its origins can be traced to the mid-thirteenth century, at the court of Frederick II in southern Italy.[16]

Based on this source, it seems clear that the most common type of lasagne was a sheet of pasta cut into squares, rectangles or lozenges (a shape that may very well derive its name from lasagne).[17] It was then boiled, drained, and layered with grated cheese. For a more flavourful dish, the recipes sometimes recommend adding spices[18] – although of course they were only for the well-to-do (which is why they never show up in tales about friars and peasants, such as the ones we saw above). To eat these noodles without burning their fingers, people would use a pointed stick, the ancestor of today's forks.

> To make lasagne, take fermented dough and make a sheet as thin as you can, then divide it into square pieces three fingerbreadths wide. After that, take boiling salted water and put the aforesaid lasagne in to cook, and when it is fully cooked, put on some grated cheese, and if you like, you may take good powdered spices and sprinkle them over the trencher. Then put a layer of lasagne over that and sprinkle again; and on top, another layer, and sprinkle; and do this until the trencher or bowl is full; then eat it using a pointed wooden stick.[19]

This specific recipe employs 'fermented dough', the

leavened kind used to make bread, but there was also a simpler version, which could be quickly made out of just water and flour:

> *For lasagne*
>
> Take good white flour, moisten it with warm water until it is thick; then roll it out thin; let it dry. It should be cooked in the broth from a capon or other rich meat; then put it in the dish with rich grated cheese, in layers, as you like.[20]

There must also have been a third kind that was not as widespread, but which closely resembled the thin sheets described in ancient times by Isidore of Seville, which were first boiled and then fried.

> You can also make lasagne 'in pavese'. Take the squares and cook them without cooking them too much, and spoon them out of the pot, and rinse them twice in cold water, and to make them as you wish, put on spices and saffron, and then you can fry them.[21]

This throwback to 'lagana' was quickly forgotten by later recipe writers, though. It did not survive the advent of the Renaissance, when pasta dishes multiplied and lasagne began to incorporate eggs, yielding a stronger, richer dough that was now truly in the category of fresh pasta.

Lasagne made with just water and flour, on the other hand, held on to a little space of its own and turns up now and then in later sources such as *L'economia del cittadino in villa* (1644) by Vincenzo Tanara of Bologna ('With water, or broth, and Flour, ordinary pasta can be made for millefanti, or for sheets from which to make tagliolini, strazzatelle, *lasagne for feast days and fast days*, tortelli for feast days and fast days'). Tanara and other seventeenth-century authors[22] also continue to cite the kind made from leavened bread dough rolled out thin and boiled, calling it *a vento* ('airy'). Vittorio Lancellotti's book *Lo scalco prattico* (1627) does not provide an actual recipe, but his description gives some sense of how different the dish was at the time compared to our own: layers of leavened dough alternated with a filling of capon breast and skin, butter, parmesan and slices of provola cheese fried in butter:

> Thin sheets of lasagne *a vento*, boiled in good capon broth, in very large dishes, with breast and skin of capons, butter, grated parmesan, slices of provola fried in butter, with sheets of pasta both over and under in a lattice, and morsels of fresh butter inside.[23]

Still, aside from a few cases that become increasingly rare after the late 1600s, the same dough began to be employed for tagliatelle, pappardelle and lasagne: flour, eggs and just a spoonful of water. The way they were served was also similar, and aside from the inevitable pairing with butter and cheese, one of the most common uses was as an accompaniment to meat dishes, especially large boiled or roasted fowl. Until well into the nineteenth century it was normal for pullets, ducks and *caponesse* – spayed hens, a speciality of Bologna – to be served under a blanket of boiled tagliatelle and lasagne, or even tortelli and macaroni, sprinkled of course with grated cheese.[24] If you're having friends over to dinner and want to try out an extraordinary Renaissance recipe (assuming your supermarket has crane meat), you could draw inspiration from this recipe by Bartolomeo Scappi, the Michelangelo of Italian cuisine:

> [. . .] crane is perfection itself when boiled with water, spices, and prosciutto, in the broth of which one then cooks lasagne to be served with grated cheese and cinnamon on top, and if the crane is cut up, then after it is cooked it can be covered with said lasagne.[25]

In other words, my fellow Italians shouldn't sneer quite so much when they visit Germany or England and someone serves them (overcooked)[26] pasta as a side to their meat. Because in the end, it may be the fault of their own great-great-great-great-grandparents.

Baked lasagne

Aside from the popular custom of eating lasagne simply boiled and sprinkled with cheese, one discovers on further investigation that even in the Middle Ages, lasagne already had a parallel history: it was the favourite noodle shape for making 'torte di pasta', baked dishes that contained much richer and more varied ingredients than cheese alone.

To get a sense of what they were, let's go back a step

and take another look at the *Liber de Coquina* (one of the recipe books from the medieval collection of Frederick II):

> If you want to make a lasagne pie, take lasagne, and
> fried or boiled or scrambled eggs, and ravioli cut
> in pieces or whole, and rich cheese either grated or
> chopped, and sufficient lard; arrange this mixture in
> layers, adding spices. And over this, with the dough,
> sculpt a snake fighting with a dove or any other animal
> you like. Then, take sausages with a good filling and
> arrange them all around like a wall. Then colour the
> layers however you please and put it in the oven. Then
> set it in front of your lord with great pomp.[27]

As usual, the medieval recipe does not provide many details about how to make the pasta or the exact ingredients for the filling: the one thing that is clear is that it must have been a rather rich dish of considerable size; an aristocratic dish, in short, to be served 'with great pomp'.

The lasagne was surrounded by a 'wall' of sausages and a pasta topping that could be decorated at whim – the suggested scene is a battle between a serpent and dove, no less. Inside, it was filled with eggs – which could be fried, hard-boiled or scrambled – ravioli,[28] cheese, lard and spices (which were also used to colour the different layers of the timbale).*

A few centuries later, in 1570, this same Bartolomeo

---

* One can't help noting the resemblance to the lasagne pies described by Apicius a millennium before, but it is almost impossible to establish whether those were really direct forerunners of the medieval recipe.

Scappi presents another recipe, a 'pie of tagliatelle or lasagne' in classic Renaissance style. This time, it is sealed within a crust of 'pasta reale' (a sort of shortcrust pastry with a bit less butter), in which the lasagne, boiled in broth or milk, is alternated with layers of provatura (a stringy cheese similar to provolone or mozzarella), butter, grated parmesan, sugar, pepper and cinnamon. A stint in the oven was then necessary to cook the pasta reale and melt the cheese:

To make a pie of tagliatelle or lasagne cooked in rich meat broth, or in milk

Take tagliatelle, or else lasagne made with white flour, eggs, warm goat's milk, or warm water, and cook it in rich meat broth, or goat's milk, or cow's milk, and when it is cooked let it cool, so that it can be cut, and then having greased the pan with butter, take a sheet of pasta reale made with white flour, rosewater, sugar and butter, and on top of this sheet place a layer of slices of provatura, sprinkled with sugar, pepper and cinnamon, with a few morsels of fresh butter, and grated Parmesan cheese, and then on top of it put the chopped tagliatelle, or lasagne, and over this lasagne make a layer of the same materials as below, and go on making layers in this way. Let it bake in the oven, or under a *testo* [an earthenware vessel heated with embers] uncovered, and when it is almost done sprinkle it with sugar, and cinnamon, and make sure there is plenty of butter. You can use this method to prepare any kind of macaroni rolled on a metal rod, cooking it in the above way; you can also layer it with mint, marjoram, and crushed garlic cloves, and serve it hot in any season.[29]

After these examples, however, something strange occurs.

Recipes for baked lasagne become increasingly rare, and baked lasagne pies, in particular, seem to fall off the culinary radar until the second half of the eighteenth century. What happened?

In Italian cuisine, the splendour of the Renaissance had come to an end. That fruitful season of creativity was followed by a long phase of subservience to French cooking that it only began to shake off in the mid-eighteenth century, edging into the modern era with a series of new ideas that put an Italian spin on French dishes.

Some good examples are the timbale recipes in which the anonymous author of *Il cuoco piemontese perfezionato a Parigi* (1766) presents an entirely Italian, pasta-filled take on the concept.[30] In two interesting baked lasagne dishes, in particular, one can see the first signs of a trend that was rapidly catching on. His lasagne with pike is quite simple, alternating layers of pasta with fish, butter, grated cheese, pepper and nutmeg; the same method is used for the version with prawn tails.[31]

Though those two dishes were not very successful at the time and never gained a true foothold in Italian cuisine, they played a trailblazing role: drawing inspiration from them, a handful of cookbooks over the next few years laid the foundations for modern lasagne, which then developed into various regional specialities.

Just five years after *Il cuoco piemontese perfezionato a*

Parigi, another anonymously authored recipe collection, *La cuciniera piemontese* (1771), suggested three new kinds of baked lasagne: two lasagne pies – one ordinary, and one made with oil for fast days – and a third dish with lasagne and butter. The first pie is what interests us most, because it uses certain ingredients – prosciutto, truffles, mushrooms, beef marrow and gravy – that became recurrent in the years that followed, forming the basis of most baked lasagne recipes up to the late nineteenth century. In this recipe, the wide noodles are simply mixed with the toppings, then sealed inside a pastry crust decorated with strips arranged on the bottom of the pan (like the latticed tops of fruit pies today). The pie was then flipped over for serving, and a hole was pierced in the middle for additional gravy to be poured in.

Lasagne pie

You will make a fairly firm dough with eggs, a little water, and some salt, rolling out four or five sheets, which you will let dry for a while, then cut to a length of two fingers; take salted boiling water, and plunge the lasagne in it for half a quarter of an hour, then drain it with a spoon; take very thin slices of prosciutto, truffles, mushrooms, minced beef marrow, fresh butter, powdered cinnamon, grated cheese and gravy; mix all of this with the lasagne in the pan, to flavour it well; then take the usual kind of pastry; rub the inside of another pan with butter, then put in strips of pastry according to your fancy, with a layer of pastry over it, as for an ordinary timbale, then place the mixture

inside, and cover with another sheet of pastry, and bake
it in the oven for an hour and a half, after which you
will turn it over on its plate, and make a hole to pour in
a good thickened gravy, and serve.[32]

You may have noticed that these early examples of lasagne are all from Piedmont, although in the decades that
followed they apparently did not find fertile ground to
put down roots and grow into a regional speciality there.
Nowadays, no Italian would expect to find lasagne with
pike or prawns in a restaurant in Turin, whereas in
Naples, Marche, Bologna and Genoa,[33] as we are about
to see, the dish flourished in all kinds of interesting ways.

Naples, Marche, Bologna

Towards the end of the eighteenth century, just a few years
after its invention in Piedmont, the lasagne timbale was
introduced to Naples by one of the greatest pioneers of
southern Italian cuisine: Vincenzo Corrado.[34] Due to his
influence, baked pasta dishes became an essential course
at gala dinners throughout the South.

As one can see from the recipe below, the lasagne presented in his best-known book, *Il cuoco galante* (1773)
is still much closer to the dish described in *La cuciniera
piemontese* than to modern-day Neapolitan lasagne –
except in one aspect: the provatura cheese, which gave
the dish its classic stringiness. Aside from that, the filling
includes parmesan, veal coulis[35] and prosciutto.

Timbales of lagane with prosciutto

Having cooked the lagane in broth, allowed it to cool, and mixed it with grated cheese, sliced provatura, and a strong Veal Coulis, and prosciutto, lay it out in a pan greased with butter, and cover it with long, wide strips of prosciutto carefully laid side by side, and bound with beaten eggs; having thus arranged everything, cover the Timbale in provatura brushed with egg, and bake it.[36]

Over fifty years later, Corrado's torch was taken up by Ippolito Cavalcanti – the new voice of Neapolitan cooking – in *La cucina teorico-pratica*, published in 1837. In the last section, devoted to 'simple home cooking,' Cavalcanti presents a number of popular recipes written entirely in Neapolitan dialect. They include a magnificent version of 'lasagne di carnevale' that features cheese (with the Renaissance-style addition of sugar and cinnamon), the gravy from a stew, meatballs and slices of mozzarella or provola:

Lasagne

For Carnival you can also make lasagne. Go to the macaroni man down in the Pennino,* get some nice wide noodles (careful, it takes extra water to cook them); after cooking them, lay them in layers in a round pan or a terracotta dish; and for every layer, put in cheese and the broth from a good stew; after that, make a layer of

---

* The Pennino, now known as Pendino, is a neighbourhood in Naples.

wee little meatballs, alternated with slices of provola, or mozzarella. And if you would like it to be sweet, mix the cheese with sugar and a little cinnamon. Then put it to cook in the testo, with a fire above and below; and what a fine dish it is![37]

Like all traditional specialities, Neapolitan lasagne has also evolved over the years, incorporating ingredients that were not in the earliest recipes. For instance, the ricotta and stewed pork used even today, which turn up for the first time in the 1927 edition of Ada Boni's *Il talismano della felicità*,[38] were probably grafted on to a tradition that was already well entrenched, but still open to changes. Over time, 'lasagne di carnevale' came to house more and more delicacies between its layers, becoming a symbol of the city's culinary opulence. This can easily be seen in the current version, which envisions, in order: ricotta, pork ragù, fried meatballs, salami or sausages from Basilicata, hard-boiled eggs and slices of fairly young caciocavallo.[39]

Just a year after Corrado's book, another classic of regional cuisine came out: Antonio Nebbia's *Il cuoco maceratese*. First published in 1779, it spotlights the cuisine of Marche, an area to which authors had not previously paid much attention. Flipping through the recipes, one finds an interesting 'Salza per i Princisgras', a sauce for the type of lasagne now known as vincisgrassi, which is still a classic in the region.

Nebbia fills its layers with diced prosciutto and truffles, binding it all with a sort of béchamel made from milk, flour and cream. This is topped off with the inevitable butter and parmesan:

Sauce for Princisgras

Take half a pound [170 g] of prosciutto, cut it in a small dice, with four ounces [113 g]* of truffles sliced thin; then take foglietta and a half of milk [670 ml], mix it in a pan with three ounces [85 g] of flour, and heat it adding prosciutto and truffles, stirring all the while until it begins to boil, and it should boil for half an hour; then pour in half a pound [170 g] of fresh cream, mixing everything until it is well combined; then make a dough for tagliolini with two eggs and four yolks, roll it out, not too thin, and cut it as they do mostaccioli in Naples [in diamonds], not too broad; cook it in half broth and half water, adjusting the salt; take the dish on which it will go to the table, and around the edge you may make a rim of frigè pastry [savoury shortcrust] to hold in the sauce and keep it from splashing out when you put it in the oven, where it must be browned a little; when you have cooked the pasta, cut it in the shape of mostaccioli; and sprinkle it with parmesan cheese, and lay it in the above dish with a layer of sauce, butter, and cheese, and another of lasagne laid out flat and smooth, and so forth until you have filled the dish; at the top, you

* The pound used here was the equivalent of 340g, divided into 12 ounces.

must take care to end with sauce and butter, and parmesan cheese, and having finished, put it in the oven to
let it form a crust.[40]

Here as well, the first recipe is by no means the definitive one. It is missing one ingredient that is fundamental
to the current version: chicken giblets. Those will turn
up a few years later, albeit in Rome, among the ingredients for 'Gattò di Lasagne alla Misgrasse'[41] in Francesco
Leonardi's *L'Apicio moderno* (1790); as one can guess
from the 'Misgrasse', this is a different version of the same
lasagne. For that matter, Leonardi was well acquainted
with giblet-based sauces, like the 'Ragù Melè'[42] or the
'Ragù of Livers'[43] that became very popular in the nineteenth century, and may have influenced the modern filling
for this unique lasagne from Marche. Despite these slight
differences from the earliest recipe, vincisgrassi remains
one of the dishes that has undergone the least variation
over the centuries, and it can be considered an enduring
monument to Italian culinary history.

The story of Bolognese lasagne – probably the best-
known and most imitated version – is a little different
from the other varieties, because back when timbales and
pies came into fashion, between the eighteenth and nineteenth centuries, Bologna still lacked the main ingredient
in the current recipe: its meat sauce.*

---

* The famous sauce must have already existed in Bologna, at least in some

Nonetheless, by the mid-nineteenth century, there was already a dish called 'lasagne alla bolognese', which is described for the first time in *Il codice gastrologico economico* (1841). Over half a century had gone by since the first published recipes for Neapolitan lasagne and vincisgrassi, dishes that by then could boast several variants. But for some reason, Bologna's name is linked here to a very odd version. Rather than cheese, ragù and béchamel, the first 'Bolognese' lasagne were filled only with boiled spinach, finely chopped and mixed with gravy (in the fast-day version, the gravy is replaced with fried onions, butter, herbs and unidentified 'spices'):

Bolognese Lasagne

For Bolognese Lasagne, use the very same method as Genoese Lasagne,* the difference lying only in the following condiment. Take tender Spinach, carefully trimmed, washed, boiled, and rinsed in cool water; squeeze it well and mince it as fine as you can, simmering it in good meat gravy, and then add sufficient gravy for the quantity of Lasagne you desire to cook, and if you want to serve it on a Fast day, then brown onions with Herbs, Spices, and Butter, and add the Spinach as above, with Butter as needed.[44]

form, but was definitely not yet famous enough to play an important role in lasagne. For more details, see chapter 7.
* That is, 'with eggs, very little salt, very little water, and if you like a touch of saffron'.

Compared to the rich, flavourful, opulent lasagne usually associated with Bologna, this version seems much more elegant (maybe even a tad austere). In any case, the dish enjoyed a degree of success and showed up four years later in two other recipe books: Giovanni Brizzi's *La cuciniera moderna* and the thirteenth edition of *Il cuciniere italiano moderno* from 1851.[45] But what did that great admirer of Bolognese cooking, Pellegrino Artusi, have to say? At the time of *La scienza in cucina* (1891), lasagne must not have been an important dish yet, and the only reference to it in the entire book is in the recipe for 'Domestic duck', which suggests using duck sauce on 'a dish of homemade ribbon noodles or lasagne.'[46] Still, one can see an indirect influence: Artusi played a key role in making ragù alla bolognese so wildly popular in the twentieth century. It was probably due to this pervasiveness that it entered the composition of Bolognese lasagne, where it is mentioned for the first time in 1908 in a recipe from *100 specialità di cucina italiane ed estere*:

Bolognese lasagnette

Clean half a kilogram of spinach, boil it for eight minutes in a little water, drain it and pass it through a sieve, then knead it into a kilogram of flour with three eggs. Roll out the pasta, as thin as you can, and cut out ribbons of lasagne, as large as you please. Having done this, prepare a good beef ragoût and a good béchamelle sauce. Then boil your lasagne in salted water and lay it out on a dishcloth. Take a copper pan, grease it with butter and arrange the

lasagne in layers, dressing each layer with cheese,
ragoût and béchamelle. When you have finished,
put the lasagnette in the oven, covered, for twenty
minutes, taking care not to let the bottom burn,
and serve.[47]

The spinach does not completely disappear, but it moves from the sauce into the pasta, along with the eggs and flour, giving it the characteristic green colour that is still a hallmark of modern-day lasagne alla bolognese. The gravy that was in almost all early versions has, however, been omitted: sacrificed on the altar of frugality and efficiency that came to characterise middle-class cooking in the twentieth century.

Reading this recipe – which is more than a hundred years old – one might think that lasagne alla bolognese has not changed in over a century. Actually, though, most recipes up to the 1940s called for a ragù incorporating chicken giblets,[48] which are now found only in a few delicious family recipes. This variant is mentioned in a wonderful anecdote from the journalist and gourmet Paolo Monelli, who in 1935 wrote:

I have read books both sacred and secular, I have
sought certainties and consolation in a thousand
volumes, but no book can rival the tome of green
lasagne that our leering Bolognese hosts set in front
of us. Page upon page, filled with an ooze of cheese,
a glimpse of truffle, a swarm of precious giblets.
Leaf through, devour each folio: it is a miniature
Decameron, a textbook of ancient philosophy, a

harmonious poem that makes us happy to be alive. A
secret melody by Rossini is hidden in these pages, but
a glass of Albana will reveal it, like an acid applied to
invisible ink.[49]

While Neapolitan lasagne di carnevale, vincisgrassi and
lasagne alla bolognese all evolved in various ways to
yield the versions enjoyed today, other local specialities
were fated to extinction. Like the lasagnes of Piedmont,
another illustrious also-ran was 'lasagne alla milanese'.
Back in 1790, Francesco Leonardi described it as a particularly fragrant dish filled with truffles, parmesan, butter,
béchamel and cinnamon.[50] And the name turns up again a
century later, on a completely different version containing
chicken, pickled tongue, truffles, mushrooms, gravy and
béchamel[51] – a bucking of trends that must have come at
a cost, since the recipe never established a clear identity
over the years, or at least not enough to survive even at
the local level.

Indeed, it's hard to say why some versions of lasagne,
like the ones with meat sauce, have become so entrenched
in the popular imagination that they turn up as Garfield's
favourite food, whereas others have vanished altogether.
But as I mentioned at the outset, lasagne seems to be the
pasta dish that more than any other tends to spawn creative new variants; history then decides what to keep.
And in the end, that's one goal of this book: I hope that
readers will try out the flavours of the past. Because
many ancient recipes, even the ones that didn't make it,
deserve another day in the sun and on the menu. Not just
in a spirit of historical re-enactment, but because they are

unquestionably fabulous dishes; the culinary equivalent, if we were talking about music, of a symphony from the distant past that still holds magic for modern ears.

9

Pesto alla genovese

Historically, Genoa has always held a special place in Italian cuisine. This may be due to the control that it exercised for centuries over maritime trade. Its ships sailed throughout the Mediterranean: from the Black Sea, via Constantinopolis, to the shores of the Near East; and then past the 'Pillars of Hercules,' circumnavigating Spain and France, to the rich ports of Flanders. Its tentacular network comprised dozens of colonies and trading hubs in all the main European harbours; they fed the coffers of its powerful bankers, the aspirations of its explorers and the creativity of its chefs.

The Ligurian capital has many specialities: its famous focaccia, farinata, cima ripiena, cappon magro and more. There is one, however, that stands out above all the rest and has become synonymous with the city of Genoa in the Italian culinary imagination, and in the world's: pesto. That green sauce whose brilliant colour and intense flavour, aided by the fact that it keeps well, have landed it on shelves all over the globe. An amazing success story for a vegetarian sauce.

And yet, while mass-produced pesto wins over more and more consumers every year, any Genoese food purist will tell you there's just one way to make it: by hand, using a wooden pestle and marble mortar. Only these sacred tools may be used to crush the basil leaves – which must be Genoese basil, mind you – and turn them, with some oil, garlic, pecorino, parmesan and pine nuts, into a fragrant, creamy, jade-green paste.

Once again, this wildly popular yet simple combination of a few choice ingredients has a history spanning almost a millennium. To retrace it, we must go all the way back to the very first pasta shape, delve into the Renaissance condiments conceived for fast days, and make the acquaintance of another extraordinary Genoese sauce that even most people in Genoa have never heard of – unless they're fans of Neapolitan cooking – yet which was, in some sense, pesto's twin.

What we are about to embark on, in short, is a voyage through this city's cuisine that will take us sailing around the whole Mediterranean, just like the Genoese fleets of yore.

Genoese tria

If you look at the medieval Italian recipes in the collection of texts that may have come from the court of Frederick II,[1] many dishes have names that indicate their place of origin. We find specialities from Rome,[2] Germany,[3]

Lombardy,[4] Provence,[5] Parma.[6] Among all these, the one that immediately catches our eye is titled 'De tria ianuensi'[7] (Genoese tria): the first instance of the city of Genoa being linked to a food, and not just any food, but the oldest form of dried pasta, 'tria'. This term is used even today in the names of certain classic dishes from Southern Italy: it turns up in the region of Puglia, for instance, with the 'ceceri e tria' of Salento and the 'tridde' of Bari, or in Sicily's 'vermicelli di tria' and 'tria bastarda'.

Like the Roman lagana that, as we have seen, was the ancestor of fresh pasta, tria has ancient origins that go back to the first records of dried pasta on the shores of the Mediterranean.[8] The word *itrion* – which in Latin then became *itria*,[9] as a generic term for doughs of flour and water – was used even by Galen, a Greek physician who lived in the second century CE. The Greek word probably spread with this meaning to the Near East, since it turns up both in the Jerusalem Talmud (fifth century CE), as *itrium*, and in the Syriac-Arabic dictionary of Isho bar Ali (tenth century CE), where the term *itriyya* means a string-like pasta that was dried before use.

Ancient sources describing this foodstuff in its earliest stages are somewhat rare, and its exact origin is difficult to reconstruct. Still, an important role in its spread must have been played by the Jewish community[10] that formed in Sicily in the second century CE, and then by Arab settlers, who must have intensified its production and trade. By the time that the Arab geographer al-Idrisi described the island in the twelfth century, he could not help but mention the flourishing trade in dried pasta as one of its marvels:

> West of Termini there is a delightful settlement called
> Trabia. Its ever-flowing streams propel a number of
> mills. Here there are huge buildings in the country-
> side where they make vast quantities of itriyya which
> is exported everywhere: to Calabria, to Muslim and
> Christian countries. Very many shiploads are sent.[11]

Al-Idrisi's chronicle is particularly important because it identifies Sicily as the first main hub of pasta production in Italy. From there, it was exported to the peninsula and further abroad. The island's position in the middle of the Mediterranean made it a natural stop on the major trade routes of the ancient world, as well as the centre of cultivation for the prized durum wheat that had already been mentioned by Pliny in Roman times, and which even then was indispensable for this kind of pasta. The climate was also perfect for drying the product – a delicate procedure, essential to ensure its stability, that was aided by the island's sun and wind. This food's extended shelf life was indeed the key to its enormous success, which has only grown over the centuries. Like cheeses or cured meats, dried pasta could be eaten long after it was made: a characteristic that made it worthwhile to select the finest grain and process it with the utmost care.

Between the thirteenth and fourteenth century, one begins to find records of durum wheat being grown and dried pasta being produced in other areas, such as Sardinia, Puglia and Naples, which already had a number of proto-factories making vermicelli, fidelini and macaroni.[12]

In Genoa, something different happened. The city didn't have its own pasta industry, yet managed to make itself a hub of the pasta trade. How? By importing it, especially from Sicily and Sardinia, and then distributing the product through its powerful mercantile network throughout the Mediterranean, all the way to the great ports of Marseille and Barcelona. Pasta thus soon became an important part of the local cuisine, even though it was not produced in the region at all. But just what was this 'tria genovese' like?

When it makes its first appearance in medieval manuscripts, tria is clearly a long, thin wheat pasta, similar to spaghettini, that is dried before use. Practically identical recipes for tria genovese show up in three different cooking treatises written in Latin. Let's look at just one:

De tria ianuensi

For Genoese tria, fry onions in oil, put them in boiling water to cook and add spices and colour and flavour them as you please; you can also add grated or sliced cheese, and if you like, you can serve it with capons, with eggs and with any kind of meat.[13]

The description is very terse – as recipes tended to be the time – and although it was probably quite enough for the court cooks of the era, seven centuries later it is anything but clear. Since the tria is mentioned only at the beginning, it is hard to determine its role in the dish, and above all the exact relationship between the pasta and the onion sauce, or the eggs[14], capon or other meat with which it could be served.

The forerunners of pesto alla genovese

If we leap ahead to the mid-fifteenth century, Maestro Martino[15] offers a much more detailed description of pasta alla genovese.

> To make *macharoni ala zenovese*, or tagliarini, make a thin pasta out of good flour, and this dough must have half an egg white in it, depending on the amount you want, and be tempered with water and a little salt; make the pasta on the firm side and roll it out rather thin, then put on plenty of flour and roll it on the rod, then take out the rod and cut it no thicker than a string, then let it dry a little or make it fresh if you prefer, then take good aged parmesan, or a provatura that is neither too hard nor too fresh, and grate it all together with said cheese, then take rocket, making sure that there are no worms left on the leaves, and grind it as well as you can, then put it together as I said with the cheese and a little saffron, then put it in dishes or bowls and mix everything together, putting a layer of macaroni, a layer of tagliarini, and any dish of pasta demands fresh butter.[16]

Maestro Martino's pasta is not the dry type made from durum wheat, but rather fresh pasta made from soft wheat, water and egg whites. This should come as no surprise, because even though dried pasta was already in use, court cooks in the fifteenth century and all through the Renaissance showed a clear preference for the kind made on the spot in their kitchens. What is instead extremely interesting is the sauce for these thin tagliatelle: a genuine rocket pesto, made with parmesan – which can be replaced with aged provatura cheese, very similar to caciocavallo – and saffron.

Even with all due caution, it's not going too far to say that the similarities to modern-day pesto are quite clear.

And yet, looking at historical sources, it is impossible to establish any real continuity between this version and the pesto we know today. In point of fact, this pasta sauce seems to have literally disappeared in the centuries that followed (or at least was no longer identified with Genoa).

It is hard to say just what happened, but it seems likely that the rocket-and-cheese recipe merged with others and was eventually overshadowed by one of the most famous condiments of the Middle Ages: agliata.

One can find dozens of different formulas for the latter, whose oldest ancestor is the *moretum* described in a Latin poem of the first century BCE, attributed to Virgil:[17] a mix of garlic, aged goat's or sheep's cheese, smallage (a kind of celery), rue and coriander, which were all ground together to form a spreadable cream.

Agliata itself began appearing in cookbooks in the Middle Ages: garlic was crushed with almonds and mixed with broth, sometimes thickened with a little bread, to make a sauce that could be used on meat.

In the fifteenth century, the types of agliata began to multiply. Maestro Martino describes one which he calls 'pavonaza',[18] tinted with purple grapes or cherries. Midway through the next century, the House of Este's cook Cristoforo di Messisbugo proposed versions that were coloured yellow (with saffron) or green (with the juice of parsley or chard). As for the possible uses, Messisbugo suggests: 'you can serve it alone, or incorporated with dishes of Meat, or large boiled Fish, and over Macaroni'.[19] Agliata thus became a perfect condiment for the fast days of Lent,[20] and was so widespread that it wiped out all other options, such as Maestro Martino's rocket pesto. In some variants, despite the name, garlic became a secondary ingredient that one could even omit, replacing it with ginger and pepper.

Meanwhile, Genoa's ties to pasta, close as they once were, had faded. From the Renaissance to the eighteenth century, the city's name was naturally associated with many other products and dishes,[21] but pasta seemed to completely disappear from the local culinary horizon. For more than three hundred years.

Yet parallel to this, in the same span of time, one of the key ingredients in modern pesto alla genovese was slowly making headway.

From the Middle Ages to the eighteenth century, basil was far from being one of the most widely employed herbs. At most, it turned up as a sporadic ingredient in sauces for roast meats. The first author to rely on it often was the Neapolitan chef Vincenzo Corrado, who in *Il cuoco galante* (1773) often uses basil mixed with other herbs and spices, especially to flavour meats or vegetables such as pumpkin or crucifers, and also the earliest examples of tomato sauce.[22]

Riffling through the many condiments described in Corrado's book, we find one – mysteriously called 'Lombard sauce' – that seems particularly close to what we are looking for:

> Mash together a clove of garlic, basil, fresh fennel, pine nuts, and spices, and after thinning with malvasia vinegar and verjuice, strain it through a sieve, and serve it over Frogs.[23]

This recipe now has quite a few ingredients in common with today's pesto, but the resulting sauce is thin and sour, still much closer to Renaissance tastes – when verjuice (unripe grape juice) and vinegar were often used instead of oil – than to modern ones.

To find a recipe that actually links basil to the city of Genoa we have to wait until 1830, when Vincenzo Agnoletti, in his *Manuale del credenziere*, a cookbook entirely devoted to cold dishes, records an 'Insalata alla Genovese':

> *Genoese salad*
>
> After arranging the lettuce, or other salad, on the plate, top it with herbs, or fruit preserved in vinegar, fillets of tarantello tuna, bottarga, salt-cured tuna, anchovies, etc.; then dress it with a sauce made from caviar, bread soaked in vinegar, a little basil and pepper, grinding all of this in a mortar, passing it through a sieve, and then thinning it with oil, vinegar and the juice of a lemon.[24]

It is not really clear whether this recipe is called Genoese due to the fish, the caviar-based sauce or the basil, but the pieces are starting to fall into place: we're getting close.

The birth of pesto

The definitive turn came eleven years later. The cookbook *Codice gastrologico economico*, printed in Florence in 1841, includes this wonderful – and above all, illuminating – recipe:

Genoese Lasagne for Feast Days and Fast Days

Both on Feast days and Fast days, make your Pasta the same way, that is with eggs, a little salt, and a little water, and if you like a little Saffron. On feast days the sauce should be from well-cooked Veal; cook the lasagne in salted water, drain it with a slotted spoon, lay it out carefully on the plate, and layer by layer dress it with said sauce and parmesan cheese. On fast days, the form is the same and one changes only the sauce, which is made as follows: put in a Mortar two cloves of garlic, a quantity of Basil, the inside of a Roman Cheese, or a Dutch cheese weighing one ounce, a little spice, and all of this should be ground well, then thinned with plenty of fine Oil, and when the Lasagne is cooked take a ladle of the pasta water and put it in the Mortar and mix well, and serve this in place of the Veal sauce with Parmesan Cheese.[25]

This recipe is pivotal to our history of Genoese pasta for at least two reasons. Let's start with the first.

As one can clearly see, the 'fast-day' version of this lasagne alla genovese is made with a sauce exactly like modern-day pesto: garlic, basil, pecorino romano or Dutch cheese – probably a sort of aged gouda – seasonings and oil, mashed together in a mortar with the addition of some water from cooking the lasagne.

Traditionalists will have noted one thing: the absence of pine nuts, a cornerstone of what is now considered the 'traditional recipe'. But the fact is that they appeared for the first time only in 1880, in the cookbook titled *Cucina di strettissimo magro*,[26] and up to the 1960s they figured only very sporadically in the composition of pesto.

In any case, the point-by-point similarity to modern-day pesto, despite many slight changes introduced by subsequent authors, leads one to suspect that this recipe had begun to be well established and deeply rooted in the area long before it was recorded by the cookbooks of the time.

One reason for this silence could lie in the fact that in the mid-to-late nineteenth century, recipe collectors had yet to devote much attention to pasta. Their primary audience was the urban middle and upper class, which preferred a French style of cooking primarily based on soups, sauces and meat dishes. To list just the most striking examples, the *Almanacco dei gastronomi* (1863)[27] presents only ten 'zuppe e minestre' (the 'soup' category that included pasta) and only one pasta dish out of 413 recipes overall; *Il moderno cuciniere universale* (1881)[28] has four pasta dishes out of 481; *La regina delle cuoche*

(1881)[29] has nine out of 511, but the record is set by *La cuciniera bolognese* (1874),[30] a brief cookbook that does not include a single pasta dish – in Bologna, no less! Just seventeen years later, Artusi's first edition – which, keep in mind, was based on field research – offers fifteen recipes for pasta in broth, and fifteen for pasta with sauces using ingredients such as minced meat, fish and cured meats. This should give some notion not only of how innovative his book was for the time, but also of how little the ones that preceded it reflected the true face of Italian cuisine.

From Genoa to Naples: the strange case of 'genovese' meat sauce

Before moving on to later stages in the evolution of pesto, let's linger at this turning point for a moment. It won't have escaped you that according to the recipe in the *Codice gastrologico economico* – the one with the first 'modern' pesto in history – there were two kinds of Genoese-style lasagne. Pesto was really just a 'fast-day' version of the richer type made with veal sauce. This 'genovese di carne' has now almost vanished from the place where it was invented, only to become the speciality of another city: Naples.

For those who may never have heard of it, genovese, today, is a sublime pasta sauce with two main ingredients: a large cut of beef and a massive quantity of onions – up to twice the weight of the meat – to which one adds, depending on the recipe, carrots, celery, white wine and just a little tomato purée. The beef is carefully browned in oil, then the onions and other ingredients are added, and everything is left to simmer on very low heat for several hours. The onions become a soft jam, the meat falls apart into long tendrils, and the sauce turns a mahogany colour. And the fragrance? Don't get me started.

Many people wonder why on earth this dish is named after Genoa, yet is known as such only in the area of Naples. That's one of the parallel histories that seem to crop up throughout this book, and it deserves to be told.

Let's begin at the beginning.

WWWWWWWWW

The first author to describe a 'Veal Loin in the manner of Genoa' in Naples was Vincenzo Corrado in 1773, a sign that by then a fruitful relationship had begun to develop between the cuisines of the two Tyrrhenian ports.* It was a very basic dish: a large cut of veal browned in lard or butter, with only water added to keep it soft and form a 'glaze', that is, a dense, dark, fragrant sauce. A few years later, Francesco Leonardi, in a recipe for 'Brisket of Veal in the manner of Périgord', speaks of cooking 'alla genovese' to describe braising meat slowly with 'a

---

* The connection between these two cities on the Tyrrhenian Sea is not surprising, because despite the physical distance between them, the modes of transport used in that era made Genoa and Naples closer than they might seem. It took just two days to sail between their ports, less time than it took to travel from Genoa to Milan before the advent of the railway. The journey by land from Genoa to Naples instead took at least eight or nine days, and only trains definitively solved the problem. Judging by accounts from the late nineteenth century, the average time it took to travel by rail from Genoa to Milan was three hours, Milan to Rome took twelve, and Rome to Naples took more than eight hours.

piece of butter, a piece of prosciutto, an onion studded with two cloves, a bouquet of herbs, a little boiling white wine; let it take on a fine golden hue, and serve it with the above sauce'.[31] This recipe is indeed still quite similar to the one we saw earlier for Leonardi's 'Maccaroni alla Napolitana',[32] so much so that to some commenters of the time the two sauces seemed interchangeable.[33]

A few decades later, genovese sauce encountered pasta: a fashion that exploded in Genoa – as we saw in the *Codice gastrologico economico* of 1841 – but also in Naples, as evidenced by this recipe from the fourth edition of Ippolito Cavalcanti's *Cucina teorico-pratica* (1844):

Beef in the manner of Genoa

Take a good piece of vacante di natica [a cut from the bottom sirloin or rump] weighing three rotoli, put it in a pot with salt, pepper, and spices, and a quarter pound of beaten lard; set the pot on the fire and let it brown slowly, putting in a little hot water every so often, and let the meat cook this way, summoning all your patience: *when you see it is done, you will put in a little more water, and do you know why? Because it will make a sauce for your pasta;* then let it thicken, slow as can be, put it in a serving dish and take it to the table.[34]

In short, in the mid-nineteenth century, people in Genoa were serving lasagne with a veal sauce very similar to the one Neapolitans put on their macaroni, made with meat, prosciutto, onions (and other optional vegetables) and a few seasonings.

At this point, the two sauces became almost inter-changeable, as we can see from this passage in the *Nuova enciclopedia agraria* (1859):

199. Genoese lasagne

Make lasagne as described in no. 196, cook the pasta in good broth, drain it, and dress it with meat sauce and parmesan cheese as you would with agnellotti (no. 198) [with the gravy from braised meat and a good grated parmesan].

200. Neapolitan macaroni

Cook macaroni in salted water, drain and serve it as you would lasagne (no. 199).[35]

The difference between the two recipes comes down to just the shape of the pasta – lasagne, in Genoa, and macaroni, in Naples – whereas the sauce and cheese are exactly the same. In *La cuciniera genovese* (1863) – a cookbook whose importance we will discuss further on – the approach is also practically identical: the 'Lasagne' is topped with veal sauce, and the 'Macaroni di napoli al sugo e al brodo'[36] with beef sauce, but both sauces are made the same way: by browning meat in butter or veal fat, with onions, carrots and a small amount of white wine, then adding several tomatoes or some purée and a few mushrooms. In a word, it was the world's first magical sauce: on lasagne, it was Genoese, while on macaroni it became Neapolitan (and later authors reprised this

281

total overlap between the two, changing the 'designation of origin' based on the shape).[37]

In short, for almost seventy years, Genoa and Naples were linked by a shared meat sauce that they used on two local kinds of pasta, respectively lasagne and macaroni.

What shook things up and definitively differentiated the two dishes was the ever more pervasive spread, in the second half of the nineteenth century, of an ingredient of prime importance for modern Italian pasta: tomatoes, which brought a corresponding decline in meat-based sauces.

In Alberto Cougnet's cookbook *L'arte cucinaria in Italia* (1910), one can see the first true split: here, in 'Maccheroni alla Napoletana', tomatoes already play a noticeable role alongside the meat, echoing the trend that led to today's ragù alla napoletana;[38] 'Altro sugo di carne stracotta alla Genovese', on the other hand, is already quite similar (except for the lack of onions) to the recipe for 'genovese' that is still made in Naples – and only in Naples.

Another stewed meat sauce, Genoese style

In a pot with 200 gr. of butter, beef marrow and a pinch of salt, brown two kilogr. of lean beef, cut in pieces; add: a few sprigs of parsley, two carrots, 150 gr. of flour, 50 g. of dried mushrooms, and let all of this cook for 20 minutes; then pour over two cups of dry

{ white wine and allow to boil for a few seconds. Lastly,
{ add enough broth to create a sauce, and let it simmer
{ until the meat is falling apart. Put everything through
{ a sieve, to obtain a sauce that can be used on many
{ dishes, especially ravioli, tagliatelle and other pastas
{ and savoury porridges.[39]

As Neapolitan ragù began to turn red, the former tomatoless version risked disappearing for good. It only managed to survive by borrowing the name 'genovese' from the sister sauce – its almost identical twin – that had existed alongside it for at least three generations of pasta eaters.

From then on, it continued down another path, adding ever larger quantities of onions which served the same purpose as the tomatoes, that is, stretching the sauce to make it cover a larger amount of pasta.

As we saw at the beginning of this digression, the modern recipe has continued to evolve, although these slight variations are the object of heated debates that have more to do with our own times than with history, so we won't get into all that. In this regard, however, the great Luciano De Crescenzo offers a delightful snapshot of family life that I would like to quote. The subject, need-less to say, is genovese sauce in Naples, but it really says something about Italian culture in general and its attitude towards 'traditional' pasta recipes: an issue that makes emotions run absurdly high, sparking disputes between different 'schools of thought' that pit cities, neighbour-hoods and even family members against each other.

In Naples there are two schools of thought about
genovese sauce, the Santa Lucia school and the Corso
Garibaldi school. In my house, as a kid, there was
a constant debate between supporters of the two
sides: those who argued that the cut of meat had to
be lacerto and those who instead used gambonci-
ello, those who claimed that the onion should never
be chopped ('the onion,' Dad said, 'must never taste
steel; if it sees the glint of a blade, it gets dejected!'
and those who instead stressed the union of onion
and meat, the reciprocal osmosis of flavours ('It's the
marriage of two souls!' Uncle Alberto would shout).
Another point of discord was the final colour: 'darkest
amber,' according to the Corso Garibaldi team, 'friar's
robe,' according to Santa Lucia. Uncle Alberto even
had a jacket that was just the right colour for making
the comparison.[40]

By now you may be wondering: if people get so worked
up about 'genovese' in Naples, what ever happened to it
in Genoa?

In Genoa, it followed the same path as Neapolitan
ragù: incorporating more and more tomatoes until it
became what is now known as 'tocco alla genovese' (or in
dialect, 'tuccu zeneize') – which, not surprisingly, still has
quite a bit in common with its southern counterpart. This
transformation left genovese cut off by itself in Naples, to
the point that no one now remembers the time when the
two cities shared the same sauce. What ended up stealing
all the attention was the 'fast-day' version: pesto.

The road to world championships

So let's get back to the main story and pick up where we left off. After the first appearance of modern pesto in the *Codice gastrologico* of 1841, the popularity of the sauce kept growing at a steady pace. The same recipe was copied shortly thereafter by two other key books, *La cuciniera moderna* (1845) and *Il cuciniere italiano moderno* (1851).[41] In 1854 a curious version appeared in the *Trattato di cucina* by Giovanni Vialardi, who served for almost thirty years as cook to the House of Savoy and was deeply familiar with the cuisine of the entire Kingdom of Sardinia – which included Liguria. His recipe for 'Lasagne o monparelle alla genovese'[42] calls for these broad noodles to be boiled and drained, then tossed with butter, cheese, pepper, nutmeg, truffles, 'a mince of herbs, such as borage, chard, chervil, burnet, garlic, parsley and a little costmary',[43] and finally fried in butter. Basil isn't mentioned anywhere. This version was definitely much richer and more complex, and perhaps not as well suited to the tables of the rising middle class.

The year 1863 was also important because it brought the publication of the first cookbook entirely focused on Genoese cuisine: *La cuciniera genovese: La vera maniera di cucinare alla genovese*, by Giovanni Battista Ratto and his son Giovanni.[44] In this collection, the 'original' names of key ingredients are even provided in dialect: an extra touch of authenticity.

Paste or seasoning with garlic (pésto)

Take a clove of garlic, basil (*baxaicò*), or, if you do
not have it, marjoram (*pèrsa*), parsley (*porsemmo*)
Sardinian cheese and grated parmesan, and mix them
together, and crush everything in a mortar with just a
little butter until it is creamy. Then thin it with plenty
of good oil. You can use this paste on lasagne, tagliolini
or gnocchi (*troffie*), adding a little warm unsalted water
if you wish to make it more liquid.[45]

As you can see, at this point in time the recipe was still
allowing variations in the herbs (marjoram and parsley)
rather than insisting on basil alone, but as we all know,
that flexibility was later lost.

The huge success of the Rattos' book necessarily
inspired imitators, with other authors sometimes echoing
– or simply lifting – entire passages. One of them was
Emanuele Rossi, who in 1865 ended up in a heated
polemic with the father and son, whom he accused of
having put together a book that was 'too succinct for the
minds of those not already acquainted with all the secrets
of cooking'. But then in his own tome, *La vera cuciniera
genovese facile ed economica*, he presented a 'new' recipe
for pesto that copies, almost word for word, the one seen
just above (the one difference perhaps being that it calls
for basil, with no alternatives).[46]

We've reached the last act and all the ingredients
are now onstage, except for the pine nuts considered so
essential today. As mentioned earlier, they come on the
scene only in 1880, in a recipe from *Cucina di strettissimo*

magro[47] that includes the nuts but still allows other variations, like the option of cooking the sauce or adding anchovies.

Genoese green sauce

In a mortar, crush some minced basil with pine nuts, garlic and some salted anchovies. Then, after thinning this paste with oil and a little boiling water, it may be used without cooking it. Or if you prefer it cooked, put it in a pot and allow it to simmer for four or five minutes.

Ingredients for six portions.
Basil: 1 small bunch
Garlic: 2 cloves
Salted anchovies: 2
Pine nuts: 30 gr.
Oil: 8 spoonfuls
Salt to taste.

Pine nuts, however, continued to be an infrequent ingredient even after this date, and most recipes do not include them, or else replace them with walnuts. They would gain a more stable foothold in the recipe only after the Second World War, but given their cost, rarely turn up in industrial formulations of the sauce.

One could say that the evolution of pesto comes to an end here. Of course, as late as 1927 there were still authors who mentioned the possibility of replacing basil with parsley,[48] or mixing basil, parsley and marjoram, or adding walnuts instead of the canonical pine nuts.[49] But by this point in the story, pesto alla genovese seems to have reached its definitive form.

Like many traditional recipes, pesto, too, got its own 'production regulations'[50] on 4 September 2002. Of course there is the usual friction between food purists and an industry that churns out jars of the stuff by the tonne, with ingredients ranging from sunflower oil to cashews. But in general, the traditional spirit of pesto and the industrial one have learned to coexist: after all, the sauce is increasingly popular, especially abroad, and has become one of Italy's key food exports.

Some people strive to preserve the old ways in spite of that, and in Genoa they've come up with their own rather unique strategy: the Pesto World Championships that are organised every two years.

The equipment? A wooden pestle and marble mortar, and that's it. The basic ingredients, which as in any proper competition are the same for everyone, are as follows:

> 4 bunches (60–70 g. of leaves) of PDO Genoese Basil, to guarantee fragrance and flavour
> 30 g. Pine Nuts
> 45–60 g. Aged Parmigiano Reggiano, grated
> 20–40 g. Fiore Sardo, grated (Sardinian Pecorino)
> 1–2 Cloves of Vessalico Garlic (from the province of Imperia)
> 3 g. Sea Salt
> 60–80 cc PDO 'Riviera Ligure' Extra-Virgin Olive Oil: sweet and fruity, to complement the fragrance of the Basil and seasonings.[51]

The competition opens to the cry of 'Ready, pestle, go.' Each participant then has up to forty minutes to prepare the best pesto of their lives. They usually crush the garlic first with a pinch of salt, then the pine nuts, and only then add the basil. Their motions must be delicate yet firm, to turn it all into a smooth cream as quickly as possible and avoid oxidisation. Finally, they top it off with cheese and oil to achieve the perfect blend.

In short, you might say – only half joking – that in Genoa, due to the (relative) stability of the recipe over time, pesto alla genovese has become not a delicacy, but a sport. The ingredients are few and certified, the instructions specific and codified. But even supposing that the recipe has reached a definitive and untouchable form, it's best to keep in mind what Gualtiero Marchesi once said, paraphrasing a famous aphorism of Gustav Mahler's: 'The recipe tells you everything, except what's most important.'

Spaghetti al pomodoro[1]

'*Maccarone*, you've pushed me too far and I'm gonna destroy you, *maccarone*! I'm gonna chew you up!'[2] I doubt there's an Italian out there who doesn't remember the famous line that Alberto Sordi – in the role of Nando Mericoni – addresses to his dish of spaghetti in *An American in Rome*, after giving up on his absurd attempt to make an 'American' dinner out of bread, jam, yogurt, mustard and milk.

The character dreamed up by the filmmaker Steno was a caricature of Italians in the 1950s who were overly eager to imitate everything that films, magazines and comic books had taught them about American life. Huge steaks with chips on the side, tins of ready-to-eat food, household appliances: these were new concepts from overseas that seemed destined to change Italian cuisine for good. Italy was slowly picking up the pieces after the war, in part through the aid of the Marshall Plan, and the average person saw Americans not just as liberators from the Nazis and Fascists, but as the essence of everything one could wish for.

This was obvious to millions of other Italians who had already emigrated to the United States in search of a better life. Most were poor farmers or labourers from the most impoverished, backward parts of the boot. In America, they found they could finally afford luxuries they had only dreamed of before. And having fled hunger, they ended up becoming the first ambassadors of Italian foodways abroad.

This development was anything but immediate, however. Like any new arrival, their cuisine had to overcome a certain initial unease on the part of Americans towards foods perceived as 'ethnic'. But by the mid-twentieth century Italian communities were increasingly well assimilated, and all wariness about their cooking was melting away.[3] This process was also helped along by the efforts of a few great Italian entrepreneurs seeking new markets for their food products. One of the most visionary was unquestionably Giovanni Buitoni.

In 1940, Buitoni was visiting the United States to investigate business opportunities there for the industrial group founded by his father, which manufactured pasta. When the outbreak of the war prevented him from returning to Italy, he founded the Buitoni Foods Corporation, with a plant in Brooklyn and another in Jersey City. But his true stroke of genius lay elsewhere. He decided to open a restaurant in the heart of New York City, right in Times Square, that was like nothing anyone had seen before. Its slogan: 'The oldest brand of spaghetti in the world served in the restaurant of tomorrow.'[4] And this was no exaggeration. Paying just one quarter, customers passed through a revolving door and found themselves in a groundbreaking eatery: not a trattoria, but a 'spaghetti bar'. Buitoni had come up with a way for his spaghetti with tomato sauce to travel straight to each table on a leather conveyor belt, from which customers could help themselves.[5] It was an 'all-you-can-eat' concept for spaghetti, decades before the conveyor belt sushi we're all familiar with today.*

In short, while Italians like Nando Mericoni were trying to imitate American customs, Italian food was rapidly coming into fashion in the United States. And just a few decades later, it had become one of the nation's most popular cuisines – maybe *the* most popular.**

Ironically enough, to tell the story of spaghetti with tomato sauce – perhaps the king of Italian pasta dishes, and the consummate symbol of Italian cooking worldwide – the Americas are the right place to start, since that's where this vegetable (or fruit, if you want to split hairs) originally came from. It was one of the first products to be brought to Europe from the New World. But just as it would later take a while for Italian food to catch on in twentieth-century America, it was no simple matter

---

* The Japanese model of conveyor belt sushi was first introduced in 1958, at the Mawaru Genroku Sushi restaurant in Osaka, so Giovanni Buitoni was far ahead of it.

** According to a 2019 survey conducted by YouGov (it.yougov.com) in twenty-four countries, Italian food is the most popular abroad after each nation's own cuisine. In the United States it was popular with 88% of people, outranked only by American food. This finding is confirmed by Italian exports to the US, which, according to the Italian Trade Agency, doubled in the decade from 2009 to 2019.

for the tomato to find its way into the Italian diet, let alone be paired with pasta.

Before the most famous alliance in Italian cuisine could be formed, centuries would have to go by.

'Red as blood, and in others the colour of gold'

The history of the tomato in Europe began in the mid-sixteenth century with a Franciscan friar, Bernardino de Sahagún, who was the first European scholar of the Aztec civilisation that the Spaniards had encountered. He compiled a wide range of information collected directly in the Nahuatl language, which he had learned during his time in the colony, recording it in his tome *Historia universal de las cosas de Nueva Espana*. Some of his observations tell us important things about how this fruit was used in its land of origin:

> The tomato seller sells large tomatoes, small tomatoes, leaf tomatoes, thin tomatoes, sweet tomatoes, large serpent tomatoes, nipple-shaped tomatoes. Also he sells coyote tomatoes, sand tomatoes, those which are yellow, very yellow, quite yellow, red, very red, quite ruddy, ruddy, bright red, reddish, rosy dawn colored. The bad tomato seller sells spoiled tomatoes, bruised tomatoes, those which cause diarrhea; the sour, the very sour. Also he sells the green, the hard ones, those which scratch one's throat, which disturb [. . .] one; which make one's saliva smack, make

> one's saliva flow; the harsh ones, those which burn
> the throat.[6]

The first thing one should note is that in America, various kinds of tomatoes were already considered a food and an item of trade. The warning about possible risks – at least when it came to unripe fruit – is characteristic of the initially cautious European attitude that continued to influence authors in the Old World for several centuries.

Around the same time that the Franciscan friar was compiling his manuscript, a few tomato plants had already made their way to Europe, and several physicians tried to describe their properties. One of the first was Pietro Andrea Mattioli of Siena, who mentions tomatoes in his *Discorsi* of 1544. As with various other exotic foods before, the journey to the table called for a stopover in the botanical garden, or at least in the pharmacist's cabinet.

> In our time another species has been brought into Italy
> which is known as *pomi d'oro*. They are flat like pink
> apples, and divided in segments that are green at first,
> but then upon ripening become in some plants red as
> blood, and in others the colour of gold. These too are
> eaten in the same way.[7]

The shape he describes is reminiscent of the 'pomodoro costoluto' (ribbed tomato) that is now primarily grown in Tuscany. But the interesting thing is that despite some wariness, Mattioli was already treating the tomato as a food and describing the manner, perhaps the only one, in which it was eaten. This is the 'same way' as aubergines

– another vegetable looked on with suspicion – which were 'simply fried in oil, with salt and pepper, like mushrooms'. It is no coincidence that both vegetables are discussed in the chapter on the mandrake, whose properties as a sedative were well known; the latter belongs to the same family as the tomato (Solanaceae) and also has yellowish-orange fruit.

For more than a century, however, the European prejudice against tomatoes did not truly fade.

In the 1600s, physicians were still the only ones writing about them. They reappear for instance in Ugo Benzo's *Regole della sanita e natura de' cibi* (1618)[8] and Giuseppe Donzelli's *Teatro farmaceutico, dogmatico, e spagirico* (1675). This Neapolitan nobleman – who also discusses tomatoes alongside aubergines, once again in a chapter on the mandrake – adds a few interesting details:

> [. . .] I am reminded of that plant that was once a foreign oddity but is now quite familiar here, especially to the Spanish, who call its fruits *Tomattes*. They are more truly called Love Apples, or Golden Apples, & even Ethiopian Apples. They are a kind of Aubergine; they have a flattened shape like Roses, and are divided in segments; they are green on first appearance, but upon ripening in some plants become red as blood, & in others the colour of Gold; you will also find some that are not segmented but instead round, like Pippin apples that are yellow in colour, or red. As a food they are slightly less cold than the mandrake: they can be eaten with Pepper, salt and garlic, cooked

> or raw: but the nourishment they give is scant
> and poor.[9]

At this point, over 130 years had gone by since the first description. The variety discussed here is a different one, round and unribbed: the kind most common today, in other words. We learn from Donzelli that in the meantime the tomato had become quite familiar in Italy, but even more so in Spain, the country that by tradition and for geographic reasons was the first stop for goods imported from the New World. Aside from a note about the 'coldness' of the fruit (which shows the influence of the Hippocratic theory of humours), the Neapolitan doctor tells us that by the end of the seventeenth century tomatoes were eaten cooked, but also raw, with oil, salt and pepper.

The first Neapolitan cookbooks

By then it was just a question of time. And sure enough, a few years later, the first significant reference to tomatoes turns up in a cookbook. We find them in a recipe for 'Spanish' sauce in *Lo scalco alla moderna*, published in Naples in 1692 by Antonio Latini. This author from Marche was one of the most famous chefs of his century. He was the first to describe the new ideas coming out of Naples, and in some sense laid the groundwork for the birth of modern Neapolitan cooking. His 'Salsa di Pomadoro, alla Spagnuola', which already seems quite modern, could be considered a prototype for all the tomato sauces that were to come.

Tomato Sauce, in the manner of Spain

Take half a dozen tomatoes, which must be ripe; put them on the coals to roast, and once they are seared, peel them with care and mince them finely with a Knife, and add Onions minced fine, at your discretion, Peparolo[10] also minced fine, a small amount of Serpollo, or Piperna,[11] and mixing everything together, season it with a little Salt, Garlic, & Vinegar, to make a Sauce that is delicious on boiled meats or other things.[12]

The mixture is still barely exposed to heat – the first step of putting the tomatoes on the coals is more of a peeling technique than an actual cooking method. They are then diced and mixed with a few choice seasonings for an almost instant accompaniment to various dishes.*

So, like Donzelli, Latini associates this fruit with Spain. And like Donzelli, he is writing his description in Naples. It is no coincidence that even today, this city has a close and special relationship with tomatoes. It is a bond that goes back centuries. By the time of this recipe, Naples had been under Spanish rule for almost 200 years, and thus enjoyed preferential channels of trade with Spanish colonies overseas. And, of course, in that era Naples was a flourishing metropolis, a hub of business and cultural ferment, the second largest city in the Mediterranean

---

* Latini also uses tomatoes in another recipe called 'Cassuola di pomadoro', which describes a sort of stew of pigeon, veal and chicken, with tomatoes and lemon juice, thickened with eggs.

after Istanbul: in short, just the kind of place that encourages new culinary experimentation.

The long pause in Italian treatises on food as French cuisine took over – for almost a century, as we saw earlier – brings us up to 1773, the year that Vincenzo Corrado's *Il cuoco galante* came out. This book, based on Corrado's experience with preparing banquets for the Neapolitan nobility, captures many new trends that were appearing on the culinary horizon and would become better established in the century that followed.

Eighty years after Latini's Spanish sauce, tomatoes were no longer a novelty, and far more than a marginal presence on aristocratic Neapolitan tables. Whether cooked and chopped, or as a sauce or coulis* flavoured in various ways, they accompanied various courses of meats, fish, eggs, and other vegetables. Although there was still no overlap between pasta and tomatoes, Corrado describes an interesting tomato soup that was eaten over toasted bread.

The fateful encounter is drawing near.

---

* At the time, the French coulis, which Corrado calls colì, was a full-bodied sauce, usually made from meat, fish or vegetables, filtered and thickened with starch, flour or a roux (the mixture of toasted flour and butter that is still used as a base for sauces such as demi-glace – heir to the ancient meat coulis – or béchamel).

Soup with Tomatoes

In Beef broth, cook a quantity of Tomatoes, with
a bouquet of aromatic herbs, and in this clarified
broth cook toasted Croutes of bread, which are to
be served with a Coulis of Tomatoes flavoured with
basil, thyme and parsley.[13]

While *Il cuoco galante* shows that there was a broad range
of tomato-based dishes in southern Italy, we don't know
just how widespread the American fruit was at the time
across the rest of the peninsula.

Still, a hint of its presence in other Italian regions
can be found, for example, in Antonio Nebbia's recipe
book *Il cuoco maceratese* (1781). Compared to Naples,
Macerata was not a particularly flourishing city from the
standpoint of trade, nor did its position encourage much
cultural exchange. Yet it seems that even there, tomatoes
had already made their way into the kitchen. Nebbia
offers us the earliest description of a 'Minestra di Riso,
e Pomi d'oro',[14] a tomato soup that is given substance by
adding rice rather than bread.

It was a preview of coming attractions, an intermediate step. The path towards pasta had now been cleared.

And indeed, that encounter arrived just nine years
later in *L'Apicio moderno* (1790), a monumental work
by Francesco Leonardi. It is anything but short on
tomato-based recipes, with pairings that are sometimes
truly unusual, like 'Tortoise with tomato coulis',[15] or
'Pear Soup with Tomato Sauce'.[16] The dish that interests us here, however, is a much less daring experiment

– or at least so it seems today: a 'Zuppa di Paste fine alla Catalana' (given the reference to Catalonia, tomatoes must still have been closely associated with Spain).

For the first time, pasta and tomatoes came together in one dish. Yet that dish is completely different from what we are used to seeing today. It is a rather thin soup of concentrated broth and tomato sauce, which the pasta is cooked in after a quick parboil in water.

Soup with thin Pasta, Catalan style

In a pot with a little oil, or butter, fry some green onions, shallots, and minced parsley, remove it from the fire and mix in two or three anchovies pulped through a sieve, then pour in half Sugo, or fast-day Suage,* and half tomato Sauce; bring it to a boil, skim it, put in pasta of Puglia that has been blanched for a moment in boiling water; let it cook slowly, and serve it well skimmed of fat after seasoning with salt. If it is made with butter you can mix in, upon serving, a handful of grated parmesan.[17]

The 'sugo di pomodoro' mentioned here is not simply tomato juice. Leonardi lists various versions of it in his treatise. In this case it is a thin sauce made from

---

* Fast-day 'sugo' and 'suage' were two kinds of broth made from vegetables, pulses, spices, fish, molluscs and frogs. As with sugo di carne (see chapter 6), the goal was to obtain a fragrant, savoury liquid that could be used to flavour a wide range of dishes. The modern equivalent in French cuisine would be a fumet.

tomatoes, other vegetables, herbs, frogs (optional) and
fast-day 'suage'.[18]

The recipe we have just seen is from the fifth volume
of *L'Apicio moderno*, entirely dedicated to 'cucina di
magro': meatless recipes suitable for fast days. Leonardi
notes, '*Magro*, and above all the kind prepared with oil,
is very important to Italians, particularly in the City of
Rome, whose inhabitants eat fast-day cooking for much
of the year.'[19]

Leonardi's recipe was quite influential for a while, and
other authors over the years followed the same approach,
presenting tomato-tinted, brothy soups to be served
with pasta, rather than over toasted bread as was the
custom.[20]

In any case, even in this embryonic form, pasta with
tomatoes already seemed to have the power to cross
Italian borders. A few years later, the same tomato soup
reached France. But instead of showing up in a cookbook, as one might expect, it appears in Grimod de La
Reynière's *Almanach des gourmands*. This annual publication, which could be considered the forerunner of
today's food guides, provided information about culinary
specialities and advice on where to purchase or sample
them. Within a broader discussion of 'potages farineux'
(a rather thin kind of soup, like the ones we've been
looking at) it mentions Italian pasta, which the author
generically calls 'vermicelli' (according to him, the most
common pasta shape).[21]

The purées and the cheese that can be mixed with
vermicelli are sometimes replaced in autumn, very
successfully, with tomatoes. The juice of this fruit
or vegetable (whatever you prefer to call it) gives the
Potage to which it is added a very pleasant acidity,
which is agreeable to almost everyone familiar with it.[22]

'Vermicielli co le pommadore'

The true culinary breakthrough, however – the
'Copernican revolution' in the world of pasta
– came thirty years later. Once again it was the doing
of a Neapolitan chef, Ippolito Cavalcanti, who in 1837
included 'Vermicielli co le pommadore' in the section
dedicated to 'Our Neapolitan style of Home Cooking' in
his book *Cucina teorico-pratica*.

Vermicelli with tomatoes

When the season is right, take three rotoli* of tomatoes,
cook them, and strain them; then take a terzo** of lard,
or two misurelle*** of oil, fry a head of garlic and put
it in the sauce. Boil two rotoli of spaghetti, drain it al
dente, and toss it with the sauce; top it with plenty of
pepper, add salt, and what a feast it will be.[23]

---

* The rotolo was an ancient measurement used in the area around Naples,
and here was the equivalent of 890g.
** This probably means a third of a pound (which in this place and time
was about 320g), hence just over 100g.
*** A misurella was about one decilitre.

The cultural leap from the previous tomato soups to this dish is huge.

The sauce is a simple tomato purée cooked with lard or oil (depending on whether it is a feast day or fast day), garlic and pepper. No broth or 'suage' has been added, so it foreshadows the middle-class fashion of simple sauces conceived especially for pasta, which would win out by the end of the century. But there is a second point worthy of note: to indicate how much the vermicelli should be cooked, the instructions in Neapolitan dialect use the term 'vierdi vierdi' (very green), as if the pasta were fruit picked while still hard. Nowadays we would say 'al dente', but the meaning is clearly the same.[24]

Why did Cavalcanti feel it was necessary to specify the right consistency for the pasta?

The answer is very simple: one need only page through recipe collections from the era to see that cooking times ranged wildly, and tended to be quite different from the ones we see today.

Even leaving out some of the oldest examples – Maestro Martino, in the fifteenth century, recommends cooking 'Vermicelli'[25] for an hour and 'Maccaroni siciliani'[26] for two (!) hours, while Bartolomeo Scappi has you boil his 'Maccaroni alla romanesca'[27] for half an hour – cooking times for pasta were still extremely long by modern standards, even in the nineteenth and early twentieth centuries. To offer some idea, here are the ones recommended by a few famous cookbooks that came out over the hundred-year span from 1832 to 1932:

Il cuoco piemontese ridotto all'ultimo gusto,[28] 1832:
     15 to 30 minutes;
La cucina facile,[29] 1844: one hour;
F. Chapusot,[30] *La cucina sana,* 1846: 45 minutes;
Almanacco dei Gastronomi,[31] 1863: 30 minutes;
E. Rossi, *La vera cuciniera genovese,*[32] (1865):
     15–20 minutes;
La cuciniera universale,[33] 1870: 30 minutes;
Il cuciniere moderno[34] 1871: 45 minutes;
Il cuoco sapiente[35] 1871: 2–3 minutes for thin pasta in
     broth, 30 minutes or longer for pasta with sauce;
Dr Leyrer, *La regina delle cuoche,*[36] 1882: 15 minutes;
V. Bossi, E. Salvi, *L'imperatore dei cuochi,*[37] 1894:
     15 minutes;
J. M. Parmentier, *Il re dei rei dei cuochi,*[38] 1897:
     20 minutes;
G. Farraris Tamburini, *Come posso mangiar bene?,*[39]
     1913: 20 minutes for 'Italian-style macaroni with
     butter and cheese' (which then undergoes an
     additional, risotto-style simmering in broth or salted
     water), up to one hour for 'macaroni with sauce';
L'arte di mangiare bene,[40] 1923: 6 to 12 minutes;
D. Fornari, *Il cuciniere militare,*[41] 1932: 18-20 minutes
     for durum wheat pasta (advising that it's better to
     take it off the heat 'a minute early rather than a
     minute late'); 5 minutes for egg taglierini in broth.

Only two of the quoted recipes include any notes about
the consistency that the pasta should have when done:
Chapusot's 'Maccheroni alla piemontese' is supposed
to be boiled until 'soft and pasty';[42] Ferraris Tamburini's

'Maccheroni all'italiana' is ready 'if it comes apart easily when pressed with a finger',[43] no less.

In addition to the inordinately long cooking times, the pasta sold up to the mid-twentieth century also contained less gluten, so it did not stand up as well to boiling and inevitably must have been softer. The 1929 edition of Renato Rovetta's book *Industria del pastificio* explained that only 'Extra Quality' pasta might use durum wheat alone, although it was usually cut with granular soft wheat flour, up to 20 or 30 per cent. 'Third Quality' pasta, on the other hand, could even be 50 per cent soft wheat flour and 50 per cent residual flours from the milling of durum wheat.[44]

This should sweep away the remaining certainties of the most intransigent food purist: even al dente pasta is a recent concept that spread out of southern Italy. And although it is now standard throughout the country, Italians can still easily experience the difference between the two cooking times. How? By eating pasta abroad, in places that still prefer a more 'melt-in-your-mouth' approach.[45] This is less and less common around the world, but when my fellow Italians come across it, they should realise it's not because 'foreigners don't know how to cook pasta' – they've just continued to cook it the way our Italian great-grandparents did. Simple as that.

But let's get back to our story. Cavalcanti's recipe is essentially the birth certificate for pasta al pomodoro. The thirty years separating it from previous recipes did not play as decisive a role as the geographic fragmentation of Italy at the time: the country had yet to be politically unified, and its cuisines were also still sharply divided. This recipe came out of Naples because Naples was the birthplace of an entire culinary culture based on tomatoes and above all on pasta, as a dignified dish unto itself. After the introduction of sugo di carne,[46] which ended the monotonous reign of cheese as the sole pasta topping, tomatoes marked both the culmination of that shift and the beginning of a new phase: making a good sauce no longer required a large cut of meat to be stewed at length, just a handful of ingredients that would yield a perfect dish of pasta. Tomatoes, in short, were at the heart of a culinary breakthrough – one that, along with the growing availability of cheap, industrially manufactured pasta, soon revolutionised the Italian meal.

Like pizza, pasta grew out of a specific social context: the necessity of feeding the vast population that swarmed the alleys of Naples, where many people lived in small rooms with no means of cooking their own meals.* It was an early form of cheap street food. A vivid picture of it is provided by Matilde Serao's extraordinary portrait of the city, *Il ventre di Napoli* (The Belly of Naples, 1884).

> As soon as they get their hands on a couple of soldi, working-class Neapolitans buy a dish of hot macaroni with sauce; in the humbler neighbourhoods, every

---

* In the nineteenth century, the population of Naples had gradually grown and the number of dwellings had grown along with it, but they were often insalubrious. In 1885 a 'Plan for the Renewal of Naples' was implemented which brought about a radical transformation of the city.

street has one of these taverns with vats and pans set up outside where the macaroni is always boiling and the tomato sauce always bubbling, alongside mountains of grated cheese, a sharp cheese that comes from Cotrone [. . .] This macaroni is sold in portions costing two or three soldi; and Neapolitans call them, for short, *nu doie* or *nu tre*, a two or a three. The portions are small and the buyer always quibbles with the vendor, demanding a little more sauce, a little more cheese, and a little more macaroni.[47]

From Neapolitan speciality to national (and international) dish

As we have seen in other chapters, the success of a dish throughout Italy – and in this case, around the world – depends on more than just an apt combination of ingredients. Very often, its spread goes hand in hand with technological and industrial advances. And the rise of spaghetti with tomato sauce was due in part to a great invention.

In 1810, the French inventor Nicolas Appert published *L'art de conserver pendant plusieurs années toutes les substance animales et végétales*.[48] Fifty years before Pasteur, this book described a method of food preservation – 'appertisation' – that involved sterilising the vessels, to vastly increase shelf life. Soon adopted in many countries (the book was also quickly translated into Italian), Appert's new concept called for using wide-mouthed glass bottles sealed with cork and then boiled – just as people still do today with homemade preserves and jams. A few years later, in England, a method was patented for preserving foods in tin-lined metal containers, which were less unwieldy and easier to store and ship.

In Italy, it was Francesco Cirio, a businessman from Nice, who first saw the potential of this method. He began applying appertisation on an industrial scale and in 1856 founded the Cirio company in Turin, which preserved and exported tinned peas; after the Unification of Italy, he also opened several plants in the south of the country, including one in Naples, and bought up vast tracts of land for growing tomatoes to process and tin.

At the same time, the cultivation of tomatoes was spreading. In the province of Parma, for instance, the crop began to be alternated every two years with corn and wheat, with excellent harvests that in this area were primarily used for tomato paste.*

While most of these industrially processed tomatoes were exported abroad, home canning became a deeply rooted tradition in Italy: a ritual performed by housewives, which many families still carry on today.

By the end of the nineteenth century, tomato sauce on pasta had become widespread throughout Italy.

The ultimate proof of this is the inclusion of the dish in Artusi's *La scienza in cucina e l'arte di mangiar bene*. His 'Spaghetti alla rustica' and 'Tagliatelle all'uso

---

* Tomato paste was initially packaged in tins and later in tubes, which were introduced in 1951 and patented by the Mutti company.

di Romagna'[49] feature a tomato sauce seasoned with a mixture of garlic, parsley and pepper, and topped off with a handful of grated parmesan.

Then at the beginning of the twentieth century, Americans, too, began to try and enjoy spaghetti with tomato sauce. On a list drawn up for the July 1907 issue of *What to Eat* by Silvio Galli (of the Chicago restaurant Mme Galli's), ranking the Italian dishes most popular with his customers, it had already reached third place:

1 Minestrone ai fagiuoli
2 Fritto misto dorate
3 Spaghetti al sugo di pomodoro
4 Timballo di maccheroni
5 Carcioffi alla giudea
6 Pollo alla cacciatora
7 Agro dolce di vitello
8 Scaloppine di cappone al madera
9 Ravioli al sugo di carne
10 Gnocchi alla Lucchese[50]

Around the same time, the first cookbooks specifically focused on regional cooking began to appear in Italy. In *100 specialità di cucina italiane ed estere* (1908) there was only one pasta dish representing Naples: 'Maccheroni o spaghetti al pomodoro'.

Macaroni or spaghetti with tomato sauce

For half a kilogram of spaghetti, take three-quarters of a kilogram of very ripe tomatoes. After cooking them down in a pot, along with a little basil, parsley, onion and celery, pulp everything through a sieve so as to make a sauce. Then melt some lard or butter over the fire – Neapolitans use lard – and cook the sauce you have prepared, but just a little, so that it stays a nice, bright red. Meanwhile, cook the spaghetti in plenty of water with a little salt, and when it is 'al dente', as people usually say, pour over the sauce, mix it well, and serve.[51]

This sauce is not very different from the one described by Cavalcanti seventy years before. Even the lard is still there, as an ingredient that remained constant up to the middle of the twentieth century, though it has now disappeared.[*]

In the 1950s, pasta with tomato sauce not only became firmly and definitively established, but came to be seen as the pasta dish most representative of Naples. One can easily tell from the recipe titles in which macaroni and vermicelli 'alla napoletana' no longer refer to ragù, but rather to ordinary tomato sauce.[52] This was the sign of a new vision of cooking, a change of attitude that was gradually gaining ground. Dishes with meat sauce held on to their own special role, but in everyday life the tomato now reigned supreme. A few decades earlier it would have been impossible to imagine such a sudden change of course.

But in the years leading up to this, all kinds of things

---

[*] Throughout the early twentieth century, Neapolitan cooking was characterised by the use of lard, as Ada Boni also reminds us in her famous *Talismano della felicità*, which tells how to make it at home, because 'in places where much cooking is done with lard – in Lazio and around Naples, for instance – it is almost a duty to have this staple on hand'. Boni, *Il talismano della felicità*, 1927, p. 553.

had changed. The 'short century' had shown its terrible face, with two global conflicts that left nothing as was before. The postwar rush to develop Italy demanded that labour be channelled into the growing industrial sector, leaving less and less time for household chores such as cooking. Pasta sauces, or at least bases for them, could now be found readymade in jars, and the spread of refrigerators meant that groceries no longer had to be bought every day. Soon the first supermarket would open. Italian homes were filling up with appliances that promised to save time and effort in the kitchen.

Spaghetti with tomato sauce responded perfectly to the needs of modern life, and was on its way to becoming a national symbol. Although it was the end of an era, it was in this very time of vast social and economic changes – when the values of traditional cooking (in the broadest sense) were at risk of being swept away – that Italian cuisine took a running leap and landed on tables around the world.

There were many reasons for this success, and many remain difficult to explain. In the space of half a century, or maybe less, Italian cooking has come to enjoy great popularity and admiration, especially abroad, and the country's food exports have steadily grown. What took place in those years is something of a miracle: as an entire model of society was beginning to crumble, an enormous collective effort made it possible to preserve Italy's food heritage and transform it into a national treasure.

It was like a library on fire, and not everything was saved. Peasant recipes – the *real* ones, the recipes of hunger – went up in smoke, to the great relief of many who remembered poverty all too well. Plucked in haste from burning shelves, some books survived instead of others, which might have told a different story; precedence was given to the unforgettable works no one could risk losing. The rebuilt library was sleeker and more modern than the previous one, and brought Italian cooking back to heights it had not known for almost half a millennium. That success was as widespread as it was sudden, due to circumstances no longer replicable today. It is in tacit awareness of this fact that Italians become so heated when they talk about pasta, and it is why, in recent years, a sort of protectionist attitude has been adopted that can sometimes be too rigid and dogmatic in its attitude towards food heritage. Excessive orthodoxy, blind obedience to the rules, and overcautiousness about irking food purists has created a climate of 'culinary correctness' that never used to exist.

Fortunately, Italian food is and will remain a vast shared legacy, added to by great chefs and grandmothers alike.

No one can tell what the next step will be. But if the history of pasta has anything to teach us, it's that the one constant in tradition is change.

ENDNOTES

1. FETTUCCINE ALFREDO

1 www.ilveroalfredo.it/storia (consulted 12 May 2020).
2 Sinclair Lewis, *Babbitt*, New York, Harcourt, 1922, p. 196.
3 George Rector, 'A Cook's Tour', *Saturday Evening Post*, 19 November 1927, pp. 14, 52, 54, 56, 58.
4 *Corriere della Sera*, 8 September 1933.
5 Giuseppe Oberosler, *Il tesoretto della cucina italiana*, Milan, Hoepli, 1948, p. 114.
6 Vera, *Annabella in cucina*, Milan, Rizzoli, 1964, p. 74.
7 Luigi Carnacina, *Il Carnacina*, Milan, Garzanti, 1961, p. 189.
8 Vincenzo Buonassisi, *Il cuciniere italiano*, Milan, Rusconi Editore, 1979, p. 478.
9 Luigi Veronelli, *I grandi menù di Luigi Veronelli*, Milan, Fabbri Editori, 1985, p. 197.
10 Myra Waldo, *Cook as the Romans Do*, Springfield, OH, Collier Macmillan, 1961, p. 69.
11 James Oseland, *Saveur: The New Comfort Food*, San Francisco, Chronicle Books, 2011, p. 76.
12 One example is on the *Saveur* website (www.saveur.com/article/ Recipes/The-Original-Fettuccine-Alfredo/, consulted 13 May 2020).
13 Recipe LXXXV, ms. 158, Biblioteca Universitaria di Bologna. The most recent study of this text can be found in Elena Bergonzoni, *Due testi*

315

medievali di cucina nel manoscritto 158 della Biblioteca Universitaria di Bologna, Bologna, CLUEB, 2006, p. 98.

14 Giovanni Boccaccio, *Decameron*, VIII.3.

15 Maestro Martino's recipes are found in various manuscripts that have been collected and analysed by Claudio Benporat in *Cucina italiana del Quattrocento*, Florence, Leo S. Olschki, 1996.

16 This title was bestowed on him by Bartolomeo Sacchi, author of the first cookbook to be printed in Italy, *De honesta voluptate et valitudine* (Rome, 1474), book I, ch. XI (quoted in Benporat, *Cucina italiana*, p. 17).

17 Urbinate Latino 1203, Biblioteca Apostolica Vaticana (quoted in Benporat, *Cucina italiana*, p. 105).

18 Vincenzo Agnoletti, *La nuova cucina economica*, vol. II, Rome, 1803, p. 132.

19 Giacomo Casanova, *History of My Life*, vol. III, trans. Willard R. Trask, Baltimore and London, Johns Hopkins University Press, 1996, p. 272.

20 'Notizie sulla Terra di Radicofani', *Nuovo giornale de' Letterati*, no. 63, 1832, p. 199. It would seem that ordinary black pepper had already fallen out of favour in the sixteenth century and been replaced by long pepper (*Piper longum*), since Galenic medicine considered it too 'hot' a food and thus suited only to the lower classes. See Jean-Louis Flandrin, 'Condimenti, cucina e dietetica tra XIV e XVI secolo', in Jean-Louis Flandrin, *Storia dell'alimentazione*, ed. Massimo Montanari, Rome and Bari, Laterza, 1996, p. 384 (English edition: 'Seasoning, cooking and dietetics in the Late Middle Ages', in Jean-Louis Flandrin and Massimo Montanari, *Food: A Culinary History from Antiquity to the Present*, ed. Albert Sonnenfeld, New York and Chichester, Columbia University Press, 2013, p. 317.)

21 I am referring to *100 specialità di cucina italiane ed estere*, Milan, Società Editoriale Sonzogno, 1908, followed by Vittorio Agnetti, *La nuova cucina delle specialità regionali*, Milan, Società Editoriale Milanese, 1909 and Alberto Cougnet, *L'arte cucinaria in Italia*, Milan, Wilmant, 1910.

22 *Guida gastronomica d'Italia*, Rome, Touring Club Italiano, 1931, p. 316.

23 See 'Vermicielli co le pommadore' in chapter 10.

24 Pantaleone da Confienza, *Trattato dei latticini*, ed. Emilio Faccioli, Bra,

Slow Food, 2001. (The English translations here are based on the Italian translation by Walter Lapini and Adriano Toti.)

25 Massimo Montanari, *Il formaggio con le pere*, Rome and Bari, Laterza, 2008.

26 Pantaleone da Confienza, *Trattato dei latticini*, p. 117.

27 Fast-day cooking has been discussed by many authors, and the most recent study of the subject is by Massimo Montanari, *Mangiare da cristiani: Diete, digiuni, banchetti: Storia di una cultura*, Milan, Rizzoli, 2015.

28 For instance, Gaspare Delle Piane, *La cucina di strettissimo magro senza carne, uova e latticini*, Genoa, Tipografia della gioventù, 1880 (2nd ed. 1931).

29 Massimo Montanari and Alberto Capatti, *La cucina italiana*, Rome and Bari, Laterza, 2005, pp. 99–101.

2. AMATRICIANA

1 From the Facebook page of the City of Amatrice (www.facebook.com/ComunediAmatrice), post dated 8 February 2015, www.facebook.com/permalink.php?story_fbid=781759585236712&id=232379030174773.

2 theguardian.com/lifeandstyle/2015/feb/09/italian-chef-cracco-ridiculed-amatriciana-secret-ingredient-garlic (consulted on 27 May 2020).

3 www.facebook.com/photo?fbid=10153002291089034&set=a.90091374033

4 *Il Messaggero*, 9 February 2015 (www.ilmessaggero.it/RIETI/amatriciana_aglio_cracco_zingaretti/notizie/1171083.shtml).

5 'L'amatriciana con l'aglio di Cracco che indigna i puristi', *Corriere della Sera*, 10 February 2015.

6 *Official Journal of the European Union*, C 393, 20 November 2019.

7 See the chapter on fettuccine Alfredo.

8 See the chapter on tomato sauce.

9 Giulia Lazzari-Turco, *Il piccolo focolare*, Trento, Monauni, 1947 (3rd ed.), p. 37.

10 Ada Boni, *Il piccolo talismano della felicità*, Rome, Colombo, 1950 (1st ed. 1949), p. 116.

11 Ippolito Cavalcanti, *Cucina teorica-pratica*, Naples, Marotta, 1837 (2nd ed. 1939), p. 279.

12 See the chapter on ragù alla bolognese.

13 Alessandro Rufini, *Notizie storiche intorno alla origine dei nomi di alcune osterie, caffè, alberghi e locande esistenti nella città di Roma*, Rome, Tipografia legale, 1855, pp. 84–5.

14 *Il gastronomo*, no. 13 (January–March 1960), p. 778.

15 Alessandro Schiavi, 'Il ventre di Roma', *La lettura: Rivista mensile del Corriere della Sera* 3, no. 9 (September 1903), p. 792.

16 Ibid.

17 The three cookbooks cited in the last chapter. See also 'Let a hundred ragùs bloom', chapter 7, where they are discussed at length.

18 Agnetti, *La nuova cucina delle specialità regionali*, p. 135.

19 Cougnet, *L'arte cucinaria in Italia*, vol. I, p. 730.

20 Ibid., p. 120.

21 Eugenio Rontini, *Briganti celebri italiani*, Florence, Salani, 1911 (1st ed. 1885), p. 524 (this addendum is missing from the first edition of 1885).

22 Amedeo Pettini, *Manuale di cucina e di pasticceria*, Casale Monferrato, Casa editrice fratelli Marescalchi, 1914, p. 138.

23 *Outing* 77, no. 1 (October 1920), p. 31.

24 Ada Boni, *Il talismano della felicità*, Rome, Preziosa, 1927, p. 84.

25 *La cucina italiana* 6, no. 7 (July 1934), p. 20.

26 *La cucina italiana* 2, no. 3 (March 1930), p. 3.

27 Giuseppe Oberosler, *Il tesoretto della cucina italiana*, Milan, Hoepli, 1948, p. 125.

28 *La cucina italiana* 5, no. 3 (March 1933), p. 4.

29 *Il talismano della massaia*, Milan, Giachini, 1955, p. 199.

30 Henri-Paul Pellaprat, *L'arte nella cucina l'eleganza della mensa*, Milan, Casa italiana del libro, 1937, p. 69.

31 Of course, there is also the one mentioned by Aldo Fabrizi in *Cameriera bella presenza offresi...*; see the next chapter on carbonara.

32 *La cucina italiana* 2, no. 3 (March 1930), p. 3.

33 *La cucina italiana* 5, no. 5 (May 1933), p. 2.

34 *La cucina italiana* 6, no. 12 (December 1934), p. 23.

35 Alberto Capatti, *La storia della cucina italiana*, Milan, Laterza, 2014.

36 Felice Cunsolo, *Gli Italiani a tavola*, Milan, Gorligh, 1959.

37 *Il gastronomo*, no. 11 (Summer 1959), pp. 663–4.

38 Ibid., p. 664.

39 *Il gastronomo*, no. 12 (October–December 1959), p. 696.

40 Ibid., pp. 699–700.

41 *Il gastronomo*, no. 13 (January–March 1960), pp. 778–80.

42 Capatti, *Storia della cucina italiana*, p. 106. In addition to its reflections on this cultural movement, the book offers a very clear-eyed analysis of the evolution of Italian cuisine from the postwar period to the present.

43 I am referring here to Eric J. Hobsbawm and Terence Ranger, *The Invention of Tradition*, Turin, Einaudi, 2002.

44 Aldo Fabrizi, *La pastasciutta*, Milan, Mondadori, 1974, p. 48.

45 Regarding the problematic aspects of certification systems, see Alberto Grandi, *Denominazione di origine inventata*, Milan, Mondadori, 2018.

46 Ministerial Decree of 18 July 2005, 'Quinta revisione dell'elenco nazionale dei prodotti agroalimentari tradizionali'.

47 Commission Implementing Regulation (EU) 2020/395 of 6 March 2020 entering a name in the register of traditional specialities guaranteed 'Amatriciana Tradizionale' (TSG).

48 Regarding *roots* and *identity* in food history, see Massimo Montanari, *Il mito delle origini*, Rome and Bari, Laterza, 2019, p. 5; Massimo Montanari, *L'identità italiana in cucina*, Rome and Bari, Laterza, 2013.

3. CARBONARA

1 This study of carbonara was originally published in Italian on my blog www.tortellinieaffini.it (now www.ricettestoriche.it) in March 2018. For this chapter I have added a few primary sources and observations that did not appear in the online version.

2 *La Stampa*, 26 July 1950.

3 Giorgio Pastina, *Cameriera bella presenza offresi . . .*, Cines, Italy, 1951.

4 Mario dell'Arco, *Lunga vita di Trilussa*, Rome, Bardi Editore, 1951, p. 101.

5 Patricia Bronté, *Vittles and Vice: An Extraordinary Guide to What's Cooking on Chicago's Near North Side*, Chicago, Henry Regnery Company, 1952, p. 34. Many thanks to Dario Bressanini and Gennaro de Gregorio for input that put me on the right track while researching the history of carbonara in the US.

6 Herbert L. Matthews, 'When in Rome You Eat Magnificent Meals in Simple Restaurants', *New York Times* (12 July 1954).

7 Elizabeth David, *Italian Food*, London, Penguin Books, 1954, pp. 88–9.

8 *Harper's Bazaar*, no. 88 (1954), p. 6.

9 Samuel Chamberlain, *Italian Bouquet, an Epicurean Tour of Italy*, New York, Gourmet Books, 1958, p. 330.

10 Carbonara is listed among the culinary specialities of Lazio, along with abbacchio alla romana and carciofi alla giudia, in the book *Italian Affairs: Documents and Notes* (Presidency of the Council of Ministers, Information Service), vol. 3 (Cities and Regions of Italy – Latium), Rome, Documentary Centre, 1954, p. 385; it also appears in Alberto Moravia's short story 'Il pensatore' (Alberto Moravia, *Racconti romani*, Milan, Bompiani, 1954, p. 75).

11 As Capatti suggests in *Storia della cucina italiana*, p. 87.

12 *La cucina italiana* 3, no. 8 (August 1954), p. 389.

13 Anita Daniel, *I Am Going to Italy*, New York, Coward McCann, 1955, p. 70.

14 Felix Dessì, *La signora in cucina*, Milan, Cino Del Duca, 1955, pp. 139–40.

15 Richard Hammond, George Martin, *Eating in Italy: A Pocket Guide to Italian Food and Restaurants*, New York, Charles Scribner's Sons, 1957, p. 97.

16 The names of film stars listed here are drawn from newspapers of the time, particularly *Il Corriere della Sera*, between 1952 and 1959.

17 *Stampa Sera*, 8 August 1957.

18 *Corriere della Sera*, 30 January 1955.

19 *Stampa Sera*, 12 March 1958.

20 Ugo Tognazzi, *L'abbuffone*, Milan, Rizzoli, 1970, pp. 110–11.

21 Tognazzi, *L'abbuffone*, 108–18.

22 The fact that Ada Boni's carbonara appears only in the 1964 edition of *Il piccolo talismano della felicità* (1964) and not in the first two of 1949 and 1950 should not be overlooked. The author was born and raised in Rome, and had become interested in cooking at a young age, due in part to the influence of her paternal uncle Adolfo Giaquinto, a well-known gourmet and author of books and magazine articles on the subject. From 1915 to 1959 she headed the magazine *Preziosa*, which gave her an excellent window on to everything happening foodwise in the capital. If carbonara had already held a place of importance among Roman specialities in 1950, it would definitely have been included in the first edition of her cookbook. Instead, one finds only 'spaghetti al guanciale', the direct forerunner of today's gricia.

ENDNOTES

23 Alberto Capatti, *Storia della cucina italiana*, pp. 88–91.

24 Luigi Carnacina, *La grande cucina italiana*, Milan, Garzanti, 1960, pp. 138–9.

25 Ada Boni, *Il piccolo talismano della felicità*, Rome, Colombo, 1964, p. 82.

26 Ibid.

27 Ibid.

28 Centro Editoriale Italiano Sviluppo Turismo (ed.), *Guida gastronomica e turistica d'Italia*, n.p., 1960.

29 Henri-Paul Pellaprat, *La cucina familiare*, Milan, Vallardi, 1965, p. 37.

30 Anna Gosetti della Salda, *Le ricette regionali italiane*, Milan, Solares, 1967, pp. 631–2.

31 Gualtiero Marchesi, *La cucina regionale italiana*, Milan, Mondadori, 1989, p. 168.

32 Alain Senderens and Eventhia Senderens, *La cuisine réussie*, Paris, J. C. Lattès, 1981, pp. 366–7.

33 Antonia Monti Tedeschi, *Il cucchiaio d'argento*, Milan, Editoriale Domus, 1986 (8th ed.), p. 161.

34 Senderens and Senderens, *La cuisine réussie*, pp. 366–7.

35 Marchesi, *La cucina regionale italiana*, p. 168.

36 Carlo Santi and Rosino Brera, *Il grande libro di cucina*, Rome, Curcio, 1966, pp. 731–2.

37 https://bressanini-lescienze.blogautore.espresso.repubblica.it/2008/02/10/le-ricette-scientifiche-la-carbonara (consulted 1 February 2020).

38 This 'scientific zabaione' is also based on Dario Bressanini's tips in *La scienza della pasticceria*, Milan, Gribaudo, 2014, pp. 91–3.

39 See 'Il cacio sui maccheroni', chapter 1.

40 Various versions of this recipe are collected in Benporat, *Cucina italiana del Quattrocento*, and come from the manuscripts Urbinate Latino 1203, p. 102, Riva del Garda, p. 178, and Bühler 19, p. 236.

41 Vincenzo Corrado, *Il cuoco galante: Opera meccanica dell'Oristano: Di varie capricciose vivande nel fine de' loro istessi trattati accresciuta*, Naples, Stamperia Raimondiana, 1773, p. 157.

42 Cavalcanti, *Cucina teorico-pratica* (1837), p. 65.

43 Cavalcanti, *Cucina teorico-pratica* (2nd ed. 1839), p. 57.

44 Francesco Palma, *Il principe dei cuochi, o la vera cucina napoletana*, Naples, Cairo, 1881, p. 25.

45 Boni, *Il piccolo talismano della felicità*, 1950, p. 116.

46 For the amatriciana recipe, see chapter 2.

47 Lazzari-Turco, *Il piccolo focolare*, p. 37.

48 Boni, *Il piccolo talismano della felicità*, 1950, p. 116.

49 *Dinámica social* 8 (1958), p. 48.

50 Giulia Lazzari-Turco, *Manuale pratico di cucina, pasticceria, credenza*, Venice, Tipografia Emiliana, 1904, p. 138.

51 Capatti, *Storia della cucina italiana*, p. 86.

52 *Corriere di Bologna*, 10 July 2009.

53 Adolfo Fabbri, *Roberto Gualandi: Peripezie di un cuoco bolognese*, Bra, Slow Food, 2006, pp. 50–51.

54 '[. . .] two new canned varieties were added: chopped pork and egg yolks, and ham and eggs. In each case the egg product was thoroughly mixed with the ground meat.' Quoted in Harold Thatcher, *The Development of Special Rations for the Army*, Historical Section Office of the Quartermaster General, s.p. [1944], p. 57. My thanks to Lorenzo Biagiarelli for suggesting this.

4. GNOCCHI

1 Migliacci is a term that has been used for many different foods over the centuries, but here it most likely means a sort of pancake made with eggs and cheese; see recipe XXX, ms. 158, Biblioteca Universitaria di Bologna.

2 Recipe LXXXV, ms. 158, Biblioteca Universitaria di Bologna (author's transcription). The most recent analysis of this text is by Elena Bergonzoni, *Due testi medievali di cucina nel manoscritto 158 della Biblioteca Universitaria di Bologna*, Bologna, CLUEB, 2006, p. 50.

3 Terence Scully, *The Opera of Bartolomeo Scappi (1570): L'arte e prudenza d'un maestro cuoco*, Toronto-Buffalo-London, University of Toronto Press, 2008.

4 See quote in 'Il cacio sui maccheroni', chapter 1.

5 In the Renaissance, a Roman pound (libbra) was just under 340g.

6 Scappi, *Opera*, f. 123 v.

7 See 'A sprinkling of parmesan', chapter 1.

8 Scappi, *Opera*, f. 123 v.

9 For more about the fast-day diet, agliata and green sauce, see chapter 9.

10 Vincenzo Tanara, *L'economia del cittadino in villa*, Bologna, Per gli Eredi del Dozza, 1651 (3rd ed., 1st ed. 1644), p. 36.

11 Tanara, *L'economia del cittadino in villa*, p. 169.

12 Tanara, *L'economia del cittadino in villa*, p. 470.

13 Antonio Latini, *Lo scalco alla moderna*, Naples, Nuova stampa delli socii Dom. Ant. Parrino e Michele Luigi Mutii, 1693, p. 277.

14 Corrado, *Il cuoco galante*, p. 162.

15 Corrado, *Il cuoco galante*, p. 164.

16 Corrado, *Il cuoco galante*, p. 210.

17 Antonio Nebbia, *Il cuoco maceratese*, Macerata, Chiapini e Cortesi, 1781 (2nd ed.), p. 152.

18 Others describe the same method: Vincenzo Agnoletti, *Manuale del cuoco e del pasticciere*, Pesaro, Tipografia Nobili, 1832–4, vol. II, p. 100; *Codice gastrologico economico*, Florence, G. Galletti, 1841, pp. 29–30.

19 Francesco Leonardi, *L'Apicio moderno*, Rome, 1790, vol. III, pp. 277–8.

20 Agnoletti, *La nuova cucina economica*, p. 89.

21 It turns up in cookbooks under a range of other names: Antonio Odescalchi, *Il cuoco senza pretese, ossia la cucina facile ed economica*, Como, Piero Ostinelli, 1834 (3rd ed.), p. 174 ('Gnocchi'); *Il cuciniere italiano moderno*, Egisto Vignozzi, Livorno, 1851, p. 66 ('Gnocchetti per le complessioni gracili'); Giovanni Felice Luraschi, *Nuovo cuoco milanese economico*, Milan, Carrara, 1853, p. 130 ('Gnocchi strisciati alla gratirola'). The 'gnocchi al latte' that the poet Giacomo Leopardi mentions in a list of forty-nine dishes drawn up during his stay in Naples from 1833 to 1837 were probably also gnocchi 'alla veneziana' (see Rolando Damiani, *Leopardi e Napoli 1833-1837*, Naples, G. Procaccini Editore, 1998, pp 65–7).

22 *100 specialità di cucina italiane ed estere*, p. 39.

23 Henri-Paul Pellaprat, *L'arte nella cucina, l'eleganza della mensa*, Milan, Edizioni Patriottiche S. A. Morat, 1937, p. 130. The tradition is still alive, as one can see from the 'Gnocchi alla parigina' that Allan Bay includes in his recent book *Gnocchi, chez moi*, Milan, Gribaudo, 2017.

24 See, for instance, chapter 10.

25 Rebecca Earle, *Feeding the People: The Politics of the Potato*, Cambridge, MA, Cambridge University Press, 2020, p. 27.

26 The reference is to Carolus Clusius (Charles de l'Écluse, one of the first botanists to offer a detailed description of the potato, after receiving several specimens from Italy, in his book *Rariorum Plantarum Historia*, published in Antwerp in 1601.

27 Ugo Benzo, *Regole della sanità et natura de' cibi*, Turin, 'heredi di Gio. Domenico Tarino', 1618, p. 623.

28 On the introduction of the potato, see: Massimo Montanari, *L'identità italiana in cucina*, Rome-Bari, Laterza, 2013, pp. 40–45; Jean-Louis Flandrin, 'I tempi moderni', in Jean-Louis Flandrin, *Storia dell'alimentazione*, ed. Massimo Montanari, Rome-Bari, Laterza, 1996, pp. 432–3; Hans Jürgen Teuteberg, Jean-Louis Flandrin, 'Trasformazioni del consumo alimentare', in Flandrin, *Storia dell'alimentazione*, p. 570.

29 On this subject, see recently: Adriano Prosperi, *Un volgo disperso*, Turin, Einaudi, 2019. An extraordinary overview of the living conditions of peasants from the Middle Ages to the modern era can be found in Piero Camporesi, *Il pane selvaggio*, Milan, Il Saggiatore, 2016.

30 Examples include: Saverio Manetti, *Delle specie diverse di frumento e di pane siccome della panizzazione*, Florence, Stamperia Moücke, 1765; Giovanni Targioni Tozzetti, *Alimurgia, o sia modo di rendere meno gravi le carestie*, Florence, Stamperia Moücke, 1767, and Giovanni Targioni Tozzetti, *Breve istruzione circ'ai modi di accrescere il pane col mescuglio d'alcune sostanze vegetabili*, s.p. [Florence], 1767.

31 The best-known is perhaps Antoine-Augustin Parmentier, who owes his fame to his studies promoting potatoes.

32 Pietro Maria Bignami, *Le patate*, Bologna, Lelio della Volpe, 1773, pp. 4–5.

33 Antonio Zanon, *Della coltivazione e dell'uso delle patate e d'altre piante commestibili*, Venice, Modesto Fenzo, 1767, p. 49.

34 Bignami, *Le patate*, p. 11.

35 Nicolò Delle Piane, *De' pomi di terra ossia patate*, Genoa, Eredi di Adamo Scionico, 1793, p. 37, note 33.

36 Vincenzo Corrado, *Trattato delle patate ad uso di cibo*, Naples, Vincenzo Orsino, 1798, p. 40. Also reprinted in the 6th edition of *Il cuoco galante*, Naples, Stamperia Raimondiana, 1820, p. 196.

37 'Gnocchi di pomi da terra, ossia triffole villane', in Odescalchi, *Il cuoco senza pretese*, pp. 54–5 and 'Zuppa di gnocchi di famiglia', in

Giovanni Vialardi, *Cucina borghese semplice ed economica*, Turin, G. Roversi, 1863, p. 49.

38 Giovanni Battista Ratto and Giovanni Ratto, *La cuciniera genovese*, Genoa, Pagano, 1863 (7th ed. 1893), p. 75.

39 Emanuele Rossi, *La vera cuciniera genovese facile ed economica*, Mendresio, s.p., p. 78 and p. 86, respectively.

40 *Il cuoco sapiente*, Florence, Moro, 1871, pp. 86–7.

41 G. Belloni, *Il vero re dei cucinieri*, Milan, Cesare Cioffi, 1890, p. 56. They also turn up in Leyrer, *La regina delle cuoche*, Milan, Manini, 1882, p. 62, with a dough made richer by the addition of butter and parmesan.

42 *100 specialità di cucina italiane ed estere*, p. 5.

43 Agnetti, *La nuova cucina delle specialità regionali*, p. 135.

44 Boni, *Il talismano della felicità*, p. 100.

45 Pellegrino Artusi, *La scienza in cucina e l'arte di mangiar bene*, Florence, Landi, 1891, p. 52.

46 Lazzari-Turco, *Manuale pratico di cucina, pasticceria, credenza*, passim.

5. TORTELLINI ALLA BOLOGNESE

1 In 1957, this radio programme became a wonderful book: Guido Piovene, *Viaggio in Italia*, Milan, Bompiani, 2017, p. 265.

2 Actually, this nickname has an interesting history that starts in the Middle Ages. See Massimo Montanari (ed.), *Bologna grassa: La costruzione di un mito*, Bologna, CLUEB, 2004.

3 Alessandro Tassoni, *La secchia rapita*, Venice, Giacomo Scaglia, 1630.

4 Specifically, it refers to the Battle of Zappolino, a bloody clash that took place on 15 November 1325 when the Modenese pushed the Bolognese army back behind its city walls, arriving at a well close to what is now Porta San Felice, where they stole the water bucket as a trophy. The stolen bucket, until recently, hung inside the Ghirlandina (the bell tower of Modena's cathedral), while the original is now in the Palazzo Comunale. Vittorio Lenzi, *La Battaglia di Zappolino e la secchia rapita*, Modena, Edizioni Il Fiorino, 1995, pp. 25 ff.

5 For a biographical note on the author, see entry no. 140, 'Giuseppe Ceri', in Zita Zanardi (ed.), *Agricoltura e alimentazione in Emilia*

Romagna: Antologia di antichi testi, Modena, Edizioni Artestampa, 2015, pp. 346–7.

6 Giuseppe Ceri, 'Origine del tortellino', in *La secchia: Contiene sonetti burleschi inediti del Tassone e molte invenzioni piacevoli e curiose, vagamente illustrate, edite per la famosa festa mutino-bononiense del 31 maggio 1908*, Bologna-Modena, A. F. Formiggini, 1908, pp. 41–4.

7 Ceri was probably not even the first to compare the shape of this pasta to a woman's navel. He would seem to have at least one forerunner, Matteo Gaspare Leonesi of Bologna (1793–1832): according to his contemporaries, an 'extemporaneous poet' who gave improvised performances in Italian theatres. His rhymes, which were never published, but were passed down orally, seem to have included one about Helen of Troy and her navel, which was described as 'the *gemello* (twin) to a little *tortello*'. Alessandro Cervellati, *All'erta umbilichi sacri*, Bologna, Sezione arti grafiche Istituto Aldini–Valeriani, 1967, p. 38.

8 Alessandro Cervellati, *Piccole storie bolognesi*, vol. 4 ('Bologna grassa'), Bologna, Tamari, 1963, p. 159. Cervellati in turn takes this anecdote from another book of Bolognese stories: Oreste Trebbi, Gaspare Ungarelli, *Costumanze e tradizioni del popolo bolognese*, Bologna, 1932, facsimile reprint by Bononia University Press, Bologna, 2011, p. 87.

9 Du Cange et al., *Glossarium mediæ et infimæ latinitatis*, Niort, L. Favre, 1883–7, vol. 8, p. 134, col. b., 'Tortellus', (http://ducange.enc. sorbonne.fr).

10 Regarding the origin of the word, see Vera Gheno, 'Il tortellino, la perfezione dell'ombelico di Venere', in Massimo Arcangeli (ed.), *Peccati di lingua: Le 100 parole italiane del gusto*, Soveria Mannelli, Rubbettino, 2015, pp. 340–45.

11 See, for instance, the categories of dough listed in Tommaso Garzoni, *La piazza universale di tutte le professioni*, Venice, Appresso Vincenzo Somasco, 1584 (1586), p. 700.

12 *Anonimo veneziano del Trecento: Libro per cuoco*, in Emilio Faccioli (ed.) *L'arte della cucina in Italia*, Turin, Einaudi, 1992, p. 88.

13 'Take an ounce of pepper and one of cinnamon and one of ginger and an eighth of cloves and a fourth of saffron' (the eighth, literally *mezo quarto* – 'half a fourth' – and fourth are both in reference to an

ounce). *Anonimo veneziano del Trecento: Libro per cuoco*, from Faccioli (ed.), *L'arte della cucina in Italia*, p. 86.

14 Recipes CVIII, CXXIIII and CVI, ms. 158, Biblioteca Universitaria di Bologna (author's transcription). The most recent analysis of this text is by Bergonzoni, *Due testi medievali di cucina nel manoscritto 158 della Biblioteca Universitaria di Bologna*, pp. 55 and 59.

15 Benporat, *Cucina italiana del Quattrocento*, p. 107. This version is from Urbinate Latino 1203.

16 *Aframomum melegueta*, a West African spice with a peppery flavour.

17 Claudio Benporat, 'Il manoscritto R 3550 della Guild of St. George, Ruskin Gallery di Sheffield', *Appunti di gastronomia*, no. 67, 2012, p. 36.

18 Pasta was already being used to accompany meat in the Middle Ages: see the recipe for 'Tria genovese' in chapter 9.

19 One example is the 1851 cookbook by Francesco Chapusot, who lists more pasta dishes as an accompaniment to meat than any other author of his time (Francesco Chapusot, *La vera cucina casalinga sana, economica e delicata*, Turin Eredi Botta, 1851).

20 Messisbugo, *Banchetti, compositioni di vivande, et apparecchio generale*, f. 10 r.

21 Scappi, *Opera*, f. 71 r.

22 Scappi, *Opera*, f. 71 r.

23 This idea is also corroborated by the title of Scappi's recipe ('Per far tortelletti [. . .] chiamate annolini') where the 'cappelletto' mentioned in the text is just still a description based on the pasta shape's resemblance to a small hat, rather than the actual name that became official later on. The word 'annolino' instead comes from a different association: the small discs of pasta that sandwiched the filling were cut out using a tool called an 'anellino' or 'annellotto', a little ring. In this regard, see also Francesco Bianco, 'Gli agnolotti: Il piacere della carne', in Arcangeli (ed), *Peccati di lingua*, pp. 17–19.

24 *Il Sovrano dei cuochi*, Naples, Bideri, 1948, p. 64.

25 Rosa Maria Grillo, *Mangiar bene e spender poco*, Bologna, L. Cappelli Editore, 1939, p. 34.

26 Grillo, *Mangiar bene e spender poco*, p. 33.

27 Antonio Frugoli, *Pratica e scalcaria*, Rome, Appresso Francesco Cavalli, 1631, p. 275.

28 Frugoli, *Pratica e scalcaria*, p. 177.

29 Aureliano Bassani and Giancarlo Roversi, *Eminenza, il pranzo è servito*, Bologna, Aniballi Edizioni, 1984, p. 125. Regarding Alvisi, see 'The origins', chapter 7.

30 The book offers three different versions of 'Cappelletti alla bolognese': with a 'Fine filling', with 'Another, simpler filling' and lastly, with 'Another filling, very simple but quite good': Lazzari-Turco, *Manuale pratico di cucina*, p. 69.

31 See 'Potatoless gnocchi', chapter 4.

32 Vincenzo Tanara, *L'economia del cittadino in villa*, p. 114.

33 Vincenzo Tanara, *L'economia del cittadino in villa*, p. 479.

34 Messisbugo, *Banchetti, compositioni di vivande*, f. 11 r.

35 Bartolomeo Stefani, *L'arte di ben cucinare*, Mantua, Appresso gli Osanna, Stampatori Ducali, 1662, p. 38.

36 The 'aiolini' are actually 'agiolini' that have lost a letter due to a typographical error, and the 'crocette' are what are now known in Liguria as 'croxetti' or 'corzetti'.

37 Stefani, *L'arte di ben cucinare*, 1685 (2nd ed.), p. 201.

38 *L'Apicio moderno* is a monumental work in seven volumes that was published in two editions, the first in 1790 and the second in 1807–8. Leonardi, relying on his vast professional experience in kitchens throughout Europe, where he rose to the highest levels and became cook to Catherine II of Russia, poured all his knowledge into this book. The French influence was obviously still quite strong and would remain so for at least another century, but this compendium of gastronomic expertise brought attention back to Italian cuisine. For an exhaustive look at Italian cookbooks and their authors from the late eighteenth century to the Second World War, see Agnese Portincasa, *Scrivere di gusto: una storia della cucina italiana attraverso i ricettari, 1776–1943*, Bologna, Pendragon, 2016.

39 Leonardi, *L'Apicio moderno*, 1790, vol. I, p. 43.

40 The word anolino comes from the Latin *anulus*, 'little ring'. See note 23.

41 Agnoletti, *La nuova cucina economica*, vol. IV, p. 55.

42 Leonardi, *L'Apicio moderno*, 1790, vol. III, p. 280. For a description of 'culì' see 'The era of timbales', chapter 6.

43 Leonardi, *L'Apicio moderno*, 1790, vol. IV, p. 236.

44 *Codice gastrologico economico*, p. 30.

45 Agnoletti, 'Cervellate alla milanese', in *Manuale del cuoco e del pasticcere*, vol. I, p. 153.

46 Giovanni Brizzi, *La cuciniera moderna*, Siena, Tipografia Di Guido Mucci, 1845, p. 68.

47 A few pages later we also find a much more canonical recipe for 'tortelli alla bolognese', with poultry, marrow and parmesan. Brizzi, *La cuciniera moderna*, p. 106.

48 *Il cuoco sapiente*, p. 83.

49 Leyrer, *La regina delle cuoche*, p. 43, and G. Belloni, *Il vero re dei cucinieri*, p. 53.

50 Regarding Artusi and the importance of his work, see chapter 7.

51 *Il cuoco sapiente*, p. 83.

52 *La cucina italiana* 6, no. 8 (August 1934).

53 Oberosler, *Il tesoretto della cucina italiana*, p. 111.

54 The 'public survey conducted by the daily newspaper *Il Resto del Carlino*, open to every sector of the entire population of the City of Bologna' is mentioned in the document registered with the Chamber of Commerce, which also contains the traditional recipe for tortellini di Bologna. See *Bologna cucina . . . Con arte*, Bologna, Camera di Commercio Industria e Artigianato di Bologna, 2004, pp. 58 and 59. Unfortunately, the other recipes sent in to the paper do not seem to have been kept on file; they would have provided an interesting window on to everyday cooking in the mid-1970s.

55 Tito Trombacco, *Bologna cuci . . . Con arte*, pp. 58 and 59 (photo of original document).

56 Alessandro Molinari Pradelli, *Il vivo ricordo*, Arcugnano, Bertagni, 2013, p. 82.

57 Giulia Ferraris Tamburini, *Come posso mangiar bene?*, Milan, Hoepli, 1913 (1st ed. 1900), p. 394. Nowadays it might sound absurd to cook tortellini for half an hour, but in the context it was perfectly normal. Because of how they were manufactured at the time, the tortellini needed a few minutes to rehydrate before they began to cook, otherwise the pasta would have inevitably broken.

58 The 'official document' can be downloaded from the Dotta Confraternita del Tortellino website, www.confraternitadeltortellino.it (consulted 26 August 2020).

59 From the website of La Cesarina, http://www.ristorantecesarina.it (consulted 18 August 2020).

60 David, *Italian Food*, p. 101.
61 The disc of pasta even shrinks to 25mm in Lazzari-Turco, *Manuale pratico di cucina*, p. 69.
62 Something similar has been done with carbonara; see 'Adding a spoonful of science', chapter 3.

6. RAGÙ ALLA NAPOLETANA

1 www.agricoltura.regione.campania.it/tipici/tradizionali/ragu.html (updated 29 August 2015).
2 *La cuciniera piemontese*, Vercelli, a spese di Beltramo Antonio Re (libraio in Torino sotto i portici della città), 1771, p. 113.
3 François Massialot, *Le cuisinier roïal et bourgeois*, Paris, Chez Charles de Sercy, 1691, foreword.
4 Charles Sorel, Paris, *La vraie histoire comique de Francion*, 1623, p. 412.
5 Massialot, *Le cuisinier roïal et bourgeois*, p. 132.
6 Guy Miège, *A New Dictionary, French and English*, London, printed by Tho. Dawks, for Thomas Baffet, near Cliffords-Inn, in Fleetstreet, 1677, 'Ragout'.
7 Stefani, *L'arte di ben cucinare*, p. 101.
8 Corrado, *Il cuoco galante*.
9 Regarding Vincenzo Corrado, see 'Potatoless gnocchi', chapter 4.
10 See chapter 8.
11 Domenico Romoli, *La singolar dottrina*, Venice, Michele Tramezzino, 1560, p. 229.
12 *Il cuoco piemontese perfezionato a Parigi*, Turin, presso Carlo Giuseppe Ricca Stampatore, vicino a S. Rocco, a spese di Beltramo Antonio Re, 1766.
13 Menon, *La cuisinière bourgeoise*, Brussels, chez François Foppes, Imprimeur–Libraire, 1760. The first edition was printed in Paris in 1746, but has no timbale recipes. The anonymous author of *Il cuoco piemontese perfezionato a Parigi* was almost certainly looking at the 1760 edition.
14 *Il cuoco piemontese perfezionato a Parigi*, pp. 470–71.
15 One example does turn up, a thin pasta meant to be served in broth or milk.

16 Corrado, *Il cuoco galante*, 1773, p. 162.

17 Corrado, *Il cuoco galante*, 1773, p. 159. For a full recipe for sugo di carne, see the one from Francesco Leonardi's *L'Apicio moderno*, quoted further on.

18 We ran into him earlier in reference to gnocchi; see 'Potatoless gnocchi', chapter 4.

19 Cristoforo di Messisbugo, *Libro novo nel qual s'insegna a far d'ogni sorte di vivande . . .* , Venice, Giovanni Dalla Chiesa, al segno di San Girolamo, 1557, p. 52 v.

20 For more about the life of this chef, see chapter 5, note 41.

21 Leonardi, *L'Apicio moderno*, 1790, vol. III, p. 284. This manner of serving pasta was common in Naples and was described for the first time in 1772 by an English journalist visiting the city, who encountered macaroni with 'meat or gravy sauce, or mixed up with butter and cheese' (*The London Magazine*, 'An account of Maccaroni', April 1772, p. 193).

22 Leonardi, *L'Apicio moderno*, 1790, vol. II, pp. 6–7.

23 Leonardi, *L'Apicio moderno*, 1807–8, vol. I, p. 1.

24 A *mongana* was a female suckling calf, a particularly prized form of veal.

25 Leonardi, *L'Apicio moderno*, 1790, vol. IV, p. 2.

26 Leonardi, *L'Apicio moderno*, 1790, vol. III, p. 291.

27 Leonardi, *L'Apicio moderno*, 1807–8, vol. III, p. 224 (italics are mine).

28 See chapter 10.

29 M. F., *La cucina casareccia*, Naples, dai torchi dei F.lli Paci, 1817 (4th ed., 1st ed. 1807).

30 M. F., *La cucina casareccia*, pp. 46–7.

31 M. F., *La cucina casareccia*, p. 31.

32 Francesco de Bouchard, *Usi e costumi di Napoli*, Naples, 1858, vol. II, p. 75.

33 Cavalcanti, *Cucina teorico-pratica*, 1837.

34 Cavalcanti, *Cucina teorico-pratica*, 1839, p. 364.

35 Regarding al dente pasta, see 'Vermicielli co le pommadore', chapter 10.

36 Cavalcanti, *Cucina teorico-pratica*, 1839, p. 367. In the first edition, from 1837, the recipe does not contain any tomatoes. This is additional proof that at this point in time, they had yet to become well established in Neapolitan cuisine.

37 Giovanni Vialardi, *Cucina borghese semplice ed economica*, Turin, Tip. G. Favale, 1854, p. 41 (with chicken roulades) and Turin 1863, p. 48 (with the addition of veal roulades); *Il cuciniere moderno*, Milan 1871, p. 43 (two versions: one without tomato sauce and the second with just cheese and cream); *Il cuoco sapiente*, Florence 1871, p. 80; *Il re dei cuochi*, Milan 1874, p. 19.

38 *Il cuoco milanese e la cuciniera piemontese*, Milan, Francesco Pagnozi, tipografo-editore, n.d., p. 299; *Il cuciniere moderno*, p. 43 (see previous note).

39 Artusi, *La scienza in cucina*, 1891, p. 49; Il cuciniere italiano moderno, p. 64.

40 *Il cuciniere italiano moderno*, p. 64.

41 Silvano Serventi and Françoise Sabban, *La pasta: Storia e cultura di un cibo universale*, Rome and Bari, Laterza, 2000, pp. 204 ff.

42 Ada Boni, *Il talismano della felicità*, 1931, p. 93.

43 See 'The *dolce vita* of carbonara', chapter 3.

44 Eduardo De Filippo, *Sabato, domenica e lunedì*, Turin, Einaudi, 1966 (first staged in 1959).

45 De Filippo, *Sabato, domenica e lunedì*, p. 5.

46 De Filippo, *Sabato, domenica e lunedì*, p. 6.

47 A sign of this shift can be found in a classic Neapolitan cookbook (Jeanne Carola Francesconi, *La cucina napoletana*, Naples, Edizioni del Delfino, 1965), whose first edition calls for a 'prime cut of beef' weighing a kilo and a half, whereas the second one, in 1977, changes this to a 'prime cut of beef or pork'.

48 Lina Wertmüller, *Sabato, domenica e lunedì*, Silvio Berlusconi Communication, Italy, 1990. (The translation here is based on the author's transcription.)

7. RAGÙ ALLA BOLOGNESE

1 There are other delicacies named after Bologna, the most famous unquestionably being mortadella. Regarding Bologna's reputation as a food mecca, see Montanari (ed.), *Bologna grassa*.

2 See 'Francesco Leonardi's revolution', chapter 6.

3 Bassani and Roversi, *Eminenza, il pranzo è servito*, pp. 112 and 136.

4 *Il cuciniere italiano moderno*, 1844 (1st ed. 1842), p. 51.

5 Giovanni Vialardi, *Trattato di cucina*, Turin, Tip. G. Favale e C., 1854, p. 41.

6 Giovanni Vialardi, *Cucina borghese semplice ed economica*, 1863, p. 48.

7 See chapter 1.

8 Palma, *Il principe dei cuochi*, p. 26.

9 Valerio Busnelli, *Il moderno cuciniere universale*, Milan, Romeo Mangoni Editore, 1881, p. 101. This recipe was quite a success and was reprinted later in Leyrer, *La regina delle cuoche*, p. 92, and in *Il cuciniere universale*, Milan, 1902, p. 151.

10 Alfredo Panzini, *Dizionario moderno*, Milan, Hoepli, 1931, 'Artusi'.

11 Artusi, *La scienza in cucina*, 1911 (15th ed.), p. 4.

12 Alberto Capatti, *Pellegrino Artusi: Il fantasma della cucina italiana*, Milan, Mondadori, 2019.

13 Some noteworthy recent examples are the proceedings from the conference held for the centennial of Artusi's death: Massimo Montanari and Giovanna Frosini, *Il secolo artusiano (Atti del convegno)*, Accademia della Crusca, 2012, especially Montanari's brief introductory essay, 'Le ragioni di un successo', pp. 7–15. The most complete and accurate critical edition of *La scienza in cucina* currently available is edited by Alberto Capatti (Milan 2010), while for Artusi's biography, see Capatti, *Pellegrino Artusi: Il fantasma della cucina italiana*.

14 Artusi, who was nonetheless a product of his time, also includes more old-fashioned pasta dishes such as 'Maccheroni alla francese', with just butter and cheese; macaroni with breadcrumbs, or with béchamel, baked in the oven; and 'Maccheroni alla napoletana'. There is only one 'Pasticcio di maccheroni', which is a sort of summation of all the timbales of the past, and only one example of a pasta dish served as a side to meat, 'Maccheroni alla balsamella'.

15 Pellegrino Artusi, *La scienza in cucina*, 1891, pp. 50–52. Readers who are feeling adventurous should give this recipe a try; I highly recommend it.

16 The failure to include tomatoes in any form is definitely no oversight on the author's part, since he uses them quite often in other recipes, even on pasta. Actually, tomatoes were so pervasive in Italian cooking by this time that Artusi tells an anecdote in his recipe for tomato sauce: 'In a town in Romagna there lived a priest who was always

sticking his nose in everyone's business [. . .] so the witty townspeople dubbed him Don Pomodoro, because tomatoes are bound to turn up everywhere.' Artusi, *La scienza in cucina*, 1891, pp. 65.

17 'Fritto composto alla bolognese', 'Coratella d'agnello alla bolognese', 'Fritto d'agnello alla bolognese', 'Fritto alla Garisenda' (named after a tower in Bologna), 'Cotolette di vitella di latte coi tartufi alla bolognese', 'Scaloppine alla bolognese', 'Tartufi alla bolognese', 'Tonno sott'olio in salsa alla bolognese', 'Baccalà alla bolognese', 'Arrosto morto di pollo alla bolognese', 'Pane bolognese', 'Maccheroni alla bolognese', 'Strichetti alla bolognese', 'Tortellini alla bolognese'. One could also add 'Girello alla brace' (a slow-cooked cut of beef) and 'Crescente' (a kind of focaccia), which are both described as Bolognese specialities.

18 Giuseppe Giacosa and Luigi Illica, *La bohème*, Turin 1896, act II.

19 Katharina Prato, *Manuale di cucina per principianti e per cuoche già pratiche*, Graz, Libreria Styria Editrice, 1893.

20 Jean Marie Parmentier, *Il re dei re dei cuochi*, Milan, Casa editrice Bietti, 1897.

21 *Il cuciniere universale, ossia la vera maniera di viver bene e spender poco*, Milan, Giovanni Gnocchi, 1902.

22 Giulia Lazzari-Turco, *Il piccolo focolare: Ricette di cucina per la massaia economa*, 1921 (2nd ed., 1st ed. 1908), p. 36.

23 *100 specialità di cucina italiane ed estere*, p. 8.

24 Cougnet, *L'arte cucinaria in Italia*, vol. I, pp. 192–3.

25 Cougnet, *L'arte cucinaria in Italia*, vol. I, pp. 199–200.

26 Cougnet, *L'arte cucinaria in Italia*, vol. i, pp. 205–6.

27 Boni, *Il talismano della felicità*, 1927, pp. 109–10.

28 'Con Nobile sull'Artide a bordo dell'Italia', *Corriere della Sera*, 19 May 1928.

29 'L'arrivo di Nobile a Verona', *Corriere della Sera*, 31 July 1928.

30 Emilia Zamara, *La cucina italiana della resistenza*, Milan, Edizioni A. Barion, 1936, pp. 49–50.

31 Petronilla, *Desinaretti per . . . questi tempi*, Milan, Sonzogno, 1944, p. 203.

32 *Il cucchiaio d'argento*, 1952 (3rd ed., 1st ed. published 1950), p. 130.

33 Trombacco, *Bologna cucina . . .* , pp. 66–9.

34 See 'The golden age', chapter 3.

35 Dario Bressanini, *La scienza della carne*, pp. 213–20. This book

contains a more detailed explanation of the procedure. The tips that follow are inspired by Bressanini's recipe and the suggestions of other Bolognese chefs.

36 An identical recipe, but with the addition of sweetbreads, can also be found in the handwritten cookbook of the Modenese Counts of Valdrighi, also from the second half of the nineteenth century. Regarding these two versions, see 'Naples, Marche, Bologna', chapter 8.

37 Oscar Tschirky, *The Cook Book, by 'Oscar' of the Waldorf*, Chicago–New York, The Saalfield Publishing Co., 1896, p. 599.

38 *The Hotel Monthly: Ideas for Refreshment Rooms*, Chicago, 1908, p. 89.

39 Massimo Montanari, *Bologna, l'Italia in tavola*, Bologna, Il Mulino, 2021, pp. 141–2. This advertisement appeared in the daily newspaper *La Stampa* on 22 April 1898, and was presented for the first time in a paper by Patrizia Battilani and Giuliana Bertagnoni, 'Il restyling di una vecchia icona pop: la storia transnazionale degli Spaghetti alla Bolognese', presented at the conference *Il cibo e la Città*, Padua, 2015.

40 Julia Lovejoy Cuniberti, *Practical Italian Recipes for American Kitchens*, Janesville, WI, Gazette Printing Co., 1917, p. 23.

41 Italians bear partial responsibility for the substitution, since for brevity's sake they would often describe tagliatelle as 'a sort of spaghetti'. See Luigi Vittorio Bertarelli, *Touring Club – Northern Italy, from the Alps to Rome (Rome Excepted)*, London, Macmillan and Company, 1924, p. CI.

42 *The Hotel Monthly: Ideas for Refreshment Rooms*, Chicago, 1923, p. 128.

43 Rian James, *Dining in New York*, New York, John Day Company, 1931, pp. 33–4.

8. LASAGNE

1 Horace, *Sermones*, I.6.110–15.

2 On the interpretation of this passage and later authors, see L. Ullmann, 'Horace "Serm." i, 6, 115 and the history of the world "Laganum"', in *Classical Philology* 7, no. 1, Jan. 1912, pp. 442–9, and Bruno Laurioux, 'Des lasagnes romaines aux vermicelles arabes', in

Bruno Laurioux (ed.), *Une histoire culinaire du Moyen Âge*, Paris, Honoré Champion, 2005, pp. 213–30. On lagana in general, see Serventi and Sabban, *La pasta*, pp. 21–52.

3 Celsus, *De Medicina*, II.22.1–2.

4 Celsus, *De Medicina*, VIII.7.6.

5 Paper-thin bread (artolaganum) is also mentioned by Cicero, *Epistulae ad Familiares*, IX.20.2 and Pliny the Elder, *Naturalis Historia*, xviii.105, but without describing how it is made.

6 Ateneus, *Deipnosophistae*, III.133d. This English translation is from *The Deipnosophists*, vol. II, trans. Charles Burton Gulick, Cambridge, MA, Loeb Classical Library, 1928.

7 Ibid., XIV.647c–648d.

8 Lagana appears in the Old Testament as a votive offering in the following verses: Exodus 29:2 and 29:23; Leviticus 2:4; 7:12 and 8:26; Numbers 6:14 and 6:18; 1 Chronicles 23:29.

9 'Laganum est latus et tenuis panis, qui primum in acqua, potea in oleo frigitur', Isidore of Seville, *Etymologiae*, XX.II.17 (Migne pl. lxxxii:708).

10 Apicius, *De Re Coquinaria*, IV.14–15.

11 'Nunquam vidi hominem qui ita libenter lagana cum caseo comederet sicut ipse.' Salimbene da Parma and Antonio Bertani, *Chronica Fr. Salimbene Parmensis Ordinis Minorum: Ex Codice Bibliothecae Vaticanae Nunc Primum Edita*, Parma, Ex officina Petri Fiaccadorii, 1857, p. 318.

12 The *memoriali bolognesi* were registers into which public documents were transcribed, and by law, to avoid later additions or tampering, no empty spaces could be left on their pages. The anonymous copyists therefore filled in the margins with proverbs, sonnets, songs and poems, often of popular origin.

13 Alessandro Andreolli and Vera Gheno, 'La Lasagna: Il successo di una forma', in Arcangeli (ed.), *Peccati di lingua*, pp. 155–9.

14 Giovanni Sercambi, *Novelle*, CXXIII, quoted by Massimo Montanari, *Convivio*, Rome and Bari, Laterza, 1989, pp. 382–3.

15 Sabadino degli Arienti, *Le porretane*, xlvi, quoted by Montanari, *Convivio*, p. 499.

16 On the dating of these manuscripts and how they are related, see Anna Martellotti, *I ricettari di Federico ii*, Florence, Olschki, 2005.

17 Sabban and Serventi, *La pasta*, p. 32.

18 The mixture could have been similar to the one described in the recipe for tortellini (see 'Round tortellini', chapter 5).

19 *Liber de Coquina*, Latin 7131, iii:10, Bibliothèque Nationale de France, Paris, quoted by Faccioli, *L'arte della cucina in Italia*, p. 35.

20 Ms. 158 from the Biblioteca Universitaria di Bologna, quoted by Bergonzoni, *Due testi medievali di cucina nel manoscritto 158*, p. 98.

21 Ingemar Boström, *Anonimo meridionale: Due libri di cucina*, Stockholm, Almqvist & Wiksell International, 1985, p. 45.

22 Vincenzo Tanara, *L'economia del cittadino in villa*, Venice, Appresso li Prodotti, 1644, p. 137; Latini, *Lo scalco alla moderna*, p. 287.

23 Vittorio Lancellotti, *Lo scalco prattico*, Rome, Appresso Francesco Corbelletti, 1627, p. 153. A simplified version can also be found in Giovanni Francesco Vasselli, *Apicio overo il maestro de' conviti*, Bologna, Per gli eredi del Dozza, 1647, p. 110.

24 See chapter 5.

25 Scappi, *Opera*, c. 43 r.

26 On the subject of cooking times, see 'Vermicielli co le pommadore', chapter 10.

27 *Liber de Coquina*, Latin 7131, v. 9, Bibliothèque Nationale de France, Paris.

28 'Ravioli' often mean small balls of meat or cheese-based filling without pasta, similar to Tuscan 'gnudi', either boiled or fried (see 'Nineteenth-century trends and Artusi's doffed hat', chapter 5).

29 Scappi, *Opera*, c. 244 v.

30 Regarding timbales, see also 'The era of timbales', chapter 6.

31 *Il cuoco piemontese perfezionato a Parigi*, pp. 473–4.

32 *La cuciniera piemontese*, p. 39. Baked dishes with a pastry crust became a true centrepiece from this point on, and although it is now increasingly rare to see pasta cooked this way, it still makes for one of the most sumptuous dishes in Italian cuisine.

33 On lasagne alla genovese, see 'The birth of pesto', chapter 9.

34 For a brief discussion of Vincenzo Corrado, see chapter 6.

35 Regarding Corrado's coulis, see 'Italian ragù', chapter 6, and chapter 10, note 16.

36 Corrado, *Il cuoco galante*, p. 163.

37 Cavalcanti, *Cucina teorico-pratica*, 1837, p. 278. This recipe is in Neapolitan dialect.

38 Boni, *Il talismano della felicità*, 1927, p. 86.

39 Lasagne alla napoletana is a dish that stands out for the vast number of variants that coexist even today as part of the same tradition. The specific recipe I am referring to comes from Luciano Pignataro's blog lucianopignataro.it (consulted 15 July 2020).

40 Antonio Nebbia, *Il cuoco maceratese*, Macerata, Remondini tipografo ed editore, 1779 (2nd ed. 1781), pp. 137–8.

41 Leonardi, *L'Apicio moderno*, 1790, vol. III, p. 317. A different version of this timbale, with macaroni, can also be found in Agnoletti, *La nuova cucina economica*, vol. II, p. 134.

42 Leonardi, *L'Apicio moderno*, 1790, vol. IV, p. 2. For the recipe for this ragù, see 'Francesco Leonardi's revolution', chapter 6.

43 Leonardi, *L'Apicio moderno*, 1790, vol. IV, p. 7.

44 *Codice gastrologico economico*, pp. 15–16.

45 Brizzi, *La cuciniera moderna, opera gastronomica*, p. 44; *Il cuciniere italiano moderno*, Livorno, 1851 (13th ed.), p. 63 and p. 75 (fast-day version). A version from around the same time that contains veal sweetbreads can be found in the handwritten recipe collection of the Valdrighi counts in Modena (Gabriele Ronzoni, *Il ricettario dei conti Valdrighi*, Modena, Edizioni il Fiorino, 2009). Regarding the recipe's popularity in the United States, see 'Francesco Leonardi's revolution', chapter 6.

46 Artusi, *La scienza in cucina*, 1891, p. 129.

47 *100 specialità di cucina italiane ed estere*, p. 5.

48 See, for instance, Cougnet, *L'arte cucinaria in Italia*, vol. I, p. 206; Dario Fornari, *Il cuciniere militare*, Novara, Cattaneo, 1930, p. 152; Pellaprat, *L'arte nella cucina*, p. 68; Ada Bonfiglio Krassich, *La cucina delle specialità regionali*, Milan, Sonzogno, 1939, p. 80.

49 Paolo Monelli and Giuseppe Novello, *Il ghiottone errante*, Slow Food Editore 2016, (1st ed. 1935) ebook pos. 1248.

50 Leonardi, *L'Apicio moderno*, 1790, vol. III, p. 291.

51 Vitaliano Bossi, *L'imperatore dei cuochi*, Rome, Edoardo Perino, 1894, p. 345.

9. PESTO ALLA GENOVESE

1 The search for the shared origins of the first Italian recipe collections is described in Martellotti, *I ricettari di Federico II*, which I refer to for the quotes that follow.

2 'Ad usum romanorum caulles', Latin 7131, I:5, Bibliothèque Nationale de France, Paris, and Palatino Latino 1768:5, Biblioteca Apostolica Vaticana.

3 'Brodium theutonicum', Latin 7131, II:6; Latin 9328, II:6; Palatino Latino 1768:53; 'Brodo todesco', Anonimo Meridionale 61, Biblioteca Internazionale di Gastronomia, Sorengo and 'compositio theutonicum', Latin 7131, v. 12; Latin 9328, v. 12.

4 'Compositio lumbardicum', Latin 7131, v. 11; Latin 9328, v. 11; Palatino Latino 1768:48.

5 'Altramente a la provençale' *Anonimo Toscano* 158:76, Biblioteca Universitaria di Bologna.

6 'Torta parmesanam', Latin 7131, v. 6; Latin 9328, v. 6; *Anonimo Toscano* 158, 122; Palatino Latino 1768, 80. The geographic meaning of this term is debated, since it could refer either to the cheese, or to the shape of a round shield (a 'parma').

7 This recipe appears in three manuscripts: Latin 7131, II:66; Latin 9328, II:66 and Palatino Latino 1768:119.

8 Regarding the invention of the first forms of dried pasta: Serventi and Sabban, *La pasta*, p. 23 ff. and Bruno Laurioux, 'Des lasagnes romaines aux vermicelles arabes', in Laurioux (ed.), *Une histoire culinaire du Moyen Âge*, pp. 213–30.

9 Galen, *De alimentorum facultatibus*, quoted in Serventi and Sabban, *La pasta*, p. 20.

10 This hypothesis is explored in Emilio Milana, *La scia dei tetraedri*, Ravenna, Danilo Montanari Editore, 2008, pp. 169–72.

11 Muhammad al-Idrisi, *Kitab nuzhat al-mushtaq fi'khtiraq al-'afaq* ('Book of Amusement for Whoever Longs to Cross the Horizons'), p. 38, quoted in Serventi and Sabban, *La pasta*, p. 57. This English translation is from John Dickie, *Delizia!: The Epic History of the Italians and Their Food*, New York, Free Press, 2008, p. 21.

12 Serventi and Sabban, *La pasta*, pp. 59–65.

13 'Ad tria ianuenssem suffrige cipolas cum olco et mite in aqua bullienti decoqui et super pone species et colora et assapora sicut vis cum istis

potes ponere caseum gractatum vel incisum et da quandocumque placet cum caponibus et cum ovis vel quibuscumque carnibus.' Latin 7131, II:66, Bibliothèque Nationale de France, Paris, quoted in Martellotti, *I ricettari di Federico II*, p. 248.

14 Based on a recipe that bears some similarities to tria genovese, 'Se vuoli tria di capponi o di carne di cavretto', from ms. 158, XXI at the Biblioteca Universitaria di Bologna, I believe that 'ovis' (uova) could be a copyist's error for 'ovibus' (mutton, goat).

15 Regarding Maestro Martino, see also 'Il cacio sui maccheroni', chapter 1.

16 Manuscript from the Archivio Storico di Riva di Garda, quoted in Benporat, *Cucina italiana del Quattrocento*, p. 182.

17 Virgil, 'Moretum', *Appendix Vergiliana*.

18 Manuscript from the Archivio Storico di Riva di Garda, quoted in Benporat, *Cucina italiana del Quattrocento*, p. 198.

19 Messisbugo, *Banchetti*, f. 45 v. The idea of using agliata on pasta is also found in later authors, for instance: Scappi, *Opera*, f. 222 r.; Giovan Battista Rossetti, *Dello scalco*, Ferrara, Appresso Domenico Mammarello, 1584, pp. 56, 187 and 206; Cesare Evitascandalo, *Libro dello scalco*, Rome, Appresso Carlo Vullietti, 1609, p. 97.

20 On fast-day cooking, see 'A sprinkling of parmesan', chapter 1.

21 Genoa was famous for a number of specialities, including capers – which were so highly prized that they were covered in a thin sheet of silver before serving (Giovanni Francesco Vasselli, *L'Apicio, overo il maestro de' conviti*, Bologna, per gli HH. Del Dozza, 1647, p. 78) – and a few kinds of fruit such as pears, plums and oranges; also mushrooms (gathered and preserved in salt), soups, dishes involving veal loin and liver, and fine pastries, with biscuits and a variant of sponge cake known as 'pasta genovese', which became famous around Europe as genoise.

22 See chapter 10.

23 Corrado, *Il cuoco galante*, 1773, p. 188.

24 Vincenzo Agnoletti, *Manuale del credenziere*, Rome, presso Angelo Ajani, 1830, p. 118.

25 *Codice gastrologico economico*, p. 15.

26 Delle Piane, *La cucina di strettissimo magro*, 1880, p. 39.

27 *Almanacco dei gastronomi*, Milan, Sonzogno, 1863 (reprinted a few years later under the title *La cuciniera universale*, 1870).

28 Busnelli, *Il moderno cuciniere universale.*

29 Leyrer, *La regina delle cuoche.*

30 *La cuciniera bolognese*, Bologna, Priori, 1874, facsimile reprint, Sala Bolognese, 1990.

31 Leonardi, *L'Apicio moderno*, 1790, vol. I, p. 206. A few years earlier, a similar version of the recipe appeared in *Oniatologia, ovvero il discorso de' cibi*, Florence, Presso J. A. Bouchard, 1785, vol. I, p. 44.

32 Leonardi, *L'Apicio moderno*, 1790, vol. iii, p. 284. On this subject, see 'Naples and tomatoes', chapter 6.

33 The entry for 'Maccheroni' in the *Dizionario universale economico rustico* of 1794 reads: 'There [in Naples] they are usually eaten without butter, but all covered in good cheese. To this is added the gravy from meat cooked in a pot or pan or roasted in the Genoese fashion.' See *Dizionario universale economico rustico*, Rome, Nella stamperia di Michele Puccinelli, 1794 (2nd ed.), vol. XI ('Maccheroni').

34 Ippolito Cavalcanti, *Cucina teorico-pratica*, Naples, Stamperia e cartiere del Fibreno, 1844 (4th ed.), p. 645 (italics are mine). In the first edition of 1837, the author includes no recipe for genovese, although the one for 'Vitello alla papigliotta' says that the veal is cooked 'alla genovese' (Cavalcanti, *Cucina teorico-pratica*, 1837, p. 92).

35 *Nuova Enciclopedia agraria*, Naples 1859, vol. VI, p. 350.

36 Ratto and Ratto, *La cuciniera genovese*, 1893, respectively p. 55 and p. 53.

37 Many recipe titles show this complete overlap. The one in Giovanni Vialardi's *Cucina borghese* leaves no room for doubt: 'Maccheroni o lasagne di Genova o di Napoli alla borghese' (Vialardi, *Cucina borghese*, 1863, p. 89), while *Il cuoco pratico ed economo* presents the same sauce for lasagne alla genovese and maccheroni alla napoletana (Milan 1867, iii ed., p. 67.), which is repeated in *Il cuoco sapiente* (1871, p. 79) and again in the three subsequent cookbooks, which bring the same recipe all the way to the beginning of the twentieth century (*Il vero re dei cucinieri*, p. 50; *Il cuoco di famiglia*, Florence, Salani, 1898, p. 83; *L'arte della cucina*, Florence, Adriano Salani Editore, 1905, pp. 52 and 54).

38 See chapter 6.

39 Cougnet, *L'arte cucinaria in Italia*, vol. I, p. 367.

40 This anecdote from Neapolitan writer, actor, director and philosopher

Luciano De Crescenzo is quoted in Rita Pane and Mariano Pane, *I sapori del Sud*, Milan, Rizzoli, 1991 (2010), p. 90.

41 *La cuciniera moderna*, p. 44 and the 13th edition of *Il cuciniere italiano moderno*, 1851, p. 75.

42 'Monparella: vermicelli pasta in long, thin, very narrow strings, a sort of lasagne'. Casimiro Zalli, *Dizionario piemontese, italiano, latino e francese*, Carmagnola, dalla tipografia di Pietro Barbié, 1830, vol. 2, 'Monparella'.

43 Vialardi, *Trattato di cucina*, p. 305.

44 From Paolo Lingua's preface to the reprint of Ratto and Ratto, *La cuciniera genovese*, 2012.

45 Ratto and Ratto, *La cuciniera genovese*, 1863 (8th ed. 1893), p. 42.

46 Emanuele Rossi, *La vera cuciniera genovese facile ed economica*, Mendrisio, n.d., 1865, p. 32.

47 Delle Piane, *La cucina di strettissimo magro*, 1880, p. 39.

48 A. Crovetto, *Cucina ed igiene*, Genoa, premiata tip. Sociale, 1927, p. 127.

49 Cesare Tirabasso, *La guida in cucina*, Macerata, Bisson e Leopardi, 1927, p. 17.

50 www.agriligurianet.it (consulted 6 November 2020)

51 www.pestochampionship.it (consulted 6 November 2020).

10. SPAGHETTI AL POMODORO

1 The history of spaghetti with tomato sauce was recently examined in Massimo Montanari's essay *Il mito delle origini* (op. cit.), which explores the theme of Italy's culinary tradition in an extremely clear and concise manner.

2 Steno, *Un americano a Roma*, Excelsa Film, Italy, 1954.

3 One of the most interesting accounts of the Italian community in New York can be found in Simone Cinotto, *The Italian American Table: Food, Family, and Community in New York City*, Urbana, Chicago and Springfield, IL, University of Illinois Press, 2013.

4 This was printed on the back of the restaurant's advertising postcards.

5 The story of Giovanni Buitoni and the connection to the character of Nando Mericoni have already been brilliantly analysed in Massimo

Capatti, *Storia della cucina italiana*, pp. 36–40, a key text exploring Italian food history from the postwar period to the present.

6 Bernardino de Sahagún, *Historia universal de las cosas de Nueva España*, 1569 (1576–7), f. 49 r. This manuscript is preserved in the Biblioteca Laurenziana in Florence. The 'Florentine Codex' is the last version, the only bilingual one (Spanish and Nahuatl) of the *Historia*, whose first version was probably completed in 1569, while the Florentine manuscript was rewritten in 1576–7. The English translation here is by Charles E. Dibble and Arthur J. O. Anderson: *Florentine Codex: General History of the Things of New Spain*, Book 10, Santa Fe, The School of American Research and The University of Utah, 1961, p. 68.

7 Pietro Andrea Mattioli, *I discorsi*, Venice 1544 (1557), p. 500.

8 Ugo Benzo, *Regole della Sanita et Natura de' Cibi*, Turin, per gli Heredi di Gio. Domenico Tarino, 1618, p. 373.

9 Giuseppe Donzelli, *Teatro Farmaceutico, Dogmatico, e Spagirico*, Naples, per Gio. Francesco Paci, Geronimo Fasulo, e Michele Monaco, 1675, part ii, p. 249.

10 This must be hot pepper, given that the previous recipe, 'Altro Fritto, di Zampe di Vitella', contains the suggestion, 'if you would like to make it spicy, you can put in minced Peparolo' (Latini, *Lo scalco alla moderna*, p. 336).

11 Serpollo (normally serpillo) and piperna are two kinds of thyme.

12 Latini, *Lo scalco alla moderna*, p. 444.

13 Corrado, *Il cuoco galante*, 1773, p. 156.

14 Nebbia, *Il cuoco maceratese*, 1781, p. 24.

15 Leonardi, *L'Apicio moderno*, 1790, vol. VI, p. 130. A recipe for 'Tortoises with peas, in the manner of Maremma' still appears among the Tuscan specialities in Agnetti, *Nuova cucina delle specialità regionali*, p. 130.

16 Leonardi, *L'Apicio moderno*, 1790, vol. VI, p. 205.

17 Leonardi, *L'Apicio moderno*, 1790, vol. V, p. 32.

18 Leonardi, *L'Apicio moderno*, 1790, vol. V, p. 9.

19 Leonardi, *L'Apicio moderno*, 1790, vol. V, p. 1. Regarding fast-day cooking, see chapter 1.

20 *Oniatologia, ovvero il discorso de' cibi*, Florence, Pagani, 1794, vol. IV, p. 156, 'Zuppa di pomodoro e pasta'; Agnoletti, *La nuova cucina*

economica, vol. IV, p. 149, 'Zuppa di qualunque sorte di paste fine in tutti i modi'.

21 Grimod de La Reynière, *Almanach des gourmands*, 5ème année, Paris, de l'imprimerie de Cellot, 1807, p. 105.

22 Grimod de La Reynière, *Almanach des gourmands*, 5ème année, p. 106.

23 Cavalcanti, *Cucina teorico-pratica*, 1837, p. 279.

24 The term 'al dente' in reference to pasta derives from the expression 'reggere al dente' ('to stand up to the tooth'), which a nineteenth-century dictionary defines as: 'used to describe firm things, like fruit, meat, or other foods, that do not easily yield to the pressure of teeth' (Giovanni Gherardini, *Voci e maniere di dire italiane additate a futuri vocabolaristi*, per G.B. Bianchi e Comp., Milano 1840, vol. II, 'dente').

25 Manuscripts from the Archivio storico di Riva del Garda e Buhler, quoted in Claudio Benporat, *Cucina italiana del Quattrocento*, respectively p. 184 and p. 237.

26 Urbinate Latin Manuscript 1203, quoted in Claudio Benporat, *Cucina italiana del Quattrocento*, p. 107. In the manuscript from the Archivio Storico di Riva, the recommended cooking time is reduced to half an hour.

27 Scappi, *Opera*, f. 51 r.

28 *Il cuoco piemontese ridotto all'ultimo gusto*, Milan, Forni, 1832, p. 45.

29 *La cucina facile*, Milan, per Gaspare Truffi, 1844, p. 23.

30 Francesco Chapusot, *La cucina sana, economica ed elegante*, Turin, Favale, 1846, p. 6.

31 *Almanacco dei gastronomi*, p. 30.

32 Emanuele Rossi, *La vera cuciniera genovese facile ed economica*, Mendrisio, n.d., 1865, p. 43.

33 *La cuciniera universale*, 1870, p. 109.

34 *Il cuciniere moderno*, 1871, p. 43.

35 *Il cuoco sapiente*, p. 65.

36 Leyrer, *La regina delle cuoche*, p. 95.

37 Bossi and Salvi, *L'imperatore dei cuochi*, 1894–5, p. 200.

38 Parmentier, *Il re dei re dei cuochi*, 1897, p. 120.

39 Ferraris Tamburini, *Come posso mangiar bene?*, 1913, p. 24.

40 *L'arte di mangiare bene: Manuale pratico per le massaie*, Milan, Sonzogno, 1923, p. 158.

41 Fornari, *Il cuciniere militare*, 1932, p. 21 and p. 151.

42 Chapusot, *La cucina sana, economica ed elegante*, p. 6.

43 Ferraris Tamburini, *Come posso mangiar bene?*, 1913, p. 24. See also the recipe mentioned in 'The origins', chapter 7, in which macaroni is boiled with a pullet, for the same amount of time.

44 Renato Rovetta, *Industria del pastificio*, Milan, Hoepli, 1929, pp. 28–31. See also the interesting studies conducted on a sample of pasta from the early nineteenth century, confirming the low percentages of durum wheat, in Marco Silvestri, Alessandro D'Alessandro, Roberto Ranieri, *Caratterizzazione di paste dell'800, oggetto di una fornitura al carcere di Parma*, in *Pasta d'archivio: Scienza e storia del più antico campione di pasta (1837–1838)*, Parma, Archivio di Stato di Parma, 2000, pp. 39–45.

45 On this subject see also Sabban and Serventi, *La pasta: Storia e cultura di un cibo universale*, pp. 287–344.

46 See chapter 6.

47 Matilde Serao, *Il ventre di Napoli*, Milan, Treves, 1884 (Naples, Francesco Perrella editore, 1906), p. 26. See also the previous quote from Francesco de Bouchard in 'Naples and tomatoes', chapter 6.

48 Nicolas Appert, *L'art de conserver pendant plusieurs années toutes les substances animales et végétales*, Paris, Chez Patris et Cie Imprimeurs Libraires, 1810.

49 Artusi, *La scienza in cucina*, 1891, respectively p. 56 and p. 39.

50 *What to Eat: The National Food Magazine* 23, no. 1 (July 1907): p. 18.

51 *100 specialità di cucina italiane ed estere*. The Neapolitan dishes in this cookbook are: Hake fillets alla Don Carlo, Omelette with anchovies, Maccheroni or spaghetti with tomato sauce, Ray alla napoletana, Beef kidneys alla napoletana, Eggs alla napoletana. The two other turn-of-the-century cookbooks of regional specialities also list pasta with tomato sauce as a local delicacy: Agnetti, *Nuova cucina delle specialità regionali*, 1909, p. 147, and Alberto Cougnet, *L'arte cucinaria in Italia*, p. 193.

52 This variation was recorded for 'Vermicelli alla napoletana' in Boni, *Il talismano della felicità*, 1946 (12th ed.), p. 105, and for 'Maccheroni alla napoletana' in *Il cucchiaio d'argento*, 1950 (2nd ed.), p. 133, which are both recipes for pasta with tomato sauce.

ACKNOWLEDGEMENTS

This book started to develop many years ago, although I still had no idea what form it would take. And now that it has acquired one, there are many people I would like to thank.

First of all, my parents, for feeding and caring for a child with little or no appetite. I don't know what role that played in all of this, but it couldn't have been insubstantial.

Federica, my loving partner and tireless reader of my drafts, who generously supported me (and put up with me) over these long months of writing, and whose abundant help and suggestions were always invaluable.

My children Sara and Jacopo, who patiently indulge my culinary obsessions.

Manuela Bonettini, who encouraged me from the start to delve into these topics, and without whom this book would not exist.

Annalisa Zordan and Massimiliano Tonelli, who offered me a one-of-a-kind opportunity for professional growth that played a fundamental role in getting me this far.

Francesco Merini, Gianluca Simoni and Michele Cogo, who helped me along when the path had yet to be found. And all my old friends, the ones I make tortellini with at Christmas.

Thanks to Giuseppe Palumbo, for always believing (and sooner or later it will happen), and to Alessandro Molinari Pradelli, for his generosity and encouragement.

To Alberto Grandi, for conversations that have always been illuminating and inspiring. To Niki Corradetti, who was of enormous help with digital sources.

To Ilaria Sita and Alessandro Salvioli, for their work putting together the data that underpin this whole story. And to Mila Fumini, for the fruitful exchange of ideas.

Heartfelt thanks to Giancarlo Gonizzi and the Biblioteca Gastronomica at Academia Barilla in Parma, for the precious work that they are doing and the kindness they've always shown. Institutions like this one, along with the Biblioteca Internazionale La Vigna in Vicenza and other libraries and archives that work to preserve and promote our cultural heritage, are the bedrock of all research. My deepest gratitude to the entire team at Il Saggiatore, the Italian publisher who believed in me from day one: Giuseppe Favi, Damiano Scaramella, Francesco Migliori and Andrea Morstabilini, who worked with me on this book from conception to promotion, and whose help proved indispensable to say the least.

Finally, thanks to the Associazione Sala d'Arme Achille Marozzo, particularly Paolo Tassinari, Marco Rubboli, Alessandro Battistini, Massimiliano Fraulini, Domenico

ACKNOWLEDGEMENTS

Giannuzzi and the other instructors at this fencing school;
once again, they've been like a second family, lending me
hours of their time and all of their support.

INDEX

NB Entries in **bold** indicate main entries